RESEARCH HIGHLIGHTS IN SOCIAL WORK 35

Effective Ways of Working with Children and their Families

RESEARCH HIGHLIGHTS IN SOCIAL WORK 35

Effective Ways of Working with Children and their Families

Edited by Malcolm Hill

Jessica Kingsley Publishers
London and Philadelphia

Research Highlights in Social Work 35
Editor: Malcolm Hill
Secretary: Anne Forbes
Editorial Advisory Committee:

Professor Joyce Lishman	Robert Gordon University, Aberdeen
Ms M. Buist	Independent researcher, Edinburgh
Mr P. Cassidy	Social Work Department, Aberdeen City Council, representing the Association of Directors of Social Work
Ms A. Connor	Independent researcher, Edinburgh
Mr D. Cox	Robert Gordon University, Aberdeen
Mr M. King	Northern College, Aberdeen
Dr F. Paterson	Social Work Services Group, Scottish Office
Dr A. Robertson	University of Edinburgh
Ms C. Smith	Scottish Council for Voluntary Organisations, Edinburgh

Robert Gordon University
School of Applied Social Studies
Kepplestone Annexe, Queen's Road
Aberdeen AB15 4PH

First published in the United Kingdom in 1999 by
Jessica Kingsley Publishers Ltd
116 Pentonville Road
London N1 9JB, England
and
325 Chestnut Street
Philadelphia, PA 19106, U S A
www.jkp.com
Copyright © 1999 Robert Gordon University, Research Highlights Advisory Group,
School of Applied Social Studies

Library of Congress Cataloging in Publication Data
A CIP catalogue record for this book is available from the Library of Congress

British Library Cataloguing in Publication Data
Effective ways of working with children and their families. - (research highlights in social work : 35)
1. Children – Services for – Great Britain 2. Family – Services for – Great Britain 3. Social work with children – Great Britain 4. Family social work – Great Britain
I. Hill, Malcolm
362.7'0941

ISBN 1 85302 619 0

Printed and Bound in Great Britain by
Athenaeum Press, Gateshead, Tyne and Wear

Contents

Acknowledgements

I would like to thank Joyce Lishman and members of the Research Highlights Advisory Board for suggesting that this volume be produced and that I should act as editor. The Board also gave helpful guidance in formulating the contents and identifying suitable contributors. Most credit for the book is due to the contributors, who worked to tight deadlines and responded with goodwill to editorial suggestions. Thanks also to Anne Forbes at the Robert Gordon University, Aberdeen, who produced the final versions of the text.

CHAPTER I

Effective Professional Intervention in Children's Lives

Malcolm Hill

Introduction

This book is concerned with professional interventions intended to make a difference to the lives of children and their families. It forms part of a long-standing Research Highlights series which originated in Scotland with a focus on research reviews relevant to social work. Over the years the scope has broadened, so that this volume encompasses a range of professional and academic disciplines, whilst retaining a particular concern for children who have serious difficulties in their lives. It is hoped that the contents will be of interest to anyone who works with children and their families, as well as to students and academics.

Children's issues have seldom been far from the headlines in recent years. Public or political concern has been repeatedly expressed about young offenders, school attainments, child abuse – both in the family and in substitute care – bullying, drug-taking and so on. Sympathy for children as victims has been expressed alongside demonisation of children as threats to the social order. Less attention has been given to chronic problems of child poverty and inequalities in child health (Townsend, Davidson and Whitehead 1992; Middleton, Ashworth and Walker 1994); indeed for a long period these were denied a place on government agendas.

Impetus to improve children's lives was provided by the UN Convention on the Rights of the Child, ratified by the UK in 1991. This emphasises children's rights to safety, healthy development, protection, provision of appropriate services and participation in key decisions affecting them. Although the Convention has not been incorporated in UK legislation, a number of its principles have informed

7

recent policy and practice. This appears to be strongest in relation to public child care law and also has implications for domestic relations, especially in post-divorce situations (Franklin 1995; Tisdall and Plumtree 1997). So far the impact on the education system has been much weaker (Sinclair 1996).

The main responsibilities for children's welfare and development lie with their families, supported by a range of government services including schools, child benefit and health provision (Hill and Tisdall 1997). An intermediate position is occupied by a range of professionals, whose activities form the focus of this book. Virtually all children have contact with certain professionals who offer a universal service – notably teachers, general practitioners and health visitors. Others provide open-access facilities which are taken up by some, but not others. These include nursery nurses and youth workers. Finally, some children with particular needs or problems encounter those with more specialist functions, such as social workers, educational psychologists and psychiatrists.

All these professions are ostensibly concerned with promoting or safeguarding children's interests, by furthering their development, learning, health or social welfare. When such help is given, it is well regarded by the majority of young people (Catan, Dennison and Coleman 1996; Farnfield 1998). Nevertheless, and to varying degrees, professional activities have a 'social control', as well as a 'social care' role, in relation to either children or their parents. The aim of encouraging individual choice and freedom is circumscribed by pressures to ensure that children abide by legal requirements and other social norms, including school rules. Indeed it has been argued that professionals use their psychological and sociological knowledge to exercise power over families on behalf of the state (Rabinow 1984; Parton 1991). This is most evident in circumstances when children are thought to be at risk in their own families; then legal action, perhaps including compulsory removal from home, may be taken by police and/or social workers, informed and supported by doctors, teachers or others. For many professionals this results in tensions, when they may be placed in the position of acting against a child's or parent's expressed wishes or in breach of confidentiality in order to protect a child from presumed danger.

The aims of any one profession are usually broad and often contested, as illustrated by debates about the meaning and nature of education and health, or indeed hybrids like health education and promotion (Bunton, Nettleton and Burrows 1995). This can make it difficult to assess whether professional activities are successful or not. If the goals are unclear, then it is not easy to say if they have been achieved. Even when aims are accomplished, it is not straightforward to determine how or why this happened or indeed whether it was due to the intervention at all. One of the classic criticisms of psychoanalysis was that although people often improved during therapy, others receiving no service were just as likely to feel better (Eysenck 1986). It is well known that people's physical and psychological health can respond to 'placebos' i.e. chemically inactive tablets, so that for medication to be deemed worth while it is necessary to demonstrate that it has a greater effect than a placebo. Similarly, people often like and benefit from personal attention, but that does not necessarily mean that professionals giving such attention are having an impact on the problems or issues their clients or patients came to see them about.

Despite these difficulties, in most professional fields there is a growing wish to ascertain what kinds of interventions are most 'effective'. This is exemplified by the emphasis on evidence-based medicine and effective schools, for instance. It has been widely recognised that 'meaning well and doing good' are not the same, since good intentions may have harmful or negligible results (McNeish and Newman 1996, p.55). This trend to assess what works and what does not is related to a wider political imperative towards accountability and the transfer into the public sector of commercially based practices like performance standards and indicators (Hutchison 1993; Clarke, Cochrane and McLaughlin 1994; Connor and Black 1994; Hegarty 1996). Services are expected to have quality assurance procedures (i.e. means of assessing whether specified standards of service delivery are adhered to), whilst various kinds of audit or evaluation are increasingly common to assess impact (Barker, Pitstrang and Elliott 1994). Politicians and managers are often particularly concerned with value for money and 'best value', but accountability to service users and the public means that they too are entitled to know whether they are likely to be helped or not when they see professionals.

This book is intended to review the state of knowledge about the effectiveness or otherwise of certain forms of intervention with respect to children and their families. As a first step it is necessary to explore rather more fully what is meant by effectiveness and how it might be assessed. This chapter considers different views about the significance of effectiveness, the feasibility of applying the concept widely and its relative importance compared with other considerations in service delivery. Finally a brief resume is offered of the following chapters which examine specific forms of service or intervention.

The meaning of effectiveness

Effectiveness generally refers to the extent to which desired goals are achieved and can be attributed to the programme itself (Rossi 1992; Schalock 1995). Goals normally involve some kind of change or improvement, such as new learning, more control over life circumstances, altered behaviour, fewer stresses or greater self-esteem. Thus two key elements are involved – assessing that change has occurred and establishing that the change would not have occurred anyway. Often it is also important to know whether a particular service made a difference compared with none or an alternative. Effectiveness thus differs from satisfaction with a service, although that may be a significant component in judging effectiveness.

One example of seeking criteria for judging effectiveness is the idea of 'effective schools'. This entails comparing how pupils in different schools fare, in terms of key educational aims such as academic achievement, orderly behaviour and social development, making allowances for the social and economic circumstances of their catchment areas. The concept of effective schools developed mainly in the United States as a response to a mix of political and social pressures, and a general trend towards greater accountability and value for money (CERI 1995). A concern to make schools more open and accountable to parents and the community has also been evident, though the views of pupils have generally taken a back seat (Macbeath 1994; Sinclair 1996). Research played a part too by demonstrating that schools in similar neighbourhoods with pupils of the same mix of class and ethnic backgrounds can produce very different levels of attendance, academic achievement, delinquency and employment (Power 1967; Rutter *et al.* 1979; Mortimore *et al.* 1988; Blyth and Milner 1997), though the capacity to offset socio-economic differences is only moderate (Scheerens 1989). A wide range of types of research evidence were used to develop profiles of effective schools. The aim was to identify a cluster of positive factors, rather than a single factor, which accounted for the apparent success of particular schools. Among the key elements were: strong leadership; a safe and orderly environment; high expectations by pupils and staff; value consensus; frequent monitoring of student progress; positive encouragement to learning; and good parent/community involvement (Scheerens 1989; Silver 1994; Reynolds *et al.* 1996). Other measures such as supporting vulnerable or inexperienced teachers and whole school behaviour policies can reduce instances of individual behaviour difficulties (Blyth and Milner 1997). Vital ingredients of success appear to be gaining joint agreement by head, staff, parents and pupils about school policies and rules. However, turning round schools which lack co-operation and a clear sense of purpose is not a simple task. Evaluations suggest that the changes 'have a much greater impact on academic performance, attendance and behaviour of pupils than on their propensity to commit offences outside school or after leaving school' (Asquith *et al.* 1998, p.19). As with residential care (Chapter 13), it is easier to alter the ways in which children act and feel within the establishment, than to produce modifications in behaviour which generalise to other contexts and last well into the future.

In general the effectiveness of an intervention is judged according to stated or intended aims, but it may also be vital to look at all the effects not only those which were wished for or anticipated. As we know from certain forms of medication, it can be important to assess whether side-effects outweigh the benefits in relation to the illness or condition. Interventions tend to have unintended consequences which need to be considered alongside the planned outcomes, as when young offenders in institutions learn skills and make friendships which assist in future law-breaking.

Further considerations are coverage and differential impact (or bias). This requires knowledge of whether a service helps most or all of the target population. Questions need to be asked if a significant proportion of potential users cannot gain access, do not take up the service or drop out. There are twin dangers. First, a service may only reach and help those who are most easily helped, because they are highly motivated to change and/or their problems are less serious. Second, the service may exclude or be much less accessible to certain groups, perhaps on grounds of poverty, language or cognitive ability (Chapter 11).

This links to another criterion for judging a service, namely *equity*. This refers to the extent to which a programme is equally available to all who need it and assists those who are initially disadvantaged as much as those who are advantaged. Thus, a key element of the effective schools movement in the 1980s was to try and ensure that children from poorer social backgrounds learned basic skills as well as their peers with higher socio-economic status (Silver 1994).

An important consideration in judging any intervention is not just whether it is working, but whether the degree of success justifies the costs: in other words are resources being efficiently used (Knapp and Fenyo 1995; Knapp and Lowin 1998)? Furthermore, benefits may include financial ones. For instance, day care enables parents to work and so improve family incomes and tax contributions. Good quality early education may increase the eventual earnings of the young participants. The availability of a range of family support services may improve the quality of child rearing and hence reduce the need for expensive long-term substitute care (Gibbons, Thorpe and Wilkinson 1990).

It is beyond the scope of this chapter and book to examine in detail the complex area of cost-benefit or cost-effectiveness analysis, but the relevance of cost assessment should be acknowledged. In cost-benefit analysis, both inputs and presumed benefits are converted into monetary values, whereas in cost-effectiveness analysis non-financial assessments of effects are considered alongside data on the costs. Something may work well but be considered too labour-intensive or too expensive to pursue. It is on-the-whole easier to estimate the financial resources required to sustain a project or agency than to put the impact into money terms (Breakwell, Hammond and Fife-Shaw 1995). Even so the costing of 'inputs' is often complex, because there are usually many indirect costs (Knapp 1997).

Ways of assessing effectiveness

Experimental and quasi-experimental designs

Evaluation is the term usually applied to research which 'is primarily concerned with describing and finding the effects of a particular approach, policy or programme' (Robson 1993, p.171).

Assessments of effectiveness need to be carried out in a way that ensures that any change or improvement which is detected can be reasonably attributed to the service, treatment or intervention being considered. *Post hoc* does not mean *propter hoc:* in other words if A follows B chronologically, that does not mean that B caused A, whether we are talking about an individual young person behaving differently after seeing a psychiatrist or an area having more leisure facilities after a new youth worker was appointed. It is necessary to use designs which rule out the possibility that apparent effects such as these are 'really' due to other factors, such as advice from a grandparent or a coincidental increase in the budget of a Recreation Department. In the natural sciences the experiment is one of the key methods for seeking to control (or rule out) the influence of competing factors and explanations, in order to show the impact of the particular factor under consideration (Breakwell *et al.* 1995).

The experimental method of assessment which is most robust and widely accepted for demonstrating effectiveness is the randomised controlled trial or RCT (Cnaan 1991; Macdonald 1996; Munro 1998; Chapters 2 and 5). This involves the random allocation of people to one of two groups. The first (experimental group) receives the service or treatment under consideration and the second (control group) receives no treatment. In some instances the control group has routine services while the experimental group has a special or additional service. The randomisation serves to ensure that the two groups should have the same range of characteristics and other influences, so that the only difference between them is the special treatment or service. Both groups are measured on relevant characteristics (ideally before and after the intervention) and any differences between the groups in the degree of change or the end-state can be attributed to the difference in intervention with reasonable confidence.

The importance of comparing the results of one group receiving a service with another group not receiving the service or receiving no service is that otherwise the improvements may be attributed to the intervention when they might have occurred anyway, perhaps as a result of other helping processes occurring at the same time, 'natural' recovery or benefits from the attention rather than the nature of the service. The further key advantage of randomisation is that it avoids potential bias, whether intended or accidental (Chalmers 1982; Juhl 1982; Oakley 1996). Otherwise, if people appear to benefit from a service, this may result from some advantage in their initial characteristics (e.g. being more highly motivated or responsive than others) which affected their exposure to that service. For example, much of the research which has purported to show why some schools and school systems do better than others has been bedevilled by criticisms that the outcomes were affected by the ability range of the intakes (good students went to good schools), which statistical controls can only partially take into account (Silver 1994). In medical trials, treatments are delivered 'blind', which means the doctor does not know which group the patient belongs to, in order to avoid deliberate or unintentional favouring of one group (Tygstrup, Lachin and Juhl 1982). In practice many social evaluations make use of assessments by people who are aware of their situation and may be biased in their reporting.

Further advantages of experimental designs include: the capacity to assess separate elements of a programme, for example by using different combinations of techniques in health education programmes; transparency and clarity of programme assessment; capacity for replication (Tones and Tilford 1994).

Where randomisation is not possible, matching the two groups on key characteristics can be used instead. Similarly it is not always possible to include pre-intervention measures, so only post-intervention comparisons are available. These methods are more open to influence by unidentified extraneous factors and so are known as quasi-experimental or sometimes pre-experimental (Campbell and Stanley 1966; Rossi and Freeman 1985; Macdonald, Sheldon and Gillespie 1992). Samples need to be of reasonable size, since the smaller the groups compared the bigger the effect which is needed to be identified as statistically significant (Page, Poertner and Lindbloom 1997). Also, interpretation of findings is seriously weakened when the groups compared are not identical in key respects (Maluccio 1997).

Even when studies are carried out following these principles, it is important to specify clearly the nature of the service being provided and its duration, so that it can be replicated. That sounds obvious, but often such details are not reported (Macdonald *et al.* 1992). Further it is valuable to know about the characteristics of those who used the service (e.g. age, gender, class, ethnicity), so that judgements can be made on whether some groups respond differently to others.

It may not be convenient to include a control or comparison group, so that in recent years single-case designs have become popular (Wilson 1995; Kazi 1998; Williams 1998). Instead of comparing differences between groups, usually across two or at most three points in time, this method charts changes in individual cases at frequent intervals as a treatment method is used. Ideally the 'treatment' is introduced, withdrawn, reintroduced and stopped again. If patterns of improvement correspond with the periods of treatment then this gives prima facie indication of the impact of that treatment. The results can be portrayed graphically, in both the literal and metaphorical senses, to show patterns of change. One of the attractions of the single-case design is that it avoids the need for random allocation or to obtain a large matched comparison sample, which is often difficult to achieve (Wilson 1995). This design has been mostly used to judge behaviour modification methods. Kazi and Wilson (1996) provide illustrations where a mother was helped to reduce the incidence of her daughter's 'bad' behaviour (e.g. ignoring requests, cheekiness, destructive actions) and in another case a child's crying in school substantially decreased. Among the measures which may be used to assess progress in relation to a target problem are administrative records (e.g. school register, immunisation record), standard scales (e.g. assessing self-esteem) and individualised criteria. The single-case design has the advantage of great adaptability to different circumstances and gives the practitioner a number of options as regards focus, measures and timing (Kazi 1996). The data can sometimes produce ambiguous results however, so the techniques should be used flexibly and critically (Levy 1996; Mattaini 1996; Rubin and Knox 1996).

An influential proponent of quasi-experimental methods is Thyer (1998), who accepts that many projects and individuals do not have the resources or circumstances which permit fully controlled comparisons. This means that they are not in a position to establish for sure that Action A definitely caused Result B, but can provide answers to more limited but nonetheless useful questions. He cites as an example knowing whether a foster placement programme was followed by an increase in placements which last. What is important is to ensure that a feasible and apt research design is chosen to acquire supportive evidence for any conclusions drawn.

Most experimental or quasi-experimental designs have been carried out on individuals or more occasionally families or groups. They are much more difficult to apply to larger groups, networks or communities. At this level of intervention, programmes tend to be complex, whilst the range of other possible factors which might influence outcomes is very large. Moreover, it will usually be prohibitively expensive to carry out measures across large populations in a sufficient number of areas to rule out the effects of geography, demography, other service inputs and so on. Often the best that can be done is to compare two or more similar neighbourhoods, generally using official statistics. Examples are given in Chapters 3, 4, and 7 of reductions in child abuse referrals and reported crime in areas subject to concerted community-based intervention, when similar nearby neighbour-hoods experienced neither the intervention nor the apparent decrease in problematic activity.

Critiques of quasi-experimental approaches

Although evaluations based on controlled quantitative comparisons are seen by many as the ideal way to judge success, they have also been criticised on epistemological, methodological, practical and ethical grounds. Some reject the basic assumptions altogether; others believe that it is wrong to rely on this approach alone.

Theoretical critiques doubt the wisdom of applying a natural science method to complex human interactions. The experimental methods derive from positivist ideas that social reality can be divided into fixed, objective and measurable elements, whose causal associations are best inferred from statistical analysis. In contrast, various kinds of social constructivist and post-modernist theoretical stances emphasise the importance of subjective meanings, the socially situated and interconnected nature of reality and the defects of abstract generalisations (May 1996; Flick 1998). The randomised controlled trial model derives very much from a clinical medical model (Cnaan 1991; Chalmers 1996) which sees problems as located in individuals whose conditions require treatment. This sits uneasily with social and anti-oppressive models of practice which regard public attitudes and social conditions as key causal influences and hence targets of action (Oliver 1996; Adams, Dominelli and Payne 1998). Furthermore, experimentation is seen as treating people as 'objects' (Tones 1997). Defenders claim that, on the contrary, parents and children can be very involved in the identification of targets and monitoring of progress in quasi-experimental research.

It is pointed out that the very tight requirements for randomised controlled trials and related designs not only make them inapplicable in many circumstances, but also restrict the notion of relevant information for judging success. Several critics have suggested that the quest for precise measurement and scientific rigour has resulted in trivial findings (Cheetham 1992; Munro 1998). Statistical rigour has been associated with results which are equivocal, confusing and of little help to policy-makers or practitioners (Brawley and Martinez-Brawley 1988).

Experiments and quasi-experimental designs also rely on standardising as far as possible all the potential influences other than the particular intervention being considered. The broader the target population and the wider the objectives, the more difficult this is to do. Moreover such activities as neighbourhood work and health promotion seek to work with the many contextual influences operating on individuals and families. Hence these approaches cannot be subjected to the same controlled assessment free of 'contaminating' influences as taking a tablet (Tones 1997). Many routine interventions are made up of a complex mix of activities often spread over a considerable period of time, and are not readily reducible to the notion of a single discrete treatment. Nevertheless quasi-experimental evaluations *have* been carried out on complex interventions. For example a combination of changes at policy, school, family and individual level were shown to produce a significant reduction in bullying (Olweus 1991).

The pragmatic objections to quasi-experimental methods using group comparisons, especially randomised controlled trials, include problems in gaining co-operation, the difficulties of achieving random allocation, small sample sizes and use of measures which may be insensitive to relevant changes. Most agencies have their own referral or eligibility criteria which they are understandably reluctant to alter to meet the needs of outside evaluation. Client and service provider preferences or matching may conflict with arbitrary allocation to one service or another (Burns 1994). The question of coverage is important – a service may help those who attend and persist, but large numbers may never gain access or may drop out (Chapter 5). Those most able to conform to randomised controlled trial requirements are likely to be special or demonstration projects which are hard to replicate in routine services (Tones 1998). Finding an appropriate control or matched comparison group can be difficult. Not uncommonly, programmes alter their goals or methods of operation during the course of evaluation. Indeed it can be argued that certain interventions should be responsive to their environment (including users' needs and wishes) which makes problematic the notion of a single uniform intervention which can be neatly judged, once and for all. This is recognised in the current emphasis on regular monitoring.

Defenders of experimental approaches acknowledge that they are difficult to achieve in routine circumstances, particularly randomised controlled trials, but nonetheless a number have been carried out, with helpful results (Macdonald 1996; Chapters 2, 5, 7, 10, 11). Proponents acknowledge that such studies need to be supplemented by a range of other evidence that has 'attributive confidence', which means that progress is carefully measured and competing explanations reasonably well explored or allowed for (Thyer 1998).

A wider point about effectiveness is the assumption, not necessarily accurate, that the intervention has explicit objectives and 'that these are clear and expressed in measurable form' (Fuller 1996, p.56). Fuller argues in favour of a pragmatic approach to effectiveness which takes into account any information which forms a vital part of the context for understanding the intervention, whether or not this fits with the idea of scientific proof.

An ethical argument is often put against experimental methods that it is not fair to deprive a control group of intervention. This may be countered by suggesting that if the positive effects have not yet been demonstrated they are not necessarily being deprived. However, in practice, professionals, users and relatives may be unwilling to forgo a service or the chance of an enhanced or additional programme.

At one level a fundamental philosophical rift can divide those who favour quantitative and especially experimental approaches and those who take a more interpretative or hermeneutic view of social reality. However, some degree of convergence can be seen in practice, since the former acknowledge the value of taking account of other kinds of study, whilst the latter can recognise that experimental studies have uses in certain areas.

Alternative approaches

Probably the most common alternative approach is some kind of survey, in which data is gained from a range of sources about measured or perceived outcomes of, for example, a number of schools or foster placements. Quite commonly the analysis takes the form of statistical association and the direction of influence is unclear. The value of surveys is strengthened when they are longitudinal, i.e. gather information at more than one point in time to plot continuities and changes. Then initial and follow-up characteristics of the children or families are assessed in relation to differences in the service input. For example, Howe (1998) reviewed evidence from a range of surveys about adoption and identified factors statistically associated with better outcomes, such as the stability of the child's previous relationships. Cohort studies have shown that parental commitment to children's education is often critical in enabling children brought up in adverse material circumstances to do well (Macdonald and Roberts 1995; Rutter 1995). On the other hand, long-term follow up of cohorts of disabled children have failed to identify any long-term effects of different types of early intervention (Beresford *et al.* 1996).

Some studies use existing administrative data, such as reported crime or examination results. With both survey and administrative data, it is often difficult to rule out the possibility that differences in outcome are affected by the nature of the samples. If sufficient information is available about the populations concerned, it is possible to take account of initial characteristics to separate their impact from that of the service itself, by using multi-variate statistical analysis. In this way it has been possible to identify the apparent impact of schools, making allowances for differences in the characteristics of their intakes (Rutter *et al.* 1979; Hutchison 1993).

Case studies set out to examine a wide range of evidence in relation to a single service or agency. Often both quantitative and qualitative data from a range of sources are obtained to provide a composite picture of how the service operates and of users' experiences. The case study approach is particularly well suited to project self-evaluation and practitioner research. Despite the evident potential problem of bias, a range of methods using agency records and generating new data can be used in a systematic way to produce useful findings (Cheetham *et al.* 1992; Connor 1993; Sommerlad and Willoughby 1995).

Comparative studies contrast two or more instances. Fuller (1992) described an interesting way of dealing with the difficulty of obtaining a comparison group. The progress of young children and young people attending an intensive family project was compared with anonymous predictions by expert assessors about what might have happened if no referral to the project had been made. Similarly, Farmer and Parker (1991) checked their own assessments of children returning home by obtaining views from a panel which included service users as well as professionals.

Both individual and comparative case studies can provide rich data about the service(s) provided, but it can be difficult to rule out competing explanations for changes apparently associated with participation. For example, if attendance at a nursery is followed by greater knowledge and sociability in the children and more self-confidence among the mothers, it cannot be demonstrated that these gains would not have occurred in families not using the centre or using some other kind of facility. It is also hard to know how a conclusion about a particular instance can be generalised to others. Nevertheless, case studies can provide useful pointers, especially if a range of studies produce convergent results. Case studies can help identify factors within a service which seem connected to success, especially those which examine 'outliers' – examples of exceptionally good or poor results (Scheerens 1989). They also provide rich detail which helps us to understand the interplay between different elements of a programme and the experiences of users. Case studies can employ some of the techniques associated with single-case design, for instance by incorporating measures of the extent of bullying or unauthorised absences in a school or levels of resident participation in local political or social activities.

Focus group discussions have been suggested as a way of assessing the effectiveness of, for example, educational materials (Lederman 1990; Holloway 1996). In the strict sense these do not demonstrate effects, but they can give access to the reported impact and provide detailed feedback about what participants believe works or does not work in a programme. Group meetings of users can contribute to definition as well as assessment of objectives. This may be best done separately from group discussion of professionals to avoid inhibition and distorting influences (Krogstrup 1997).

Evidence-based practice

In recent years the notion of 'evidence-based practice' has become common, especially in medicine but increasingly in other fields too. The basic tenet is that good practice ought to derive from research evidence about either the nature, causes and typical pathways of social problems or about the success of particular methods used to deal with those problems. For example, Chapter 6 includes a model for family mediation based on research findings about children's cognitive and emotional development. In relation to intervention, evidence is valued which demonstrates change, 'health gain' or some other kind of improvement (Tones 1998). The evidence-based practice movement also urges practitioners to seek out and assess relevant research literature, making judgements about the rigour of the sampling, methods and analysis (Evidence-based Medicine Working Group 1992; Reid 1994). This is not meant to replace practitioner or clinical judgements, but to support them. In addition, evidence-based practitioners should themselves collect data systematically, specify outcomes in measurable terms and systematically monitor and evaluate their interventions (Thyer and Wodarski 1998).

It is possible to obtain widespread support for the idea that professionals should ground their work in empirical evidence and few would disagree that account should be taken of good research. Also few would wish to defend activities which have no apparent effect.

However, some have expressed qualms about making research evidence the *sole* basis for developing or sustaining services. In many instances research may only give guidance about some aspects of intervention and not necessarily the most important ones. Also, it is argued that other considerations, including professional values, theoretical rigour, legislation and reflective processes, are just as important. Furthermore, total reliance on the tried and tested may inhibit innovation. An excessive reliance on research, especially quantitative research, can lead to neglect of the meaning, values and aims embodied in practitioner–user interactions (Shaw 1996; White 1998). Concentration on the impact of services on social problems may divert attention from tackling root causes of those problems.

Critics of the evidence-based movement also object to the viewpoint expressed by some that the randomised controlled trial is the 'gold standard' and that other forms of evidence are inferior or even worthless (Cheetham 1992; Tones 1998). This relates to the arguments noted above about what quasi-experimental approaches leave out of consideration, even though their value for carefully assessing specific elements of practice is acknowledged. Within social work the debate has also focused on the extent to which evidence is or should be mainly behaviourist (Reid 1994). Among others, Cheetham (1992) has argued in favour of having available a wide range of evaluation designs and methods, since 'the experimental method does not have a monopoly on disciplined analysis' (p.272). Munro (1998) argues that intuition, reflection and practice wisdom are not only inadequate but sometimes fallible and dangerous guides for action, as demonstrated in child abuse inquiries. She argues that it is important to seek evidence about daily practice which is valid and reliable, though using forms of assessment which extend beyond behavioural measures. The chapters in this book all reflect a commitment to the use of evidence, but vary in the kinds of evidence used and the weighting given to them.

One criticism of the emphasis on evidence about effectiveness is that the focus on actions or targets which are readily specified and measurable may cover only a limited part of the overall goals. It is important to know about examination results, which are most readily and increasingly used as an indicator of school success (CERI 1995), but they tell us little about other goals of education. They may also lead to policies based on measures which tackle 'symptoms' rather than root causes. For instance, pre-school or school-based strategies for dealing with poverty and social exclusion can be seen as leaving the reasons for disadvantage essentially untouched. 'The new climate, with its measurement- and outcomes-oriented policies for schools, meant the marginalising of concerns relating to schools' social environments, pointing away from the problems of impoverished families and neighbourhoods and at-risk children' (Silver 1994, p.157). Although the 'successful interventions' help some children overcome current adversity, they may do little to prevent future children and families being poor. This pre-supposes a largely structural explanation of poverty, for which research provides considerable support (Alcock 1993). Such ideas do not necessarily invalidate pleas to develop services with proven good outcomes, but suggest that they are not sufficient. The counterargument is that programmes like enriched pre-school education or effective schools provide the necessary employment and interactional skills to enable the next generation to avoid material and parenting difficulties.

An asset of outcome-based evidence is that it has chimed with trends toward greater accountability and notions of best value in public sector services. It is now expected that expenditure should be justified by measures of achievement rather than conviction that something is useful. At the same time, many practitioners are sceptical about or hostile to what they perceive as crude managerialism, with oversimplified performance indicators (Clarke *et al.* 1994; Shaw 1996). Some point to the fact that these are not merely neutral measures but have an impact themselves. For example, in education the pressure on schools to produce good results is thought to have contributed to the rise in exclusions (Blyth and Milner 1993; Berridge *et al.* 1996).

Research on effectiveness does carry weight in itself, since it appeals to those who put faith in systematic evidence, but its influence is also affected by the receptiveness of policy-makers, managers and practitioners. 'Research evidence is only one fragment of evidence available to those who make judgements' (Silver 1994, p.162). Research evidence itself indicates that many front-line professionals (e.g. in nursing, teaching and social work) make little use of formal research evidence and are resistant to quantitative approaches (Graham 1996). Instead they rely on a complex mix of reflection on cumulative experience, identified changes in individual clients, observations of commonly recognised good practitioners and informal feedback (Elks and Kirkhart 1993; Shaw and Shaw 1997; Cheetham *et al.* 1998).

A final point is that if practice were to rely on experimental evidence alone, the evidence is often meagre or absent altogether. As Fitz-Gibbon (1996) observed in relation to education research 'You would hardly have any reading to do if you read only randomised trials' (p.104).

Measuring outcomes

Assessing effectiveness entails making judgements about the outcomes of professional activities. The term outcome is rather ambiguous. On the one hand it may refer to something which simply follows intervention, and may or may not be caused by it. In this sense it is legitimate to talk about the long-term outcomes of most careers of children in public care as being poor, since many encounter poverty, unemployment and relationship problems (Quinton and Rutter 1988; Biehal *et al.* 1995). Yet these problems may owe as much to the factors which led the children to be placed away from home in the first place, including poverty, poor education and disturbed attachment histories, as to the care experiences themselves (Heath, Colton and Aldgate 1994). On the other hand the word outcomes may appear to presuppose or imply *causation*, so that reference to the outcomes of, say, counselling or an education campaign can easily be taken to mean their effects. Nevertheless, the word is now widely used in this context and will be retained here to refer to an achieved state at the end of or some time after intervention, even though the issue of causation may be uncertain or the subject of investigation.

Whatever design is used, it is still necessary to use one or more means of measuring what happened, that is, the outcome. The form of measurement need not be quantified, since in some circumstances the presence or absence of something might be sufficient. For example, if an objective of professional activity is to set up a school council or young people's forum, the creation of such a body may be an adequate indicator of success. Usually, though, it is desirable to go beyond that – perhaps to identify how representative membership is or to assess the activities of the council or forum and their impact on participants. Similarly a nursery place may be said to fulfil its function of providing care while parents work as long as children are attending, but indications of the quality of care or indeed the consequences for parents are also of vital interest. By and large numerical data add precision in ascertaining impact, whereas qualitative data add depth to understanding how or why the effects occurred (Vaughn, Schumm and Sinagub 1995).

Commonly a distinction is made between client and service outcomes. The former refers to the results for populations or samples of clients, whereas the latter correspond to the global products of a programme, project or agency – which include but are not confined to client impacts. Neighbourhood studies may entail a mix of criteria by which baseline data about needs, informal relationships and formal services are compared with subsequent developments (Barr, Hashagen and Purcell 1996).

Service outcomes refer to 'the nature, extent and quality of what is provided' (Cheetham 1992, p.276). For example, in relation to family placements away from home, Sellick and Thoburn (1996) cite as examples of service outcome measures:

- the proportion of requests for respite care which led to receipt of a service
- the proportion of adoption placements which break down within a specified time scale
- the frequency of children's comfortable contacts with family and friends.

An important component of service outcomes is the extent to which the target populations are served. Conversely, it is valuable to know how far certain groups may be under-represented.

Four main types of criteria have been used to assess outcomes at the client level (See also Parker *et al.* 1991; Hill *et al.* 1996):

1. Are aims achieved?

2. Is the development or functioning of the child improved?

3. What are the views of participants?

4. What is the status or living situation of the child subsequently?

The first concerns stated *goals or expectations* (e.g. to help a depressed adolescent become happier or to reduce bullying levels in a school). Here success occurs if the aims have been fulfilled.

Two questions immediately arise from this – who decides what the goals are and how? Are the relevant goals those of service managers, professionals, external agencies (like the courts), children, parents or some combination of these? It is important to assess programmes at least partly in terms of an agency's aims and objectives, which may of course include notions of empowerment at different levels. Identifying precisely what a service or programme is intended to achieve is often not straightforward. Even official goals may not be stated clearly at the outset; they may be multiple, and different members of the organisation may have diverse and even conflicting expectations. Funders or councillors, senior managers and other staff may well hold different views. A further common problem is that often goals change over time, for example in response to the wishes of referral agencies or as a result of learning from experience.

If only the views of service providers count as valid, however, there are dangers that the aims and outcomes are assessed in terms of compliance to authority. Behaviourism has been criticised for imposing conformity, although defenders assert that, normally, behavioural targets are reached by agreement. For instance, children can be helped to learn communications skills which enable them to be more sociable or resist unwanted overtures (Wodarski 1998). Parents of pre-school children can gain in confidence and self-esteem when they have learned skills and techniques which help them to better manage emotional or behavioural difficulties in their children (Page *et al.* 1997).

Rather than seek an illusory common set of objectives, it may often be more appropriate to acknowledge that multiple perceptions and objectives co-exist, even within one organisation and even more so when the views of service users and other interested parties are taken into account (Smith and Cantley 1985). Many now recognise the value of obtaining the perspectives of key stakeholders besides agency representatives, and establishing their views about what should be achieved. 'Evaluations should serve the interests not only of the sponsor but also of larger society, and of various groups within society, particularly those most affected by the program under review' (House 1993, p.128). Children's lack of power and status (Qvortrup *et al.* 1994) may mean that their contribution to defining goals is ignored, devalued or difficult to express. However, certain interventions like youth work place high priority on working to a young person's agenda (Williamson 1993).

Many of the helping professions define their goals in terms of producing changes in children, parents or families, hopefully for the better. It is also important to recognise that desired outcomes may take other forms. For instance, the goal may be a change in public policy (e.g. as regards corporal punishment), the local environment (e.g. provision of safe play areas) or public attitudes (e.g. about racism). Targeting action at wider influences on a large number of families may be more effective in the long run than tackling each manifestation of a common problem individually.

Nor should ideas about outcome dominate assessment of success at the expense of considering the processes by which goals are established and achieved. Empowerment models of evaluation are partly about process and partly about outcomes. User participation in determining the nature and aims of a service or a research study is seen as an important consideration in itself (Barr *et al.* 1996; Fetterman, Kaftarian and Wandersman 1996; Drewitt 1997). This approach is based partly on notions of citizen's rights (everyone is entitled to respect and participation) and partly on well-documented findings that individuals who feel good about themselves and in control of their lives tend to have more satisfying and healthier lifestyles (Tones 1998). Small-scale but exciting developments have taken place which involve children and young people in setting research agendas and helping carry out studies (Alderson 1995; Liverpool 8 Children's Research Group 1997). Furthermore, indicators of empowerment such as greater self-confidence, enhanced independence and capacity to exercise choices and make important decisions can constitute the criteria for success, as in relation to health promotion or community work initiatives (Tones and Tilford 1994). Writing particularly in relation to children with disabilities, Mithaug (1996) argues that schools should be judged not simply according to children's scholastic achievements, but also in terms of enhanced opportunities, capacities and self-determination. Among the advantages and conclusions of qualitative evaluation is that understanding of processes may be very valuable to key stakeholders and that participants may benefit in unexpected ways from involvement in a project or indeed in an evaluation (Patton 1990; 1998).

The second kind of criteria are those which refer to a child's *developmental progress*. In some instances, it is the main aim to enhance the child's development. The Assessing Outcomes Project promoted by the Department of Health in the late 1980s identified seven core dimensions which have now been developed in the Looking After Children programme (Ward 1995; 1996). These dimensions are:

- health
- education
- emotional and behavioural development
- family and social relationships
- self-care
- identity
- self-esteem.

A number of standardised and validated scales are available which can be used to compare a child's progress with the 'normal' population of a similar age. Besides identifying children with achievements which fall well behind the average for their age, these also serve to indicate those whose behaviour causes concern to others, for example as a result of aggression or stealing. Amongst the scales most commonly used are the Rutter and Achenbach scales designed to identify emotional and behavioural difficulties (Rutter, Tizard and Whitmore 1970; Achenbach and Edelbrock 1981). The 'Strengths and Difficulties' scale is shorter and more even-handed in identifying positive aspects of children as well as problems (Goodman 1997). Likewise, measures of self-esteem range considerably in length and complexity (Rosenberg 1979; Coopersmith 1990). These are intended for school-age children and alternatives are available for younger children (Richman, Stevenson and Graham 1982). Rapid assessment tools have been developed which are specific and reliable (Wodarski 1998). Also 'one of the most remarkable advances in health status measurements in the last few years has been the development of Quality of Life Measurement scales for children and adolescents' (Rodriguez and Bowen 1998, p.26), though these often do not take good account of people's own health priorities.

Some scales are completed by the children themselves, notably those assessing self-esteem and fears. Others are completed by teachers, psychologists, psych-iatrists or social workers, either based on their existing knowledge of the child or by means of a one-off assessment. Parents or other carers may also provide information or ratings. When the views of different parties converge, this gives greater confidence in the measures used (Millham *et al.* 1986). On the other hand, sometimes very different assessments are provided, and then interpretation is difficult (Triseliotis *et al.* 1995). Either a judgement has to be made about who is the best informed or else the absence of an agreed objective reality recognised. Similarly it is often difficult to assess the accuracy of self-reports on behaviour such as criminal activity or substance misuse, which have been used in a number of evaluations.

The third set of criteria refer to *client or user evaluations*. These include but are not confined to indicators of satisfaction. It is well known that the majority of users of most services tend to report satisfaction and that this often bears little relationship to whether they have been helped or not, so this in itself is an unreliable guide to success (Rees 1992; Breakwell *et al.* 1995). Parents and children may be asked to give more specific evaluations, such as whether an intervention benefited the child, met his or her needs and lasted as long as appropriate (Rowe, Hundleby and Garnett 1989; Triseliotis *et al.* 1995). A study of youth provision asked young people what attracted them to different youth facilities, what they thought they learned and how much involvement they had in making decisions (Love and Hendry 1994). Feedback about particular professionals can provide illuminating data about what qualities young people find helpful, including empathy, confidentiality, being listened to and the use of ordinary language (Farnfield 1998; Hill 1998). It is also important to invite comment on negative experiences. Evidently, these invite fairly broad subjective appraisals, but nonetheless represent the views of the key participants.

The fourth criteria comprise various kinds of *service and placement measures* (Parker *et al.* 1991). Thus it is generally considered a poor outcome if a young person ends up in prison or secure accommodation. Likewise needing to access special rather than mainstream schooling may be seen as a sign of difficulties. For young people in foster or residential care, the breakdown of a placement has often been used as a negative indicator (Chapters 12 and 13). In North America a standardised Restrictiveness Scale has been developed, which classifies living situations like parental home, foster home and residential school according to the presumed freedom and access to normal community activities (Hawkins *et al.* 1992). Although this has some merit in helping to chart careers, the restrictiveness approach is an oversimplification. The same kind of setting may be experienced as restrictive or not depending on the particular child or regime. Equally important, restrictive settings like secure units and/or psychiatric in-patient units, although not desirable as long-term residences, have proved helpful for some young people who have fared poorly in less open settings (Harris and Timms 1993).

Since each type of outcome criterion has merits and drawbacks, it seems sensible to advocate that wherever possible evaluations should use multiple measures which take account of more than one view point.

Processes and outcomes

A common distinction is commonly made in evaluation between a summative evaluation (which assesses inputs and outcomes) and a formative evaluation (which assesses the processes entailed in the intervention) (Robson 1993). The word 'process' in this context simply refers to all the events and factors affecting how a service operates. On the one hand it may entail qualitative understanding of the social interactions involved. On the other hand, it may also refer to key elements or inputs to a service which can be expressed quantitatively, for example, length of wait until service starts; frequency of user–professional contacts (Pietrzak *et al.* 1990; Crombie and Davies 1998). It is also possible to estimate how often particular techniques like giving encouragement or teaching impulse control are used. For instance one study established a statistical association between the usage of certain techniques (problem clarification, crisis intervention and conflict management) and success in enabling children in foster and residential care to return home (Lewis, Walton and Fraser 1995).

Understanding of processes helps show which elements are contributing to the assessed results or not. It is also important to know the extent to which a service is actually being provided in a way which corresponds with official plans or accounts. Services and treatments are sometimes not operating as they should, as when faulty assessments are made or inappropriate prescription of drugs occurs. Lack of success does not always mean that the nature of the intended service is wrong, if it has not been provided in the required manner as a result of inadequate resources or training. For all these reasons, it can be valuable to carry out studies to establish exactly what happens and how.

The quality of the processes may form part of the explicit or implicit goals. For example, it is part of the ethical codes of caring professions that people should be treated with dignity and respect. In certain activities like youth work and community work part of the aim is to empower people and ensure that participation is optimised throughout (Barr *et al.* 1996). Hence any project needs to be assessed on the extent to which the relevant population were enabled to participate in setting and implementing goals and to develop such characteristics as confidence, leadership skills and useful knowledge. A 'ladder of participation' is sometimes used as a set of criteria for measuring the degree of involvement. The ladder can apply to any service users (e.g. parents), but one version (see Figure 1.1) has been applied to children's rights to involvement (Arnstein 1969; Hart 1992).

Thus the creation of clubs, groups and organisations which are run or partly run by young people themselves can be seen as an achievement within community work (Hulyer 1997), though clearly it is important to then go on and assess whether the participants experience benefits in their lives, as well as who gains and who does not.

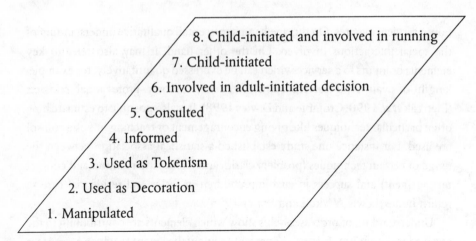

Figure 1.1 The ladder of participation

Other considerations

Even if evaluation uses a good design and appropriate and precise measures of outcomes and processes, that is not the end of the story. Timing of assessment is a major issue. Often immediate benefits are not sustained. The history of custodial measures is replete with evidence that reductions in law-breaking associated with removal from home soon give way to renewed or even greater levels of criminal activity on return (Cornish and Clarke 1975). Likewise, some children who returned home from residential and foster care initially appeared to do well, but later experienced abuse or neglect (Farmer and Parker 1991). The Portage system and other early intervention programmes to assist disabled children have been shown to have positive short-term benefits, but the long-term impact on intellectual development and academic achievements is much less apparent (Beresford *et al.* 1996). Such short-lived results in which early gains do not last are sometimes known as wash-out effects. It is also possible for sleeper effects to occur whereby benefits become apparent only in the longer run. For example, a Tasmanian evaluation of parent education programmes found that attendance was associated with increased self-confidence compared with non-attendance, but the impact on parent–child interaction only became noticeable some months later (Barber 1992). Moreover, effects may be mediated by later events. For instance the experiences of a sample of women brought up in residential care depended greatly on their access to a partner or confidant in early adulthood (Quinton and Rutter 1988). Assessment of long-term outcomes is difficult for both practical reasons and because of the effects of intervening events.

Methods or programmes of intervention may have unintended consequences. Thus it is important not only to assess whether planned results occurred, but also to examine the wider impact. In the use of medication, unpleasant side-effects may offset any benefits gained in relation to the problem or disorder being treated (Anthony, Lancashire and Creed 1991; Chapter 10).

A feature of service provision which has received relatively little attention is the question of which kinds of people use the service and also who drops out. Commonly research on 'what works' has tended to reach blanket conclusions, without specifying whether something works less well or perhaps not at all for some individuals or categories of people. It is important that consideration is given to identifying who 'drop out', i.e. stop attending, and why (see for example Chapter 10). A facility may work well for those who attend, but others may have difficulty gaining access. It may 'fail' a number of people who do attend initially but then stop using the service and so may not be taken into account in evaluation. This means that close attention should be made to the selection, referral and access processes of a service (Hudson and Williams 1991). One of the problems traditionally faced by family therapy has been that many potential clients have been put off by its mode of operation and so have not taken up the service, hence current attempts to develop a more 'user-friendly' approach (Reimers and Treacher 1995; Chapter 8).

Feedback from young people, especially those with histories of relationship difficulties, indicates that they often find it hard to trust formal services or specialist professionals and so refuse to comply with a referral or to keep in contact after one or two appointments (Triseliotis *et al.* 1995; Farnfield 1998). For this reason, sometimes the best option to reach some alienated young people will be through youth, community and outreach work using skills to build up trusting mutual relationships, which can form the basis for either direct counselling or referral elsewhere (Chapter 9). Consumer surveys have shown that young people think they gain a number of practical and recreational skills from attending youth facilities. However, the most vulnerable (e.g. offenders, school non-attenders) are least likely to participate in organised youth activities (Love and Hendry 1994; Powney *et al.* 1997).

The discussion so far has highlighted the need for evaluation of effectiveness to take account of varied types of evidence, criteria of success and viewpoints. This is reflected in the chapters that follow, both individually and collectively.

Summary of following chapters

The topics covered by the ensuing chapters were chosen to give a broad range of approaches, service types and targets of intervention. Some relate to ways of working directly with children or young people, some to work with families as a whole, whilst others combine the two. No claim is made to comprehensiveness, though hopefully a good spread of the major forms of intervention is included. Certain issues or categories of children were not included since these have been dealt with in recent volumes of the same series, for example crime (Asquith 1996) and children affected by disability (Stalker and Robinson 1998).

Given the varied aims and functions of professional activity, the diversity of views about effectiveness and also the uneven availability of research findings, it was considered important to include contributors from a range of backgrounds and to take an inclusive view of what might constitute evidence for effectiveness. Amongst the disciplines represented are psychology, social work, psychiatry, education, community work and family mediation.

The book as a whole is intended to include material about working with individual children, groups of children and/or members of children's families (nuclear and extended). The term 'children' embraces young people up to the age of 18, as in the UN Convention on the Rights of the Child.

Each contributor was asked to concentrate within their topic area on ways of working which appear to succeed or work well. No precise prescription was given about what might constitute evidence for success, but authors were encouraged to draw on systematic external evaluations whenever possible and to be clear about the sources of their claims. As far as possible emphasis has been placed on demonstrated benefits, but in a number of areas the literature and precise evidence is largely lacking, so on some topics other kinds of research and practice evaluations are drawn on. In general terms, carefully controlled positivist evidence is available mainly with respect to interventions targeted on individuals with very specific aims, whereas methods of working on a larger canvas with families and especially networks and communities are harder to assess in this way, so other kinds of evidence have been brought to bear.

In order to give some degree of standardisation and comparability between chapters, it was suggested that each cover the following:

- a summary of the key elements of the method, service or approach under consideration and the contexts in which it is relevant
- a brief account of theoretical underpinnings of the approach
- discussion of the types of evidence available, noting limitations
- key findings of relevance to practitioners
- if possible, indications about which kinds of child or family the approach might be most suitable for
- implications for practice, service delivery and policy.

Earlier chapters deal with more general approaches to working with children and their families, while later chapters concentrate on particular kinds of children.

First, in Chapter 2, Roberts and Macdonald review work with families in the early years. Whilst acknowledging the value of qualitative research, they emphasise the need to maximise the use of robust evidence, particularly by means of the randomised controlled trial. The authors note that certain kinds of early years nursery centres have been shown to have long-lasting benefits, though they stress these should also be valued for the here-and-now pleasure children experience. The interventions with the most clear-cut effects were those which were carefully targeted, used well structured programmes and covered a significant period of a child's life. The observed benefits extend beyond education and social skills to include, in the longer term, reduced likelihood of criminal activity and enhanced employment achievements.

As well as children's attendance at centres, another form of intervention involves supportive and educational visiting to parents – usually mothers. These have been able to address both general parenting skills and specific issues, like diet and immunisation. Again it seems that enduring contact is most effective. Parent training programmes based on social learning and skill development principles are helpful, but families with the greatest difficulties are the least likely to attend or respond well.

Chapter 3, by Gilligan, stresses the value of considering and involving children's wider social networks in assessment, planning and intervention. Agencies and projects which work individually or collectively with network members beyond the nuclear family are not common, and even fewer have been evaluated, so the chapter reviews evidence about the significant and often positive role that people other than parents or professionals can have for children. American research has demonstrated how children brought up in very adverse social and economic circumstances can nevertheless do well if they have encouragement, help and support from one or more relatives or other significant adults. Gilligan reviews network functions, for example to prevent, moderate or alleviate stress; provide information, advice and support; enhance children's sense of identity and belonging. He also examines the implications of structural characteristics like size, connectedness and perceived support.

Largely anecdotal accounts suggest that network meetings can be successful in resolving family problems and avoiding the need for court action, though there are dangers of idealising networks which can of course include negative and destructive relationships. A survey of family group conferences indicated that the majority produced stable plans in response to professional concerns about child care and were positively regarded by both professionals and family members. A Canadian project which strengthened the networks of vulnerable parents was associated with reduced levels of reported child abuse compared with a similar neighbourhood. Certain organisations seek to simulate naturally-occurring support by linking young people or families to others who take on mentoring or befriending roles.

Whereas Gilligan reviewed the role of personal networks of individual children, Henderson considers, in Chapter 4, the relationships and activities of children and young people within a community or neighbourhood context. Community work has traditionally promoted bottom-up collective action, especially amongst poor people, but has also responded to opportunities arising from central and local government regeneration initiatives. Little evaluative research has been done in this area, although a number of case studies have been carried out. Such ethnographic research is more consistent with the holistic philosophy of community work than more quantitative forms of evaluation. An early study highlighted the complexity of needs and interests which can be involved, since a project which was positively regarded by young people aroused hostility from some local residents.

Henderson notes that a number of writers simply assume that projects like play schemes are worthwhile and argues that there is a need to produce more systematic outcome assessments, though this should be done in a way which does justice to the multiple, integrated goals which community workers typically pursue. Furthermore, it follows from community work principles that as far as possible relevant community members should be engaged in defining research aims and in subsequent stages of evaluation, as has happened in Liverpool 8. Thorough studies using standard measures have demonstrated the value of neighbourhood-oriented family centres and shown how areas with varied and open facilities can reach a wider section of the population and increase voluntary activity. Participative work with the local community has been accompanied by reduction in child abuse registrations, though other factors may have played a part in this. Children value being consulted about developments in their area. This can be seen as a positive benefit in itself, although it may raise further expectations about changes in services which may or may not be fulfilled. Henderson sets out a research agenda which should focus on social, organisational and policy barriers and opportunities affecting children's well-being and participation.

In contrast, Chapter 5 examines forms of intervention targeted directly on children and families themselves, for which there is a comparatively rich supply of systematic research evidence, some using randomised controlled trials or matched comparison groups. Here Gough considers a range of approaches derived from psychological theories of how individuals learn, think and behave. These form the basis of a range of techniques aimed at helping children or their parents modify 'maladaptive' behaviour or learn to act in a more socially acceptable way. Although often seen as directive, many programmes seek to define their goals in partnership with family members. Gough notes that both the resulting treatments and the associated research share a commitment to precise identification of targets and tasks. The evidence is in many ways clear and impressive that such interventions can be very effective, though Gough cautions that the findings tend to focus on statistical rather than clinical significance and that studies have more often investigated special rather than routine practice. Also benefits observed in one setting do not necessarily generalise to others, whilst drop-out rates can be high (see also Chapter 10).

Problem-solving and social skills training have been shown to work well, especially with older children and with those whose problems are not deep-rooted. Programmes which teach parents how to manage their children better have been shown to be effective in many cases. Again, less 'promising' parents who are severely disadvantaged or isolated are least likely to respond well. Combining attention to both children's and parents' skills seems most successful. Certain specific problems can be relieved using appropriate methods (e.g. cognitive-behavioural treatment for depression; relaxation and modelling for phobias). It seems that sometimes combining methods increases the impact, whilst in other instances the effects of individual techniques may be diluted.

Learning methods have sometimes been applied to (nuclear) families as a whole, but are most often used with individuals or pairs. The next two chapters deal with approaches whose primary focus is the family unit. In Chapter 6 Robinson discusses mediation services which have become increasingly available to assist families dealing with parental separation or divorce. Services originally concentrated on the parents, although often with plans for the children as a central consideration. Nowadays children may be more directly involved, though usually that depends on parental initiative or willingness. Guidelines emphasise that parents retain responsibility for communication with their children.

A study carried out in Newcastle established the value of having regular stages in the mediation process: to establish the arena for discussion; clarify what the key issues are; explore each issue; develop a plan; and secure agreement. Canadian research has indicated that mediation can achieve positive results, but is not likely to work when one or both partners exhibit overwhelming distress, extreme rigidity or obsessive preoccupation with a rejecting spouse. Based on a combination of clinical experience and empirical evidence (including child development research), Robinson outlines a stage-related framework for understanding children's reactions to divorce. In line with evidence about resilience given in Chapter 3, it has been demonstrated that children's adaptation following parental divorce is related to the availability of support within their social networks. Shared parenting following divorce works best when parents have a low level of conflict and are committed to each partner having a substantial caring role.

Vetere defines family therapy as seeking to modify family relationships as a whole (Chapter 7). Although a wide range of models exist, they have in common an emphasis on the interconnectedness of family relationships, their evolving nature and the interactions with wider social systems, including the therapist. Since the family is the context for sustaining problems, this is seen as the appropriate level of intervention. Nonetheless, a comparatively small proportion of family problems are referred to family therapists. Higher proportions of children with identified behaviour problems are referred than those with emotional problems. It is interesting that few children refer themselves and many parents who are referred do not accept conventional family therapy but want other kinds of information or help, suggesting a mismatch between what is on offer and what family members want. As a result, efforts have been made recently to develop more 'user-friendly' approaches.

It has been shown that family therapy can produce beneficial changes compared with individual approaches and with control groups receiving no service. Knowledge is more limited about the differential effects of the varied ways in which family therapy operates. Families where there is much self-blame tend to respond better to supportive than challenging therapist styles. Feedback from young people indicates that most value having individual attention alongside family sessions.

Vetere concurs with Gough (Chapter 5) that parent-training management has produced sustained improvements at home and school for families with pre-adolescent children who have behaviour problems. However, she adds that where behaviour or other problems are embedded in a wider mix of issues, a more systemic approach is needed and has indeed been shown to enhance effectiveness (e.g. in relation to anorexia). Vetere notes that some forms of therapy are very expensive, because of the intensive deployment of staff, use of special equipment and/or operating from a residential or hospital base. Thus, comparative costs need to be considered together with treatment outcomes.

Outside the home, the main place where children spend time and where difficulties may manifest themselves is the school. In Chapter 8 Lloyd and Munn explore the results of schools' strategies for dealing with pupils who have social, emotional or behavioural difficulties. As with community work, the main form of evidence available has been the case study. Whilst other chapters concentrate on serious difficulties like depression or anorexia, it is pointed out that many teachers find it hardest to cope with minor but persistent actions by pupils who are in most respects little different from their peers. Consequently, whole school or whole class approaches are at least as likely to make a difference as measures which single out individual pupils.

Systems for rewarding positive behaviour and achievements appear to be successful. Special units and support staff can be helpful not only in giving additional assistance to particular students, but also in influencing the wider school ethos. Some teachers welcome behavioural packages which assert directive discipline, whilst others prefer more humanistic approaches aiming to develop children's self concepts, self-esteem and hence, it is hoped, self-control. The use of circle time in primary school has been observed by parents and teachers to reduce 'difficult' behaviour. The authors describe concerns about the growing use of medication to control behaviour like overactivity. They conclude with a plea for strategies which are inclusive (i.e. do not stigmatise and segregate certain pupils) and for assessing effectiveness through the eyes of parents and pupils, as well as teachers and external experts.

Youth work has a diversity of forms and functions, but is primarily concerned to engage with young people outside the home and outside school. In Chapter 9, Bradford begins by outlining tensions within youth work. Its ideals embrace voluntary, participatory practice to promote personal development and education. In particular it seeks to engage with those who are seen by adults as 'at risk' and/or alienated, many of whom are generally suspicious of adults in formal roles. Aims also include increasing social responsibility and countering discriminatory attitudes – goals which may conflict with the wishes and views of some young people.

The diffuseness of youth work's aims mean that evaluation is not straight-forward. Information, advice and counselling are integrated with everyday conversations and activities in ways which make it hard to distinguish their effects, though many young people do seem responsive to this approach. Survey evidence about young people's views indicate they value youth services for providing three main things which are otherwise difficult to obtain: safe space for peer interaction; relationships with adults who accept them on their own terms; and enjoyable activities. Settings which provide entertainment and social interaction are much more attractive to them than educational or treatment settings. In such places youth workers can broach lifestyle topics and health promotion issues like drugs and sex which many young people are only prepared to discuss in this kind of context. Much hope and speculation has been expressed about youth work's preventative role in relation to crime, but little hard evidence exists. Nevertheless at least one project has been accompanied by reduced self-report and police crime figures, as well as a reduction in community fears about crime.

Whereas youth work operates on an outreach and open access basis for a wide range of young people, child and adolescent psychiatry services (Chapter 10) usually respond to external referrals for individuals whom professionals identify as having significant mental health problems. As a result of the medical tradition, much evidence is available from randomised controlled trials or approximations to them. Whilst acknowledging their value, Barton also points out the limitation that many of the studies were not carried out on typical practice, did not provide a comprehensive assessment of outcomes and omitted important perspectives, including those of children. They are also difficult to apply and expensive.

Barton documents the strong evidence that cognitive-behavioural therapy, which alters thinking patterns and habitual actions, is very effective in tackling children's overactivity, aggression and anxiety. As indicated in Chapters 2 and 5, behaviourally based parenthood training and pre-school programmes are effective, especially if intensive and sustained. The results of psychotherapy are inconclusive. Like Lloyd and Munn (Chapter 8), Barton acknowledges the controversial nature of drug treatments. These do reduce overactivity, though not general aggressiveness. Antidepressants have poor results and a question mark is also put against the effects of stimulants. Given the risks of side-effects and the efficacy of other methods, any use of drugs needs to be very circumspect.

In general, evidence about specific psychiatric interventions is quite good (less so with adolescents), but Barton notes the difficulties in assessing 'whole service' strategies, multiple programmes and inter-agency collaboration. Thus these medical services combine some of the convincing techniques of behavioural psychology in relation to certain particular behaviours (Chapters 5 and 11) with the under-assessment of more complex and wider goals witnessed in community work, youth work and whole-school approaches (Chapters 4, 8 and 9).

In Chapter 11, Murray turns our attention to a group of children whose serious difficulties and needs have only received concerted attention in the last ten years or so – those who have been sexually abused. She notes that child sexual abuse is sadly much more common than many people realise and can have severe effects on many aspects of a child's life, though most of the children affected do recover well. Delayed effects are not uncommon. Approaches to helping children overcome the emotional and behavioural effects are based on a number of psychological theories concerned with learning, cognition, development and attachment. Children themselves value adult responses which are experienced as warm, honest and inclusive. Murray notes that one of the advantages of cognitive approaches is that children and parents can decide whether to take part or not on the basis of clear, explicit information.

According to Murray, much of the research evidence in this area has not compared interventions with proper control groups and so is inconclusive. Even when results show differences in group means or trends in support of a general approach to treatment, this may be of little help to practitioners who need to know more about individual variations in responsiveness to particular elements of programmes. Nonetheless, the evidence suggests that the ill-effects of abuse are reduced if children participate in group work. Both individual and group approaches appear to work well when they help children to think differently about the abuse and its causes, particularly to recognise that it is the abuser and not the child who is responsible. Involvement in the treatment of the non-abusing parent (usually the mother) also helps children. It seems however that treatments which stress cognition may be of little help to children with learning difficulties or communication problems, whilst in one study black parents found a service did not fit with their expectations and so were reluctant to co-operate.

The following two chapters of the book consider children who are placed away from home. In Chapter 12, Berridge starts by saying that foster care has received comparatively little research and policy attention in recent years compared with residential care. Since the children placed in foster care tend to include higher proportions who are older and have significant difficulties than in the past, earlier evaluations may not be relevant to the current situation. In view of the paucity of external evaluations of effectiveness, Berridge argues that developments should be based on a combination of available research knowledge and the experience of reflective practitioners.

The outcome measures used in fostering research have usually consisted of percentages of placement breakdowns and the perceptions of key participants. These have their limitations, but can act as partial markers of success or failure. Influences on these outcomes are usually grouped into child, carer and agency factors. Studies have repeatedly shown that placements of older children and those with behaviour difficulties are more prone to premature endings and reports of dissatisfaction. The risks of breakdown are also high when two children of the same age are in the same foster household. Fostering by relatives has a good record – a point which supports Gilligan's plea to attend more to the wider family when considering resources for children in need (Chapter 3). Frequent contact between fostered children and their birth parents is a good predictor of both well-being and the likelihood of return home, though of course this is likely to reflect a better parent–child relationship in the first place. It appears that pre-placement preparation and in some circumstances a prior residential placement can increase the chances of a placement lasting as long as planned. There is no simple recipe for successful foster carers, as they are a diverse group, but research indicates that flexibility and resilience are helpful characteristics. Feeling supported by social workers and having adequate financial remuneration are also important.

Bullock echoes Berridge in commenting that young people entering residential care nowadays nearly always have significant emotional or behavioural problems (Chapter 13). Often time spent in a residential unit or school is part of a sequence of living situations within a complex care career so it is hard to differentiate the impact of one particular placement. Most research has considered long-stay homes. The majority of those who experience residential care give positive feedback about it. At its best, it provides stable care and remedial education, though this can be diminished by staff discontinuity. Like day schools, different residential units have persistent differences in outcomes, suggesting the importance of intake and regime. In general, caring regimes appear to produce better results than punitive ones, though the near absence of rules and controls is also unhelpful.

Bullock stresses the importance of distinguishing immediate and longer-term outcomes. The latter are often more negative, partly because of the lack of sustained support on leaving residential care (this also applies to other kinds of intervention). Although many young people are content and make progress while in residential units, they frequently struggle afterwards. Even if their initial problems are partly remedied, they often face unemployment, poverty, isolation and homelessness when they leave. Behavioural improvements may not be maintained, though controlled evaluations do show that the impact on serious but short-lived crime can be lasting. Also patterns can reverse. For instance girls who are unsettled and challenging in residential care often do well later, whereas withdrawn boys may appear to cope all right until they leave, but then have difficulties.

Recent research suggests that a good residential unit (in some ways like a school with a good ethos) is one with a welfare commitment, clear and concordant structures, positive staff–resident relations and definite leadership. Caring staff and opportunities to gain educational or practical skills and qualification are equally important. Bullock concludes that establishments should seek to respond to individual needs related to the reason for the young person being there, rather than general needs related to the secondary phenomenon of living in a residential group.

In the final chapter an attempt will be made to synthesise some of the key implications of these individual chapters.

References

Achenbach, T.M. and Edelbrock, C.S. (1981) 'Behavioural problems and competencies by parents of normal and disturbed children aged four through sixteen.' *Monographs for the Society for Research in Child Development 46*, 1.

Adams, R., Dominelli, L. and Payne, M. (eds) (1998) *Social Work: Themes, Issues and Critical Debates.* London: Macmillan.

Alcock, P. (1993) *Understanding Poverty.* London: Macmillan.

Alderson, P. (1995) *Listening to Children: Children, Ethics and Social Research.* London: Barnardo's.

Alderson, P. *et al.* (eds) (1996) *What Works?* Barkingside: Barnardo's.

Anthony, P., Lancashire, S. and Creed, F. (1991) 'Side effects of psychiatric treatment.' *Sociology of Health and Illness 13*, 4, 530–549.

Arnstein, S.R. (1969) 'Eight rungs on the ladder of citizen participation.' *Journal of the American Institute of Planners 35*, 4, 216–224.

Asquith, S. (ed) (1996) *Children and Young People in Conflict with the Law. Research Highlights in Social Work 30.* London: Jessica Kingsley Publishers.

Asquith, A., Buist, M., Loughran, N., Macauley, C. and Montgomery, M. (1998) *Children, Young People and Offending in Scotland.* Edinburgh: Scottish Office Central Research Unit.

Barber, J.G. (1992) 'Evaluating parent education groups: Effects on sense of competence and social isolation.' *Research on Social Work Practice 2*, 1, 28–38.

Barker, C., Pistrang, N. and Elliott, R. (1994) *Research Methods in Clinical and Counselling Psychology.* Chichester: John Wiley and sons.

Barr, A., Hashagen, S., and Purcell, R. (1996) *Monitoring and Evaluation of Community Development in Northern Ireland.* Glasgow: Scottish Community Development Centre.

Beresford, B., Sloper, P., Baldwin, S. and Newman, T. (1996) *What Works in Services for Families with a Disabled Child?* Barkingside: Barnardo's.

Bernstein, B. and Brannen, J. (eds) (1996) *Children, Research and Policy.* London: Taylor and Franklin.

Berridge, D., Brodie, I., Barrett, D., Henderson, B. and Wenman, H. (1996) *Hello – Is Anybody Listening? The Education of Young People in Residential Care.* Luton: University of Luton.

Biehal, N., Clayden, J., Stein, M. and Wade, J. (1995) *Moving On: Young People and Leaving Care Schemes.* London: HMSO.

Blyth, E. and Milner, J. (1993) 'Exclusion from school: First step on exclusion from society.' *Children and Society 7*, 3, 255–268.

Blyth, E. and Milner, J. (1997) *Social Work with Children: The Educational Perspective.* London: Longman.

Brawley, E.A. and Martinez-Brawley, E.E. (1988) 'Social programme evaluation in the USA: Trends and issues.' *British Journal of Social Work 18,* 391–413.

Breakwell, G.M., Hammond, S. and Fife-Shaw, C. (1995) *Research Methods in Psychology.* London: Sage.

Bunton, R., Nettleton, S. and Burrows, R. (eds) (1995) *The Sociology of Health Promotion.* London: Routledge.

Burns, B.J. (1994) 'The challenges of child mental health services research.' *Journal of Emotional and Behavioural Disorder 2,* 4, 254–259.

Campbell, D.T. and Stanley, J.C. (1966) *Experimental and Quasi-Experimental Research.* Chicago: Rand McNally.

Cannan, C. and Warren, D. (eds) (1997) *Social Action with Children and Families.* London: Routledge.

Catan, L., Dennison, C. and Coleman, J. (1996) *Getting Through.* Brighton: The Trust for the Study of Adolescence.

CERI (Centre for Educational Research and Innovation) (1995) *Schools Under Scrutiny.* Paris: OECD.

Chalmers, I. (1996) 'Assembling the evidence – the Cochrane collaboration.' In P. Alderson *et al.* (eds) (1996) *What Works?* Barkingside: Barnardo's.

Chalmers, T. (1982) 'The randomized clinical trial as a basis for therapeutic decisions.' In N. Tygstrup, J.M. Lachin and E. Juhl (eds) *The Randomized Clinical Trial and Therapeutic Decisions.* New York: Dekker.

Cheetham, J. (1992) 'Evaluating social work effectiveness.' *Research on Social Work Practice 2,* 3, 265–288.

Cheetham, J., Fuller, R., McIvor, G. and Petch, A. (1992) *Evaluating Social Work Effectiveness.* Buckingham: Open University Press.

Cheetham, J. and Kazi, M.A.F. (1998) (eds) *The Working of Social Work.* London: Jessica Kingsley Publishers.

Cheetham, J., Mullen, E.J., Soydan, H. and Tengvald, K. (1998) 'Evaluation as a tool in the development of social work discourse: National diversity or shared preoccupations? Reflections from a conference.' *Evaluation 4,* 1, 9–24.

Clarke, J., Cochrane, A. and McLaughlin, E. (eds) (1994) *Managing Social Policy.* London: Sage.

Cnaan, R.A. (1991) 'Applying clinical trials in social work practice.' *Research on Social Work Practice 1,* 2, 139–161.

Connor, A. (1993) *Monitoring and Evaluation Made Easy.* Edinburgh: HMSO.

Connor, A. and Black, S. (1994) *Performance Review and Quality in Social Care. Research Highlights in Social Work 20.* London: Jessica Kingsley Publishers.

Coopersmith, S. (1990) *Self Esteem Inventories.* Palo Alto, CA: Consulting Psychologists Press Inc.

Cornish, D.B. and Clarke, R. (1975) *Residential Treatment and its Effects on Delinquency.* London: HMSO.

Crombie, I.K. and Davies, H.Y.O. (1998) 'Beyond health outcomes: The advantages of measuring process.' *Journal of Evaluation in Clinical Practice 4,* 1, 31–38.

Drewitt, A. (1997) 'Evaluation and consultation: Learning the lessons of user involvement.' *Evaluation 3,* 2, 189–204.

Elks, M.A. and Kirkhart, K.E. (1993) 'Evaluating effectiveness from the practitioner perspective.' *Social Work 38,* 5, 554–563.

Evidence-based Medicine Working Group (1992) 'Evidence-based Medicine: A new approach to teaching and the practice of medicine.' *Journal of the American Medical Association 268*, 17, 2420–2425.

Eysenck, H.J. (1986) *Decline and Fall of the Freudian Empire.* Harmondsworth: Pelican.

Farmer, E. and Parker, R. (1991) *Trials and Tribulations.* London: HMSO.

Farnfield, S. (1998) 'The rights and wrongs of social work with children and young people.' In J. Cheetham and M.A.F. Kazi (eds) *The Working of Social Work.* London: Jessica Kingsley Publishers.

Fetterman, D.M., Kaftarian, S.J. and Wandersman, A. (eds) (1996) *Empowerment Evaluation.* Thousand Oaks, CA: Sage.

Fitz-Gibbon, C. (1996) 'Experiments, qualitative data and feedback.' *Evaluation 2*, 1, 103–106.

Flick, U. (1998) *An Introduction to Qualitative Research.* London: Sage.

Franklin, B. (ed) (1995) *The Handbook of Children's Rights.* London: Routledge.

Fuller, R. (1992) *In Search of Prevention.* Aldershot: Avebury.

Fuller, R. (1996) 'Evaluating social work effectiveness: A pragmatic approach.' In P. Alderson *et al.* (eds) *What Works?* Barkingside: Barnardo's.

Gibbons, J., Thorpe, S. and Wilkinson, P. (1990) *Family Support and Prevention: Studies in Local Areas.* London: NISW/HMSO.

Goodman, R. (1997) 'The strengths and differences questionnaire.' *Journal of Child Psychology and Psychiatry 38*, 5, 581–586.

Graham, P. (1996) 'The thirty year contribution of research in child mental health to clinical practice and public policy in the UK.' In B. Bernstein and J. Brannen (eds) *Children, Research and Policy.* London: Taylor and Franklin.

Harris, R. and Timms, N. (1993) *Secure Accommodation in Child Care.* London: Routledge.

Hart, R.A. (1992) *Children's Participation: From Tokenism to Citizenship.* Florence: Unicef International Child Development Centre.

Hawkins, R.P., Almeida, M.C., Fabry, B. and Reitz, A.L. (1992) 'A scale to measure restrictiveness of living environments for troubled children and youths.' *Hospital and Community Psychiatry 43*, 1, 54–59.

Heath, A.F., Colton, M.J. and Aldgate, J. (1994) 'Failure to escape: A longitudinal study of foster children's educational attainment.' *British Journal of Social Work 24*, 4, 241–260.

Hegarty, S. (1996) 'NFER Jubilee: a half century of research.' *Educational Research 38*, 3, 243–257.

Hill, M. (1998) 'What children and young people say they want from Social Work Services.' *Research, Policy and Planning 15*, 3, 17–27.

Hill, M. and Aldgate, J. (eds) (1996) *Child Welfare Services.* London: Jessica Kingsley Publishers.

Hill, M. and Tisdall, K. (1997) *Children and Society.* London: Longman.

Hill, M., Triseliotis, J., Borland, M. and Lambert, L. (1996) 'Outcomes for teenagers on supervision and in care.' In M. Hill and J. Aldgate (eds) *Child Welfare Services in the United Kingdom and Ireland.* London: Jessica Kingsley Publishers.

Holloway, I. (1996) *Qualitative Research for Nurses.* Oxford: Blackwell.

House, E.R. (1993) *Professional Evaluation.* London: Sage.

Howe, D. (1998) *Patterns of Adoption.* Oxford: Blackwell.

Hudson, J. and Williams, M. (1991) *Evaluation Models of Child Sexual Abuse.* Calgary: University of Calgary.

Hulyer, B. (1997) 'Long-term development.' In C. Cannan and D. Warren (eds) *Social Action with Children and Families.* London: Routledge.

Hutchison, D. (1993) 'School effectiveness studies using administrative data.' *Educational Research* 35, 1, 27–47.

Juhl, E. (1982) 'Clinical elements of the randomized control trial.' In N. Tygstrup, J.M. Lachin and E. Juhl (eds) *The Randomized Clinical Trial and Therapeutic Decisions.* New York: Dekker.

Kazi, M.A.F.(1996) 'Single case evaluation in the public sector using a combination of approaches.' *Evaluation 2*, 1, 85–98.

Kazi, M.A.F. (1998) 'Putting single-case evaluation into practice.' In J. Cheetham and M.A.F. Kazi (eds) *The Working of Social Work.* London: Jessica Kingsley Publishers.

Kazi, M.A.F. and Wilson, J. (1996) 'Applying single-case evaluation in social work.' *British Journal of Social Work 26*, 6, 699–717.

Knapp, M. (1997) 'Economic evaluation and intervention for children and adolescents with mental health problems.' *Journal of Child Psychology and Psychiatry 38*, 1, 3–25.

Knapp, M. and Fenyo, A. (1995) 'The cost effectiveness of intermediate treatment.' In A. Netten and J. Dennett (eds) *Unit Costs of Community Care.* Canterbury: Personal Social Services Research Unit.

Knapp, M. and Lowin, A. (1998) 'Child care outcomes: Economic perspectives and issues.' *Children & Society 12*, 3, 169–179.

Krogstrup, H.K. (1997) 'User participation in quality assessment: A dialogue and learning oriented evaluation method.' *Evaluation 3*, 2, 205–224.

Lederman, L.C. (1990) 'Assessing educational effectiveness: The focus group interview as a technique for data collection.' *Communication Education 38*, 117–127.

Levy, R.L. (1996) 'Data analysis problems in single-case evaluation: Much ado about nothing.' *Research on Social Work Practice 6*, 1, 66–71.

Lewis, R.E., Walton, E. and Fraser, M.W. (1995) 'Examining family reunification services: A process analysis of a successful experiment.' *Research on Social Work Practice 5*, 3, 259–282.

Liverpool 8 Children's Research Group (1997) *Listen to the Children.* Liverpool: Liverpool 8.

Love, J.G. and Hendry, L.B. (1994) 'Youth workers and youth participants: Two perspectives of youth work.' *Youth and Policy 46*, 43–55.

Macbeath, J. (1994) 'A role for parents, students and teachers in school self-evaluation and development planning.' In K.A. Riley and D. Nuttall (eds) *Measuring Quality.* London: Falmer Press.

Macdonald, G. (1996) 'Ice therapy: Why we need randomised controlled trials.' In P. Alderson *et al.* (eds) *What Works?* Barkingside: Barnardo's.

Macdonald, G. and Roberts, H. (1995) *What Works in the Early Years?* Barkingside: Barnardo's.

Macdonald, G., Sheldon, B. and Gillespie, J. (1992) 'Contemporary studies of the effectiveness of social work.' *British Journal of Social Work 22*, 6, 615–643.

Maluccio, A.N. (1997) 'Assessing child welfare outcomes: The American perspective.' *Children and Society 12*, 3, 161–168.

Mattaini, M.A. (1996) 'The abuse and neglect of single-case designs.' *Research on Social Work Practice 6*, 1, 83–90.

May, T. (1996) *Situating Social Theory.* Buckingham: Open University Press.

McNeish, D. and Newman, T. (1996) 'Evaluating child welfare interventions.' *Research, Policy and Planning 14*, 1, 53–58.

Middleton, S., Ashworth, K. and Walker, R. (eds) (1994) *Family Fortunes: Pressures on Parents and Children in the 1990s.* London: Children's Poverty Action Group.

Millham, S., Bullock, R., Hosie, K. and Haak, M. (1986) *Lost in Care.* Aldershot: Gower.

Mithaug, D.E. (1996) 'Fairness, liberty and empowerment evaluation.' In D.M. Fetterman, S.J. Kaftarian and A. Wandersman (eds) (1996) *Empowerment Evaluation.* Thousand Oaks, CA: Sage.

Mortimore, P., Sammons, P., Stoll, L., Lewis, D. and Ecob, R. (1988) *School Matters: The Junior Years.* Wells: Open Books.

Munro, E. (1998) *Understanding Social Work: An Empirical Approach.* London: Athlone Press.

Oakley, A. (1996) 'Who's afraid of the randomised controlled trial? The challenge of evaluating the potential of social interventions.' In P. Alderson *et al. What Works?* Barkingside: Barnardo's.

Oliver, M. (1996) *Understanding Disability: From Theory to Practice.* London: Macmillan.

Olweus, D. (1991) 'Bullying among schoolchildren.' In V. Peters, R. McMahon and V. Quinsey (eds) *Aggression and Violence Throughout the Life Span.* Newbury Park, CA: Sage.

Page, M., Poertner, J. and Lindbloom, R. (1997) 'Promoting the preschooler's chances for success: A program efficacy review for behaviourally disordered or emotionally troubled children.' In J.T. Pardeck and M.K. Markward (eds) *Reassessing Social Work Practice with Children.* Amsterdam: Gordon and Breach.

Pardeck, J.T. and Markward, M.K. (eds) (1997) *Reassessing Social Work Practice with Children.* Amsterdam: Gordon and Breach.

Parker, R., Ward, H., Jackson, S., Aldgate, J. and Wedge, P. (1991) *Assessing Outcomes in Child Care.* London: HMSO.

Parton, N. (1991) *Governing the Family.* London: Macmillan.

Patton, M.Q. (1990) *Qualitative Evaluation and Research.* London: Sage.

Patton, M.Q. (1998) 'Discovering process use.' *Evaluation 4*, 2, 225–233.

Peters, V., McMahon, R. and Quinsey, V. (eds) (1992) *Aggression and Violence Throughout the Life Span.* Newbury Park, CA: Sage.

Pietrzak, J., Ramler, M., Renner, T., Ford, L. and Gilbert, N. (1990) *Practical Program Evaluation: Examples from Child Abuse Prevention.* London: Sage.

Power, M.J. (1967) 'Delinquent schools?' *New Society 10*, 542–543.

Powney, J., Furlong, A., Cartmal, F. amd Hall, S. (1997) *Youth Work with Vulnerable Young People.* Edinburgh: SCRE.

Quinton, D. and Rutter, M. (1988) *Parenting Breakdown.* Aldershot: Avebury.

Qvortrup, J., Bardy, M., Sgritta, G. and Wintersberger, H. (eds) (1994) *Childhood Matters.* Aldershot: Avebury.

Rabinow, P. (ed) (1984) *The Foucault Reader.* Harmondsworth: Penguin.

Rees, S. (1992) 'The impact of consumer based research and the importance of its dissemination for education and practice.' *Issues in Social Work Education 12*, 1, 69–83.

Reid, W.J. (1994) 'The empirical practice movement.' *Social Service Review 68*, 165–184.

Reimers, S. and Treacher, A. (eds) (1995) *Introducing User-friendly Family Therapy.* London: Routledge.

Reynolds, D. *et al.* (1996) *Making Good Schools.* London: Routledge.

Richman, N., Stevenson, J. and Graham, P. (1982) *Pre-school to School: A Behavioural Study.* London: Academic Press.

Riley, K.A. and Nuttall (eds) (1994) *Measuring Quality.* London: Falmer Press.

Robson, C. (1993) *Real World Research.* Oxford: Blackwell.

Rodriguez, E. and Bowen, K.A. (1998) 'New developments and challenges of health status measurement for outcomes evaluation.' *Evaluation 4,* 1, 25–36.

Rosenberg, M. (1979) *Conceiving the Self.* New York: Basic Books.

Rossi, P.H. (1992) 'Assessing family preservation programs.' *Children and Youth Services Review 14,* 77–97.

Rossi, P.H. and Freeman, H.E. (1985) *Evaluation: A Systematic Approach.* Beverly Hills: Sage.

Rowe, J., Hundleby, M. and Garnett, L. (1989) *Child Care Now: A Survey of Placement Patterns.* London: British Agencies for Adoption and Fostering.

Rubin, A. and Knox, K.S. (1996) 'Data analysis problems in single-case evaluation: Issues for research on social work practice.' *Research on Social Work Practice 6,* 1, 40–65.

Rutter, M. (1995) 'Psychosocial adversity: risk, resilience and recovery.' *Southern African Journal of Child and Adolescent Psychiatry 7,* 2, 75–88.

Rutter, M., Maughan, B., Mortimore, P. and Ouston, J. (1979) *Fifteen Thousand Hours: Secondary Schools and their Effects on Children.* London: Open Books.

Rutter, M., Tizard, J. and Whitmore, K. (eds) (1970) *Education, Health and Behaviour.* London: Longman.

Schalock, R. (1995) *Outcome Based Evaluation.* New York: Plenum.

Scheerens, J. (1989) *Effective Schooling.* London: Cassell.

Sellick, C. and Thoburn, J. (1996) *What Works in Family Placement.* Barkingside: Barnardo's.

Shaw, I. (1996) *Evaluating in Practice.* Aldershot: Arena.

Shaw, I. and Shaw, A. (1997) 'Keeping social work honest: Evaluating as profession and practice.' *British Journal of Social Work 27,* 6, 847–870.

Silver, H. (1994) *Good Schools, Effective Schools.* London: Cassell.

Sinclair, R. (1996) 'Children's and young people's participation in decision-making: The legal framework in Social Services and Education.' In M. Hill and J. Aldgate (eds) *Child Welfare Services.* London: Jessica Kingsley Publishers.

Smith, G. and Cantley, C. (1985) *Assessing Health Care: A Study in Organisational Evaluation.* Milton Keynes: Open University Press.

Sommerlad, E. and Willoughby, S. (1995) 'Self-evaluation and practitioner evaluator.' *Evaluation 1,* 1, 105–118.

Stalker, K. and Robinson, C. (eds) (1998) *Growing Up With Disability.* London: Jessica Kingsley Publishers.

Thyer, B. (1998) 'Promoting evaluation research on social work practice.' In J. Cheetham and M.A.F. Kazi (eds) *The Working of Social Work.* London: Jessica Kingsley Publishers.

Thyer, B. and Wodarski, J.S. (1998) 'First principles of empirical social work practice.' In B. Thyer and J.S. Wodarski (eds) *Handbook of Empirical Social Work Practice. Volume 1 Mental Disorder.*

Tisdall, E.K.M. and Plumtree, A. (1997) *The Children (Scotland) Act 1995.* Edinburgh: Stationery Office.

Tones, K. (1997) 'Beyond the randomized controlled trial: a case for judicial review.' *Health Education Research 12,* 2, i–iv.

Tones, K. (1998) 'Health education: Effectiveness and efficiency in promoting child health.' In R. Weston and D. Scott (eds) *Effectiveness of Health Promotion.* London: Stanley Thornes.

Tones, K. and Tilford, S. (1994) *Health Education: Effectiveness, Efficiency and Equity.* London: Chapman Hall.

Townsend, P., Davidson, N. and Whitehead, M. (1992) *The Health Divide.* Harmondsworth: Penguin.

Triseliotis, J., Borland, M., Hill, M. and Lambert, L. (1995) *Teenagers and the Social Work Services.* London: HMSO.

Tygstrup, N., Lachin, J.M. and Juhl, E. (eds) (1982) *The Randomized Clinical Trial and Therapeutic Decisions.* New York: Dekker.

Vaughn, S., Schumm, J.S. and Sinagub, J. (1996) *Focus Group Interviews in Education and Psychology.* Thousand Oaks, CA: Sage.

Ward, H. (1995) *Looking After Children: Research into Practice.* London: HMSO.

Ward, H. (1996) 'Constructing and implementing measures to assess the outcomes of looking after children away from home.' In M. Hill and J. Aldgate (eds) *Child Welfare Services.* London: Jessica Kingsley Publishers.

White, S. (1998) 'Analysing the content of social work: Applying the lessons from qualitative research.' In J. Cheetham and M.A.F. Kazi (eds) *The Working of Social Work.* London: Jessica Kingsley Publishers.

Williams, A. (1998) 'Experience of single-case evaluation in a small agency.' In J. Cheetham and M.A.F. Kazi (eds) *The Working of Social Work.* London: Jessica Kingsley Publishers.

Williamson, H. (1993) 'Youth policy in the United Kingdom and the marginalisation of young people.' *Youth and Policy 40*, 33–48.

Wilson, S.L. (1995) 'Single case experimental designs.'In G.M. Breakwell, S. Hammond and C. Fife-Shaw (eds) *Research Methods in Psychology.* London: Sage.

Wodarski, J.S. (1998) 'Social problems: A cost-effective psychosocial preventive paradigm.' In J.S. Wodarski and B. Thyer (eds) *Handbook of Empirical Social Work Practice. Volume 2 Social Problems and Practice Issues.*

CHAPTER 2

Working with Families in the Early Years

Helen Roberts and Geraldine Macdonald

Introduction

The majority of caring and support to children in the early years is provided by parents, usually mothers, and most family support is provided through informal kin and friendship networks. This caring work, even when carried out in extreme adversity, normally has good results. So while this chapter identifies some of those professional interventions in health, education and welfare in which we can have confidence, we need to acknowledge from the start that professional interventions and professional evidence are not the only forms of knowledge. There is a special expertise on childhood and parenting which resides with children and parents themselves. Families have huge reservoirs of knowledge which experts have yet to tap fully (Roberts 1997a; 1997b).

The nature and aims of early years services are varied, with a range of services designed to have short- and longer- term desired outcomes. These services may be provided by statutory health, welfare and education agencies, as well as voluntary bodies. Despite some good examples of co-ordination, services are frequently piecemeal and fragmented. Their aims include the provision of basic care, promoting the well-being of children, monitoring or improving child health, enhancing cognitive or educational achievements and protecting children from harm. Some interventions are centre based, others directed at the home. Some focus on children, some on parents, and some on families or entire neighbourhoods. Differences in approach reflect different philosophies about intervention, and different wished-for outcomes (Cannan 1992; Cannan and Warren 1996; Lloyd 1996; Lloyd *et al.* 1997). A common feature of good early

49

years services is that they recognise that there is no quality without equality. Valuing a child's social, cultural, spiritual and ethnic background is not an optional extra (Siraj-Blatchford 1996), nor is the inclusion of disabled children in mainstream services (Beresford, Sloper and Newman 1996).

Agencies whose purpose is to provide support for young children and their families cover a vast field. In what follows, we confine ourselves almost entirely to service interventions, while recognising that changes in fiscal and social policies may have wider ranging effects. What works in social policy to support children and families is addressed only peripherally here, though there is an increasing case for evidence-based policy addressing the corrosive effects of family poverty on child welfare (Wilkinson 1994; Holterman 1995; Roberts 1997c). A persuasive and well-designed study from the United States, for instance, demonstrates the positive benefits of negative income tax for lone mothers with a high risk of having a low birthweight baby (Kehrer and Wolin 1979; Arblaster *et al.*1997).

A growing body of scholarly evidence indicates that the early years provide a crucial opportunity for future development. If intervening during this period is so powerful, we need to be sure that there is at best convincing evidence that our well meaning interventions will do some good, and at the very least a commitment to submit unproven interventions to scrutiny (Alderson *et al.* 1995; Macdonald 1997; Newman and Roberts 1997). While this chapter concerns itself with those interventions in the early years where there is good evidence of beneficial outcomes, we would not want to lose sight of the fact that enhanced childhood experiences are important for the here-and-now. It would be a mistake to base our interventions only on the promise of some good outcome at a later date.

The link between interventions and outcomes and the need to test their validity has long been understood. The Book of Daniel describes an experiment in which children were given pulses to eat and water to drink, rather than the king's wine and meat. Present day nutritionists might be surprised to know that after only ten days, the experimental group given a vegetarian diet did better than the children given the king's food, but good nutrition was clearly established as a helpful early intervention policy (Holy Bible, Daniel i, vv 10–16).

Different kinds of research evidence

Many good research studies explore child welfare issues using qualitative or mixed methodologies (e.g. O'Flaherty 1995; Thoburn, Lewis and Shemmings 1995).

There is also a rich stream of work focusing on children's own experiences (Alderson 1995; Little and Kelly 1995; O'Flaherty 1995).

Without the understanding gained from qualitative studies we could not begin to conceptualise interventions which might be acceptable, let alone effective. But the development of effective services requires other kinds of evidence. We look below at a range of research methods used to evaluate interventions, and describe a number of health, education and child welfare interventions in the early years which suggest good outcomes. The example which follows provides an illustration of the kinds of problems we face in evaluating services.

The challenge of evaluation

Suppose a family centre wants to evaluate a discussion group aimed at improving the parenting of a group of parents whose children have been placed on the Child Protection Register because of neglect. Suppose the programme runs for eight weekly sessions and is considered by the workers and parents to have been a success for those who did not drop out. These judgements are based on the self-reports of the parents, the workers' observations of parents' increasing self-esteem, and improvements in the apparent well-being of the children (who have been cared for in a crèche during the parents' group). Before asserting that 'discussion groups work' we need to know whether:

1. improvements *have* taken place and

2. they can be attributed to the group.

It is difficult to do this if we cannot rule out competing explanations such as:

- The parents might have improved simply with the passage of time. There is evidence that many problems improve spontaneously (Rachman and Wilson 1980).

- The children might have become more manageable as a result of weekly sessions with skilled crèche workers.

- Other factors might be responsible for changes such as improved income support or additional help from social services (e.g. extra day care), due to the children's registration.

- The perceived improvement in the parents might be due to their having learned the right things to say, having been asked the same kind of questions at the beginning and end of the programme.

- The parents who stayed might have been highly motivated and would have improved anyway. Alternatively, those parents who dropped out might have done just as well as those in the programme. The research method which gives the best chance of untangling the challenges described here is the randomised controlled trial.

Randomised controlled trials (RCTs)

Randomised controlled trials can settle disputes about the relative efficacy of two forms of intervention, or of intervention versus non-intervention. The starting point for randomisation is that we frequently do not know what works, or what works best. Much innovative (and not so innovative) practice is, in effect, uncontrolled experimentation.

An example of an instructive RCT was the Alameda Project. This research project aimed to tackle the problem of 'decisional drift' of children languishing in an unplanned way in foster care (Stein and Gambrill 1977). The majority of children in the study were accommodated away from home for reasons of neglect. The researchers wanted to assess whether an intensive service, aimed at birth parents, could improve outcomes for children. Four hundred and eighty two children were randomly assigned to one of two groups. Families of children in the *experimental* group received intensive help directed at problems that were identified as preventing rehabilitation. The starting point for workers in the experimental group was to focus attention on the birth parents and involve them actively in deciding what outcomes they wanted for their children and themselves. In order to involve parents, experimental workers took a firm stance on visiting: they required contact and facilitated it. They made use of detailed contracts, characterised by clear, specific goals, and precise identification of objectives needed to meet these goals which were then agreed with parents. In order to help parents meet their goals, appropriate help was offered or arranged. Families of children in the *control* group received a normal service from workers in the Child Welfare Department. The results were:

- Overall, almost half (48%) of the children in the experimental group were returned home compared with 11 per cent of the controls.

- There was a significant difference between the groups in favour of the experimental group in three out of ten problem areas, namely parent–child interaction; personal parental problems; and marital problems.

Depressingly, this study is little referred to in the UK literature despite good results. A randomised controlled trial which has attracted much wider attention, from policy makers and politicians as well as practitioners, is of the children who were randomised to the Highscope approach to pre-school education, and who have been followed up well into adulthood. This is described in the section on education below.

Studies with quasi-experimental designs

Where it is not possible randomly to allocate clients to different services, it is essential that alternative approaches to evaluation are designed, analysed and interpreted in ways that maximise our knowledge of the relationship between what is done, and improvements seen. Studies which have one or more control groups, but to which subjects are not randomly allocated are known as quasi-experimental studies. Some clients receive a service, whilst others do not, or receive a different service. Instead of random allocation, researchers take clients occurring 'naturally' and establish a control group matched on characteristics thought to be important: socio-economic status, severity of problem, duration of problem, and so on.

An example of a quasi-experimental design investigated a therapeutic day care programme addressing the developmental delays associated with child abuse and neglect. Culp, Heide and Richardson (1987) assessed the impact of the programme on the developmental scores of 35 children who had been mistreated by their parents, by comparing them before and after the programme with the scores of a matched group who had not yet been enrolled in such a programme. All the children were under six years of age. The researchers selected a control group matched for age, sex, race and diagnostic category (abuse, neglect, abuse and neglect, sibling abused). In the treatment programme children participated in group activities for six hours a day, five days a week. There was a high adult to child ratio (1:2) with the major focus on the development of strong teacher–child relationships. The environment was designed to facilitate the development of self-esteem, caring peer relationships, and to help children recognise and deal with their feelings. The programme included typical pre-school learning activities. In addition, individual child treatment, parental counselling and parent education services were integrated with the group programme, as well as a 24 hour crisis telephone line. Children were assessed before the programme (pre-test) and afterwards (post-test). Post-test scores for the experimental children were significantly higher than those of their matched controls. The authors observe that because of the nature of the treatment programme, it was not possible for the effects of the classroom intervention to be separated from the family intervention provided by the programme.

Studies with non-experimental designs

Research designs within this category are evaluated interventions but with no random allocation and no pre-intervention matching of groups, if indeed a comparison group is used at all. Taken singly, results based on studies using these designs are, at best, suggestive. Our confidence in the results of these studies can be enhanced in two ways. If a number of such studies produce similar results, then one can feel more confident that the intervention is influencing the changes. Such a pattern would indicate that it might be worth investing the time and resources involved in experimental research.

CLIENT-OPINION STUDIES

Client opinion or 'user' studies give us insight into what it feels like to be on the receiving end of a service (Brown 1984), what side effects are produced, and the ways in which clients attribute patterns of change or deterioration to the actions of staff (Fisher 1983). This approach to evaluation is one in which the British have a good track record. Unfortunately the correlation between satisfaction (or dissatisfaction) and the achievement of pre-intervention goals is loose, to say the least (McCord 1981), and time and time again the message comes that clients usually like professionals, appreciate their endeavours and value their support, but rarely have (or are provided with) a clue as to *what* they are endeavouring to achieve and how they expect to do it.

COHORT STUDIES

Cohort studies interview subjects or otherwise obtain data at more than one point in time. The UK has a number of major cohort studies from which we can obtain data on the early years and link it to later outcomes. Data from the cohort studies indicate what might be protective for children who have a difficult start. For example, parental interest in, and enthusiasm for, education, has been shown to provide good protection in the long term from the adverse consequences associated with a start disadvantaged by poverty (Wadsworth 1985, 1986; Pilling 1990). Children fortunate enough to have this help tended strongly to do better in cognitive tests, and in educational attainment (Douglas 1986). In due course, such children as adults are more likely to be enthusiastic about their own children's education. The importance of educational attainment is seen in all aspects of the findings on adult life. Those who gained qualifications at 'A' level (or training equivalents) or above had much better chances in health (Wadsworth 1991; Mann, Wadsworth and Colley 1992; Kuh and Wadsworth 1993) as well as in occupation and income.

Effective interventions in the early years

In what follows, we provide some examples of interventions which seem to have promising beneficial effects in education, health, family support and child protection. Evidence will be briefly reviewed which includes examples of each of the research designs discussed above.

Education

A number of US and UK studies have demonstrated the value of structured, participative pre-school programmes. Early educational interventions which show promising effects include Highscope, a pre-school intervention involving an active learning curriculum, trained staff and parent participation (Macdonald and Roberts 1995). The UK has a particularly strong history in developing early childhood education, though we have been less strong in universal provision. Highscope shares many of the elements of other good quality pre-school interventions, but has some distinct elements in its curriculum, notably activities which involve 'plan/do/review' sequences as part of the daily routine. A randomised controlled trial of Highscope in which the participants have been followed up over a long period indicates that at age 27, those attending the programme had significantly higher monthly earnings, a significantly higher proportion of home ownership and significantly fewer arrests including for crimes of drug-taking or dealing, compared with a control group who did not participate in the programme (Schweinhart and Weikart 1993).

Parent-led Saturday school is a different kind of educational initiative which is of interest in the light of the evidence from cohort studies about parental interest. It also shows the importance of providers listening to parents. One Saturday school was set up by a group of African-Caribbean parents using Barnardo's premises. Reading, writing, number work and Black history were emphasised. A client opinion study (Brown and Ware 1994) highlights the value parents placed on this.

> I was not aware of his capabilities until the Saturday School showed me that there was hope.

> He's achieved a great deal in a very short space of time. His mainstream school has also noticed the difference, awarded lots of stars, for his work and behaviour, all because of the Saturday School.

Health

DIET

Children born into poverty are at considerably heightened risk of poor health. Within that context, the most important protective factors for children in terms of health seem to be those things which optimise growth and development before birth and in early childhood including favourable diets (Barker 1994). For some workers, interventions which concentrate on providing basics such as food smack of Victorian paternalism. For the families concerned, services which help to ensure an adequate diet are likely to have lasting beneficial effects. Recent research indicates that nutrition in foetal life and the very early months may critically influence later behaviour and learning. While a number of interventions have been developed in promoting healthy diets as well as changes to drinking and smoking patterns during pregnancy, these have met with varying degrees of success, and require further evaluation (DoH 1995, p.55). The value of such interventions is illustrated by the following example of good practice.

The Govan Healthy Eating project in Glasgow redeems welfare milk tokens. Using the profit component of the tokens, they pass part of the profit back to the community, in partnership with local food co-ops by giving fruit and vegetables as an extra along with the milk (Laughlin and Black 1995, p.90).

SOCIAL SUPPORT

Most social support in the early years is provided through informal networks of kin and friends. Some families do not have access to such networks and, in other cases too, the networks are supported or supplemented by professional services. The introduction in 1995 of mandatory Children's Services Plans which must take account of the links between health, education and social services has the potential to encourage a holistic, flexible and comprehensive approach to children's needs, in line with the provisions of the UN Convention on the Rights of the Child. Support such as early care and education, parenting programmes and action on domestic violence are essential specialised components of a comprehensive family support system which is responsive to need (Lloyd 1996).

A promising social support intervention is the Child Development Programme whose fundamental goal is to help and encourage parents (Barker, Anderson and Chalmers 1992; 1994). This programme offers monthly support visits to new mothers, antenatally and for the first year of life. Most of the visits are undertaken by specially trained health visitors. Perhaps the most radical development of this programme is the Community Mothers intervention in which mothers were recruited to provide support. An RCT demonstrated that children in the intervention group were more likely to have received all of their primary immunisations and to be read to daily. They were less likely to begin cow's milk before 26 weeks. Mothers as well as children in the intervention group also had a better diet than the controls. At the end of the study, they were less likely to be tired or feel miserable (Johnson, Howell and Molloy 1993). Since that study was published, the programme has expanded to incorporate breast-feeding support, mother and toddler groups and attention to the special needs of travellers. In one Dublin suburb a peer-led nutrition intervention programme is being developed which draws on the model of the Community Mothers programme in terms of involving volunteers (Johnson and Molloy 1995).

Evaluation has indicated that on almost every outcome measure, families using the programme scored more highly than those not involved, even though the former were generally more disadvantaged.

Two studies have shown how social support in pregnancy improved the health of women and their babies. In Birmingham, Judy Dance (1987) looked at the effect of 'linkworkers' on the care of Pakistani women who had already had one low-birthweight baby. Of 50 women in the study, 25 were allocated at random to have linkworker support. The linkworkers were women of childbearing age with some formal Western education, and were fluent English speakers who also spoke at least one of the local minority languages. They visited the women three to five times during pregnancy to give information on health needs, facilities and services and to advise, befriend and support. The effect of this scheme was to increase the birthweight of babies born to the intervention group compared with the control group. Also, the women involved reported fewer medical problems and more happiness in pregnancy, shorter labours, less analgesia and fewer babies with feeding problems (Oakley 1992, p.57).

A second study demonstrated the effectiveness, appropriateness and safety of a social support intervention provided by midwives in 'high risk' pregnancy (Oakley, Rajan and Grant 1990). A total of 509 women with a history of low-birthweight were randomly assigned to receive either social support intervention in pregnancy in addition to standard antenatal care (the intervention group) or standard antenatal care only (the control group). Social support was given by four research midwives in the form of 24 hour availability by telephone and a programme of home visits, during which the midwives provided a listening service for the women to discuss any topic of concern to them, gave practical information and advice *when asked*, carried out referrals to other health professionals and welfare agencies as appropriate, and collected social and medical information. The babies of intervention group mothers had a mean birthweight slightly higher than control group babies, and there were fewer very low birthweight babies in the intervention group. Women's attitudes to the social support intervention were found to be very positive, with 80 per cent of those who filled in the postnatal questionnaire singling out the fact that the midwife 'listened' as important. Interestingly, as follow-up has continued, differences between the intervention and control groups have been maintained, with more positive results in the intervention group. At seven years, there were fewer behaviour problems among the children and less anxiety among the mothers in the intervention group (Oakley, Rigby and Hickey 1997).

In an Edinburgh study, women identified as depressed were randomly allocated either to normal treatment or to eight weekly counselling sessions by health visitors who had received a short training in counselling for postnatal depression. Standardised psychiatric interviews and a 10 point self-report scale were used to identify depression before and after the intervention. After three months, 18 (69%)

of the 26 women in the treatment group had fully recovered compared with 9 (38%) of the 24 in the control group. The authors conclude that counselling by health visitors is valuable in managing non-psychotic postnatal depression (Holden, Sagovsky and Cox 1989). Since postnatal depression is a major source of unhappiness which affects both family and maternal health, this appears a promising, and relatively low cost/high benefit intervention.

ACCIDENT PREVENTION

Accidents are the main cause of death in childhood in the UK, and a cause of considerable morbidity in children and anxiety in adults. There is a steep social class gradient in child accident deaths and the gap between the most and the least disadvantaged children is widening (Roberts and Power 1996).

The emphasis of road safety work tends to be focused on the child's behaviour, rather than that of motorists (Ampofo-Boateng and Thomson 1989). A common intervention in child accident prevention has been the use of leaflets, pamphlets, and health education. There is scant evidence that these are effective in reducing child accidents, and some evidence that they are harmful, increasing anxiety among mothers, without reducing risks to children (Roberts, Smith and Bryce 1993). While there is considerable public expense and attention directed at addressing child protection within the private domain of the home and the family, children's services plans do not usually consider the dangers to children in the wider public domain, through accidental injury (McNeish and Roberts 1995). There is a need to develop children's plans which protect children from accidental injury as well as abuse. A number of studies suggest that parents' levels of awareness of accidents to children in general, and of specific local risks, is high (Colver, Hutchinson and Judson 1982; Roberts, Smith and Bryce 1995). We have relatively poor data on how parents manage to keep their children safe most of the time, and why these strategies sometimes fail. Even in a high risk area, safety, and in particular child safety, is a priority for local people. Good practice will draw on this commitment to safety, and specialist local knowledge. The local authority of Rochdale has built the prevention of child accidents into its children's plan (McNeish, Roberts and Power 1996). In order to understand 'what works?', the approach they have taken has been to commission research in a part of the town with a high child accident rate, turning the question of what prevents child accidents on its head. Instead of asking: Why did that accident happen?, it looks at what children and parents are doing right in areas with so many risks, and how we can learn from it. The acid test, of course, will be whether accident rates go up, go down, or stay much the same after relevant sections of the children's plan are operationalised.

CHILD PROTECTION INTERVENTIONS

Work in the child protection field points to the need for research of better quality and rigorous design, and for care when taking the most promising of findings and implementing them in practice. The good evaluative study spells out its assumptions, says how the intervention is expected to address the problems, and how we can tell that it has. Unfortunately – given the large investment of professional time and resources that have been devoted to the problems presented by parents who provide less than adequate care for their children or who abuse them physically or sexually – such studies are few and far between.

Primary prevention

Programmes concerned to reduce the incidence of abuse and neglect by primary prevention are targeted either at the general population (for example 'Don't shake the baby'), or at populations of about-to-be parents or new parents thought to be at high risk. The studies we discuss in this section are from this last group. Studies which target families known to be at risk, or who have already been abusive, are referred to as studies concerned with secondary and tertiary prevention respectively.

Promising approaches to primary prevention have been identified by MacMillan *et al.* (1994). MacMillan and her colleagues concluded that among the perinatal and early childhood intervention programmes, long-term home visiting was effective in the prevention of child physical abuse and neglect among families with one or more of three risk factors: single parenthood; poverty; and teenage parent status (Olds *et al.* 1986; Hardy and Streett 1989). With regard to the effectiveness of short-term home visits, early and extended postpartum contact, intensive paediatric contact, use of a drop-in centre, classroom education and parent training the evidence remained inconclusive (MacMillan *et al.* 1994; p.852).

Secondary and Tertiary prevention

What of approaches to preventing abuse and neglect in families where it has already become a problem, or who have been identified as high risk? It is now generally accepted that child abuse and neglect are the result of a range of biological, psychological and social variables. In reviewing the effectiveness literature, where there is a tendency to concentrate on micro-social and psychological variables such as social isolation and personal skill deficits, it is important that we do not lose sight of the influence of macro-social variables such as poverty and inadequate resources.

A review by Macdonald, Sheldon and Gillespie (1992) examined studies of the effectiveness of social work. The first 13 studies were explicitly concerned with families in which the children had been abused or were thought to be at high risk of abuse. A second group of 25 studies were concerned with social work with children and families where child protection issues were not the central focus, although many of these were relevant to the preventative end of child protection. The review concluded that behavioural and cognitive behavioural interventions accounted for the lion's share of positive results.

Parent training programmes aim to improve parents' abilities to manage their children's behaviour and to reduce conflict and confrontation whilst increasing co-operation and pleasant interaction. A further goal is to alter the balance of reward and punishment in favour of the former. Physical abuse may occur in the context of disciplinary incidents, in which the boundary line between discipline and violence becomes confused (Reid *et al.* 1987; Reid 1985). An inability to end children's troublesome behaviour successfully through non-physical methods leads to escalation via threats to physical measures. As the emotional temperature rises, the punishments are likely to become more severe, and for young children in particular, more dangerous. Whilst parent training will not always be sufficient, it will in all probability have a role to play with most parents who physically abuse their children (as well as the majority who do not). Working with parents behaviourally can present difficulties in so far as the emphasis on a detailed assessment and monitoring of progress may lead parents to feel that they are providing evidence 'which may be used against them' in the future. Further, many parents are constrained to accept advice or help for behaviour they may not themselves perceive as problematic. Whilst few families are formally obliged to attend programmes, the American experience suggests that families who are unwilling can be worked with successfully (Wolfe, Sandler and Kaufmann 1981; Reid 1985).

Parent training with families with young children has at its core the following strategies:

- emphasising the importance of establishing the ground rules and boundaries of acceptable family behaviour

- helping parents to acquire an understanding of what they can reasonably expect from their children

- teaching parents to give clear, unambiguous instructions – 'James, I want you to'

- training in contingency management skills – to recognise and reinforce desired behaviour and to respond appropriately to unwanted behaviour.

In general, studies indicate that parent training has good results with a wide range of child behaviour problems, particularly when skill deficits are identified (Dumas 1989; Miller and Prinz 1990). It has been successfully deployed by social workers working in the home, in groups, and in family centres (Bourne 1993). However, problems have been reported. Some studies record high drop-out rates (Griest *et al.* 1980) and a failure of successful results to last for any appreciable length of time beyond the end of the intervention or to generalise to new problems (Griest and Forehand 1982). The reasons for these failures have been the subject of investigation, and intervention failures appear to be attributable to too narrow an approach in response to complex problems. Families for whom parent training is unlikely to be a *sufficient* response to child management difficulties are those where there is one or more of the following:

- poor parental adjustment, particularly when associated with maternal depression (Rickard *et al.* 1980; McMahon, Forehand and Griest 1981)

- maternal stress and low socio-economic status (Dumas and Wahler 1983; Kazdin 1990)

- social isolation of the mother (Wahler 1980)

- relationship problems (O'Leary and Emery 1983)

- extra-familial conflict (Wahler 1980)

- severe and/or longstanding problems (McAuley and McAuley 1980)

- parental misperception of the deviance of their children's behaviour (Lobitz and Johnson 1975; Griest *et al.* 1980; Larrence and Twentyman 1982; Reid, Kavanagh and Baldwin 1987).

Three things follow from these data:

1. Because these compounding problems are the rule rather than the exception (for example couple relationships are often poor in families complaining of child behaviour problems (Webster-Stratton 1989)), parent training is unlikely to be adequate by itself unless problems are purely about child management. Unfortunately, workers too rarely have scope for this work, but it could form a component of community-based approaches.

2. Given the dependence of these programmes on the active participation of at least one parent, this intervention is inapplicable where parents are unwilling to participate.

3. The complexity and entrenchment of many of these difficulties indicate the importance of a move away from time-limited approaches with multi-problem families. The development of longer-term therapy has shown dividends in work with families of pre-adolescent antisocial children in contrast with time-limited programmes (Patterson, Chamberlain and Reid 1982).

Another promising approach is that of anger control. Families in which child abuse is a problem are often characterised by low levels of pleasant exchanges and high rates of aggressive behaviour on the part of parent and child (Patterson 1965; Patterson 1982). This can result in a pattern in which, in response to a child's misdemeanour: his mother shouts; he continues, she threatens; he goes on in either the same way or his behaviour gets worse; mother smacks him, he retaliates with verbal and/or physical abuse; mother 'lets fly'. It is worth noting that this sequence identified by Patterson and others highlights a problem that bedevils so much research in this area – the predominant focus on mothers and the apparent invisibility of fathers.

Ordinary parent training aims to break this cycle early on by equipping parents with more effective management strategies. However, sometimes the problem lies less with skill deficits of this kind, than in a parent's poor self-control, which is what anger management sets out to tackle. In most cases, what distinguishes child-abusing families from non-abusing families is not angry feelings or impulses, but that most of the time the majority of parents can contain these. Some parents can't, or fail to on one or more occasions. One of the aims of anger-management strategies is to equip the parent with impulse or anger control – usually in combination with child-management skills. Anger control training does not yet enjoy the empirical support that parent training does, but offers a promising avenue for continued research (Barth *et al.* 1983).

As programmes with abusing parents so often include a number of intervention strategies (reflecting an appreciation of the urgency and multifaceted nature of the problem) it is often difficult to say which procedures are in fact (the most) effective or responsible for the successful outcomes reported.

Implications of an evidence-based approach to practice

Practice should wherever possible be based on evidence that a particular intervention is:

- better than doing nothing, and
- better than alternative approaches.

Certain kinds of research designs produce more secure findings than others. It follows that:

1. When sound studies show interventions provide no greater benefit than occurs with the passage of time, or appear harmful to those on the receiving end, then these approaches should be discontinued. However, it is difficult to find published studies with clear negative results, whether due to publication bias or because people choose not to publish such findings.

2. It seems reasonable to suggest that we should not persist with a particular approach in circumstances where others have proved their (greater) worth.

The difficulties faced by those who work in the personal social services are not unique to them. Medicine has been struggling with the question 'what shall count as evidence?', and only recently has the Department of Health adopted a systematic approach to the dissemination of good quality research findings to those who need them. What it has achieved in a relatively short time is impressive. Attention has now turned to the field of social welfare.

Nowhere is this trend more to be welcomed than in the fields of child care and child protection, particularly with the renewed emphasis on prevention currently taking place. If we are to intervene in the lives of children and families, we *must* adopt a more accountable stance in relation to *what* we do, as well as to *how* we do it. There has been a great deal of excellent research in the field of child care, but by far the lion's share has been concerned with the life experiences and life chances of those children and families for whom prevention has failed and who are therefore placed in substitute care. If we are to make more room for preventative work, then the research agenda must make room for more rigorous evaluations of what works.

As we have seen, there is good evidence that a range of early interventions effect change. While the accumulation of risks for poor later outcomes is cumulative, the benefits of early intervention are considerable though such investment cannot fully overcome disadvantage (Power and Hertzman 1997). Providing opportunities for improved cognitive and emotional functioning to socio-economically dis- advantaged children will improve their life chances, but will not put them on an even playing field with their more advantaged peers. It is for this reason that we also need to emphasise evidence-based social and economic policies.

Meanwhile, intervention at practice level, and in particular early years education is clearly worth while in affording children and young people the opportunity to experience a good childhood. Just as early insults may have long- term effects, early interventions enable children and young people to accrue some of the social capital needed for good long-term outcomes.

Note

A fuller discussion of some of the interventions described above can be found in Macdonald and Roberts (1995).

Acknowledgements

We are grateful to Malcolm Hill and Eva Lloyd for their comments on earlier drafts. The responsibility for the outcome is ours.

References

Alderson, P. (1995) *Listening to Children: Children, Ethics and Social Research.* Barkingside: Barnardo's.

Alderson, P., Brill, S., Chalmers, I., Fuller, R., Hinkley Smith, P., Macdonald, G., Newman T., Oakley, A., Roberts, H. and Ward H. (1995) *What Works? Effective Social Interventions in Child Welfare.* Barkingside: Barnardo's/SSRU.

Ampofo-Boateng, K. and Thomson, J.A. (1989) 'Child pedestrian accidents: a case for preventive medicine.' *Health Education Research 5,* 265–274.

Arblaster, L., Entwhistle, V., Fullerton, D., Forster, M., Lambert, M. and Sheldon, T. (1997) *A Review of the Effectiveness of Health Promotion Intervention Aimed at Reducing Inequalities in Health.* CRD report. York: NHS Centre for Reviews and Dissemination.

Barker, D.J.P. (1994) *Mothers, Babies and Disease in Later Life.* London: British Medical Journal Publications.

Barker, W.E., Anderson, R. and Chalmers, C. (1992) *Child Protection: The Impact of the Child Development Programme.* Evaluation Document No. 14. Bristol: Early Childhood Development Unit, Department of Social Work.

Barker, W.E., Anderson, R. and Chalmers, C. (1994) *Health Trends Over Time and Major Outcomes of the Child Development Programme.* Bristol: Early Childhood Development Unit and Belfast: Eastern Health and Social Services Board.

Barth, R.P., Blythe, B.J., Schinke, S.P. and Schilling, R.F. (1983) 'Self control training with maltreating children.' *Child Welfare LXII,* 4, 313–324.

Beresford, B., Sloper, P. and Newman, T. (1996) *What Works for Families with a Disabled Child?* Barkingside: Barnardo's.

Bornstein, P.H. and Kazdin, A.E. (eds) (1985) *Handbook of Clinical Behaviour Therapy with Children.* Homewood, IL: The Dorsey Press.

Bourne, D. (1993) 'Over-chastisement, child non-compliance and parenting skills: A behavioural intervention by a family centre social worker.' *British Journal of Social Work 5,* 481–500.

Brown, B. and Ware, C. (1994) *What the Parents Say.* Barkingside: Barnardo's London Division.

Brown, C. (1984) *Child abuse parents speaking–parents' impressions of social workers and the social work process.* Working Paper 63, Bristol: School of Advanced Urban Studies.

Cannan, C. (1992) *Changing Families, Changing Welfare: Family Centres and the Welfare State.* New York/London: Harvester Wheatsheaf.

Cannan, C. and Warren, C. (eds) (1996) *Social Action with Children and Families: A Community Development Approach to Child and Family Welfare.* London: Routledge.

Colver, A., Hutchinson, P. and Judson, E. (1982) 'Promoting children's home safety.' *British Medical Journal 285,* 1177.

Culp, R.E., Heide, J. and Richardson, M.T. (1987) 'Maltreated children's developmental scores: treatment versus non-treatment.' *Child Abuse and Neglect 11,* 29–34.

Dance, J. (1982) *A social intervention by linkworkers to Pakistani women, and pregnancy outcome* (unpublished), described in Oakley (1992), op cit.

Department of Health (1995) *Improving the Health of Mothers and Children: NHS Priorities for Research and Development.* Report to the NHS Central Research and Development Committee. London: Department of Health.

Douglas, J.W.B. (1986) *The Home and the School.* London: MacGibbon and Kee.

Dumas, J.E. (1989) 'Treating anti-social behaviour in children: Child and family approaches.' *Clinical Psychology Review 9,* 197–222.

Dumas, J.E. and Wahler, R.G. (1983) 'Predictors of treatment outcome in parent training: Mother insularity and socioeconomic disadvantage.' *Behavior Assessment 5,* 301–313.

Fisher, M. (ed) (1983) *Speaking of Clients.* Sheffield: University of Sheffield, Joint Unit for Social Services Research/Community Care.

Griest, D.L. and Forehand, R. (1982) 'How can I get any parent training done with all these other problems going on?: The role of family variables in child behaviour therapy.' *Child and Family Behaviour Therapy 4,* 1, 73–80.

Griest, D.L., Forehand, R., Wells, K.C. and McMahon, ? (1980) 'An examination of the difference between non-clinic and behaviour problems, clinic referred children and their mothers.' *Journal of Abnormal Psychology 89,* 497–500.

Hardy, J.B. and Streett, R. (1989) 'Family support and parenting education in the home: an effective extension of clinic-based preventive health care services for poor children.' *Journal of Paediatrics 115*, 927–931.

Holden, J.M., Sagovsky, R. and Cox, J.L.(1989) 'Counselling in a general practice setting: a controlled study of Health Visitor intervention in the treatment of postnatal depression.' *British Medical Journal 298*, 223–226.

Holterman, S. (1995) *All Our Futures: The Impact of Public Expenditure and Fiscal Policies on Britain's Children and Young People*. Barkingside: Barnardo's.

Holy Bible (1611) Authorized version, Daniel, i, vv10–16.

Johnson, Z., Howell, F. and Molloy, B. (1993) 'Community mothers' programme: randomised controlled trial of non-professional intervention in parenting.' *British Medical Journal 306*, 1449–1452.

Johnson, Z. and Molloy, B. (1995) 'The community mothers programme – empowerment of parents by parents.' *Children and Society 9*, 2, 73–83.

Kazdin, A.E. (1990) 'Premature termination from treatment among children referred for anti-social behaviour.' *Journal of Child Psychology and Psychiatry 31*, 3, 415–425.

Kehrer, B.H. and Wolin, V.C.M. (1979) 'Impact of income maintenance on low birthweight, evidence from the Gary experiment.' *Journal of Human Resources XIV*, 434–462.

Kuh, D.J.L. and Wadsworth, M.E.J. (1993) 'Physical health status at 36 years in a British National Birth Cohort.' *Social Science and Medicine 37*, 905–916.

Larrence, D.T. and Twentyman, C.T. (1982) 'Maternal attributions and child abuse.' *Journal of Abnormal Psychology 92*, 449–457.

Laughlin, S. and Black, D. (1995) *Poverty and Health: Tools for Change: Ideas, Analysis, Information, Action*. Birmingham: Public Health Alliance.

Little, M. and Kelly, S. (1995) *A Life without Problems? The Achievements of a Therapeutic Community*. Aldershot: Arena.

Lloyd, E. (1996) 'The role of the centre in family support.' In C. Cannan and C. Warren (eds) *Social Action with Children and Families: A Community Development Approach to Child and Family Welfare*. London: Routledge.

Lloyd, E., Hemingway, M., Newman, T., Roberts, H. and Webster, A. (1997) *Today and Tomorrow: Investing in Children*. Barkingside: Barnardo's.

Lobitz, G. and Johnson, S. (1975) 'Normal versus deviant children.' *Journal of Abnormal Child Psychology 3*, 353–374.

Macdonald, G. (1997) 'Social work: Beyond control?' In A. Maynard and I. Chalmers (eds) *Non Random Reflections on Health Services Research*. London: BMJ Publishing Group.

Macdonald, G. and Roberts, H. (1995) *What Works in the Early Years? Effective Interventions in Health, Social Welfare, Education and Child Protection*. Barkingside: Barnardo's.

Macdonald, G. and Sheldon, B. with Gillespie, J. (1992) 'Contemporary studies of the effectiveness of social work.' *British Journal of Social Work 22*, 6, 614–643.

MacMillan, H.L., MacMillan, J.H., Offord, D.R., Griffith, L. and MacMillan, A. (1994) 'Primary prevention of child physical abuse and neglect: A critical review. Part 1.' *Journal of Child Psychology and Psychiatry and Allied Professions 35*, 5, 835–856.

Mann, S.L., Wadsworth, M.E.J. and Colley, J.R.T. (1992) 'Accumulation of factors influencing respiratory illness in members of a national birth cohort and their offspring.' *Journal of Epidemiology and Community Health 46*, 286–292.

Martin, S.E., Sechrest, L.B. and Redner, R. (eds) (1981) *New Directions in the Rehabilitation of Criminal Offenders.* Washington: National Academy Press.

Maynard, A. and Chalmers, I. (eds) (1997) *Non Random Reflections on Health Services Research.* London: BMJ Publishing Group.

McAuley, R. and McAuley, P. (1980) *Child Behaviour Problems.* London: Macmillan.

McCord, J. (1981) 'Consideration of some effects of a counselling programme.' In S.E. Martin, L.B. Sechrest and R. Redner (eds) *New Directions in the Rehabilitation of Criminal Offenders.* Washington: National Academy Press.

McMahon, R.J., Forehand, R. and Griest, D.L. (1981) 'An assessment of who drops out of therapy during parent behavioural training?' *Behavior Counselling Quarterly 1,* 79–85.

McNeish, D. and Roberts, H. (1995) *Playing it Safe.* Barkingside: Barnardo's.

McNeish, D., Roberts, H. and Barrett, A. (1996) *The Prevention of Child Accidents in Wardleworth, Rochdale.* Barkingside: Barnado's and Rochdale Borough Accident Prevention Group.Miller, G.E. and Prinz, R.J. (1990) 'Enhancement of social learning family interventions for childhood conduct disorders.' *Psychological Bulletin 108,* 291–307.

Newman, T. and Roberts, H. (1997) 'Assessing social work effectiveness in child care practice; the contribution of randomized controlled trials.' *Child: Care, Health and Development 76,* 6, 487–489.

Nutbrown, C. (ed) (1996) *Children's Rights: Respectful Educators – Capable Learners.* London: Paul Chapman.

Oakley, A. (1992) *Social Support and Motherhood.* Oxford: Basil Blackwell.

Oakley, A., Rajan, L. and Grant, A. (1990) 'Social support and pregnancy outcome.' *British Journal of Obstetrics and Gynaecology 97,* 155–162.

Oakley, A., Rigby, D. and Hickey, D. (1997) 'Social support in pregnancy: does it have long term effects?' *Journal of Reproductive and Infant Psychology*

O'Flaherty, J. (1995) *Intervention in the Early Years – An Evaluation of the High/Scope Curriculum.* London and Dublin: National Children's Bureau and Barnardo's.

Olds, D.L., Henderson Jr, C.R., Chamberlin, R. and Tatelmaum, R. (1986) 'Preventing child abuse and neglect: a randomized trial of nurse home visitation.' *Paediatrics 78,* 65–78.

O'Leary, K.D. and Emery, R.E. (1983) 'Marital discord and child behaviour problems.' In M.D. Levine and P. Satz (eds) *Developmental Variation and Dysfunction.* New York: Academic Press.

Patterson, G.R. (1965) 'Responsiveness to social stimuli.' In L. Krasner and L.P. Ullaman (eds) *Research in Behaviour Modification.* New York: Holt, Reinhart and Winston.

Patterson, G.R. (1982) *Co-ercive Family Processes.* Eugene, OR: Castalia.

Patterson, G.R., Chamberlain, P. and Reid, J.B. (1982) 'A comparative evaluation of a parent training program.' *Behaviour Therapy 13,* 638–650.

Pilling, D. (1990) *Escape from Disadvantage.* Brighton: Falmer Press.

Power, C. and Hertzman, C. (1997) 'Social and biological pathways linking early life and adult disease.' *British Medical Bulletin 53,* 210–221.

Rachman, S.J. and Wilson, G.T. (1980) *The Effects of Psychological Therapy.* Oxford: Pergamon.

Reid, J.B. (1985) 'Behavioral approaches to intervention and assessment with child abusive families.' In P.H. Bornstein and A.E. Kazdin (eds) *Handbook of Clinical Behavior Therapy with Children.* Homewood, IL: The Dorsey Press.

Reid, J.B., Kavanagh, K. and Baldwin, D.V. (1987) 'Abusive parents' perception of child behaviour problems: an example of parental bias.' *Journal of Abnormal Child Psychology 15,* 457–466.

Rickard, K.M., Forehand, R., Wells, K.C., Griest, D.L. and McMahon, R.J. (1980) 'Factors in the referral of children for behavioral treatment: A comparison of mothers of clinic-referred deviant, clinic-referred non-deviant and non-clinic children.' *Behavioral Research and Therapy* *19*, 201–205.

Roberts, H. (1997a) 'Qualitative methods in child health research.' *Archives of Disease in Childhood,* June.

Roberts, H. (1997b) 'Listen to the parents' (editorial). *British Medical Journal 313*, 954–955.

Roberts, H. (1997c) 'Socio-economic determinants of health: children poverty and health.' *British Medical Journal 314*, 1122–1125.

Roberts, I. and Power, C. (1996) 'Does the decline in child injury mortality vary by social class? A comparison of class specific mortality in 1981 and 1991.' *British Medical Journal 313*, 784–786.

Roberts, H., Smith, S.J. and Bryce, C. (1993) 'Prevention is better...' *Sociology of Health and Illness* *15*, 4, 447–463.

Roberts, H., Smith, S.J. and Bryce, C. (1995) *Children at Risk: Safety as a Social Value.* Buckingham: Open University Books.

Schweinhart, L. and Weikart, D. (1993) *A Summary of Significant Benefits: The High-Scope Perry Pre-School Study through Age 27.* Ypsilanti, MI: High Scope UK.

Siraj-Blatchford, I. (1996) 'Language, culture and identity: challenging inequality and promoting respect.' In C. Nutbrown (ed) *Children's Rights: Respectful Educators – Capable Learners.* London: Paul Chapman.

Stein, T.J. and Gambrill, E.D. (1977) 'Facilitating decision making in foster care.' *Social Services Review 51*, 502–521.

Thoburn, J., Lewis, A. and Shemmings, D. (1995) *Paternalism or Partnership, Family Involvement in the Child Protection Process.* London: HMSO.

Wadsworth, M.E.J. (1985) 'Parenting skills and their transmission through generations.' *Adoption and Fostering 9*, 28–32.

Wadsworth, M.E.J. (1986) 'Effects of parenting style and preschool experience on children's verbal attainment: a British longitudinal study.' *Early Childhood Research Quarterly 1*, 237–248.

Wadsworth, M.E.J. (1991) *The Imprint of Time: Childhood, History and Adult Life.* Oxford: Oxford University Press.

Wahler, R.G. (1980) 'The insular mother: Her problems in parent–child treatment.' *Journal of Applied Behaviour Analysis 13*, 207–219.

Webster-Stratton, C. (1989) 'The relationship of marital support, conflict and divorce to parent perceptions, behaviours and childhood conduct disorders.' *Journal of Marriage and the Family* *51*, 417–430.

Wilkinson, R.G. (1994) *Unfair Shares: The Effects of Widening Income Differences on the Welfare of the Young.* Barkingside: Barnardo's.

Wolfe, D.A., Sandler, J. and Kaufmann, K. (1981) 'A competency based parent training program for child abusers.' *Journal of Consulting and Clinical Psychology 49*, 633–640.

CHAPTER 3

Working with Social Networks
Key Resources in Helping Children at Risk

Robbie Gilligan

This paper argues that children's own social networks must be considered as central in developing effective interventions in children's lives. While primary attachment relationships with parents or parent-figures are clearly very important, an excessive preoccupation with these may obscure the significance of other key relationships in vulnerable children's lives (Lewis 1994). Similarly professionals engaged in the delivery of formal services to children may overestimate the significance of such formal services relative to the meaning and impact of informal supports from within naturally occurring social networks. As Hill (1989, p.210) observes, 'children's lives are not merely the result of actions by parents and the state, but are embedded within a more complex web of relationships.'

While full empirical evidence or even investigation is awaited on the power of their networks as sources of help, it seems reasonable to suggest that children's own social networks are likely to be important because through them, and from individual members of their networks, may flow vital social support which may help a child under social stress of whatever kind. Emerging research evidence suggests that this is so. An American study of 667 two- to five-year-olds and their maternal caregivers living in adverse social circumstances found that social support and integration into local networks distinguished the 13 per cent who were doing well from the majority who were not. Measures of church affiliation, perception of social support and support within the neighbourhood were the direct measures of 'social capital' which influenced the children's social functioning. The authors suggest that this social capital may be most potent for families with fewer financial and educational resources (Runyan *et al.* 1998). A study of post-divorce adjustment among 102 pre-teen children in the US shows how social support, not just from parents but from friends, siblings and other adults may be valuable in assisting the child's adjustment (Cowen, Pedro-Carroll and Alpert-Gillis 1990).

Thus informal help and relationships within social networks may be effective in assisting children's development, both in normal and adverse circumstances. It seems plausible also that such help may be more acceptable, meaningful and enduring than usually scarcer and remoter help from formal services. If children's problems are often complex, then responses to these problems are likely to need to mirror this complexity.

The picture, however, is not all rosy and uncomplicated. If positive support can flow through the relationships which constitute networks, so too may negative energy which undermines, damages or criticises the child or draws him or her into anti-social rather than pro-social behaviour. It is well to remember for instance that abuse and bullying may also occur within key relationships in a child's social network. Peer relationships, for example, may be a source of friendship and support, but they also may be a source of problematic experiences such as sexual harassment (Fineran and Bennett 1998). In reality, networks tend to contain simultaneously elements which prove helpful and others which do not. The key point however is that it is unwise to ignore social networks since they may have such influence for good or ill. Interventions with children and young people should take account of their social networks, be alive to ways of incorporating an appropriate role for relevant network members, and, where necessary, consider desirable network changes.

This paper explores the importance of children's own social networks in intervening in children's lives. It considers key aspects of social networks and social support and their inter-relationships. It also reviews some of the available evidence on the importance as sources of support to a child both of individual categories of network member (e.g. siblings, peers, teachers etc.) and of the network operating as a collective entity.

Why consider children's social networks independently of their parents'?

While children's needs and interests are often close to those of their parents, they must be seen as separate and distinct, especially by child care professionals working with children and young people at risk. When compared to those of their parents, children are likely to have different needs for support and quite possibly different potential sources of support in their specific personal social networks. These differences are due to many factors including the child's developmental stage and power status, relative to their parents and other adults. While there may be overlap between children's and parents' networks and sources of support, we must avoid simplistic merging of the two in our thinking. This chapter focuses primarily on children's networks because of the need to render children's networks less invisible, and because the extensive literature on the importance of parental social networks has received much more coverage elsewhere. In the case of younger children, of course, they may be more reliant on accessing support through their parents' agency and network. Accordingly, the question of parental networks and younger children is discussed briefly towards the end of the chapter.

Why may social networks be important?

The informal social support which children can access for themselves through their network may be an important resource that can help protect children against stressors in their lives. Support may prevent moderate or counteract stress. Support can influence self-esteem or a young person's sense of having control in response to stress (Sandler *et al.* 1989). This may have a crucial impact on a child's functioning.

Social networks may play a significant part in social intervention by acting as a source of:

- key information about needs and resources in the life of the child
- essential help to the target child or child's family
- a mandate for professional or other intervention
- a dynamic for positive change.

Network members may be able to relate information about the child's history, needs and circumstances which can assist in assessing the strengths and resources available to a child and his or her family. When gathered together in a structured way, as in a family group conference, they may provide ideas about options to resolve a child's unmet needs (Marsh and Crow 1998, p.145). Network members may generate fresh perspectives, offer to take responsibility or endorse what an agency plans to do, thus minimising the risk of subsequent sabotage of agency efforts by network members who might otherwise have felt alienated from the process of planning and decision making. They may also help to attune a proposed intervention to the cultural or other realities of a child's life.

The network can be the context within which are found key individuals whose relationship and commitment to the child may be a vital or central ingredient of intervention, for instance a sibling who keeps close contact with an otherwise isolated younger sibling in care or a grandparent who takes on the role of kinship carer for a child who would otherwise be placed in foster care with a stranger. The network may also be a focus for intervention. This may involve professionals meeting with significant members collectively in order to influence relationships and mutual perceptions and responsiveness within it. Alternatively the intervention may be aimed at adding new resources to the network or trying to deepen the commitment of selected individuals to the member of concern. The network becomes a source of empowerment as the anchor child or person comes to realise, value or use the full range of supports and linkages he or she has (Fuchs 1990; 1995). As Cleaver (1996, p.32) reminds us, even where network members are unable to play a particularly active or positive role, their relationship with the vulnerable young person may be significant because of its symbolic value – as in the case of the ties a young person in care may have to wider family. A sense of having even passive or remote network members may be helpful to a young person who yearns for some sense of belonging to some other human beings or who can refer to them when in conversation with friends.

What factors may influence a child's capacity to access support through the social network?

Clearly both child factors and network factors may be among those affecting the availability of support and the child's capacity to access it. The accessibility and impact of social networks and social support may be influenced by a child's age and gender, and by their 'internal working model' of 'help' (Marris 1996). Taking the issue of age, for instance, Bryant (1985) suggests from an American study comparing 72 seven-year-olds with 96 ten-year-olds that the ten-year-olds were better able to make more effective use of social support resources in their social ecology than were the seven-year-olds in the same community, presumably because of their greater mobility and autonomy.

Key features of social support and social networks include the concepts of *network size* (the number of people in the network), *social embeddedness* (frequency of contact with network members), *enacted support* (the amount of help received) and *perceived quality of support* (the recipient's evaluation of the support received). Coping with stress may be influenced by an expectation that support will be available to be called on, irrespective of whether this is borne out in practice. People who perceive themselves as having this support to call on may feel stronger and more confident in the face of stress. Network size of itself does not tell us about the quality of support available, although small networks are likely to have fewer resources. In an American study of child psychiatric in-patients, researchers found that children who reported fewer supportive persons in their lives appeared to be at risk of higher levels of hopelessness and behavioural problems. They were less attentive, more withdrawn, harmful to others, damaging to property and unco-operative (Kashani *et al.* 1994). While this study suggests an association between perceived low numbers of supportive adults and behaviour problems and hopelessness, the direction of any possible causation is not clear.

Under normal developmental conditions, children and young people may be thought of as having hierarchies of attachment relationships, that is, relationships which are of special importance to them. In one Canadian study of young adults (college students), the respondents were asked to nominate people whose support, companionship or presence for good or ill was very significant to them. Five categories emerged in the following order of importance: partner (where relevant), mother, father, sibling and best friend (Trinke and Bartholomew 1997). Similarly, other research stresses the importance for children in adversity of having confidants and helpers within and beyond the nuclear family. A British study of children in residential care highlighted the value of access to a range of potential sources of support. The young people studied 'wanted more contact with siblings, grandparents, friends and other relatives as well as parents' (Sinclair and Gibbs 1996, p.13). This wish on the part of the young people seems soundly based according to American research on resilient young people who have transcended adversity growing up. These resilient youngsters drew on the support of grandparents, other relatives, peers, teachers and other willing adult mentors. In their study of children whose parents misuse alcohol, Hill, Laybourn and Brown (1996, p.164) found that usually the children did have at least one confidant, 'most often the other parent, a sibling or a grandparent'. Westcott and Davies (1995) reported on a study of 98 boys and girls aged eight to seventeen years about their views on how to seek help in the face of bullying or parental arguing. Parents, friends and teachers emerged as the most likely people from whom to seek help. The quality of the helper rather than the degree of need seemed to influence any decision to seek help. A sense of the coherence of the network and the relationships within it may be important for a young person enduring adversity. Bennett, Wolin and Reiss (1988) use the term 'deliberate family process' to describe the pattern they found whereby children were more protected from paternal alcoholism when their family was still intact enough to be able to plan and carry off rituals – ceremonies, traditions and routines, which symbolised a vital order for the child presumably.

The key non-parental members of the child's social network

For the purposes of this discussion, the focus is largely on the informal network, that is people whose role or relationship within the network (a) occurs naturally rather than by special professional intervention and (b) is not defined by a primary professional obligation to offer help. Thus categories of informal network members can include non-parental relatives, whether residing with the child or not, peers, non-relative adults, including neighbours, sports coaches and so on. Teachers can be included because they appear 'naturally' in children's lives (and not usually by special arrangement or referral) and their primary obligation is educational rather than therapeutic or practically supportive. It is worth noting that the main physical sites within which social network support operates in the child's life are the school and the neighbourhood (Holman 1988; Gilligan 1998).

Siblings

Siblings are likely to grow closer to each other in the face of shared adversity. In the face of family break up, siblings may act as a 'potent supportive network' and offer relationships which model 'loyalty, intimacy and enduring love' (Werner and Smith 1992, p.12). Intense feelings between siblings are likely to emerge where they have 'high access' to each other and where there is a 'vacuum of parental care' (Banks 1992, p.145). The sibling relationship may be a source of 'protection, warmth, comfort' in non-harmonious homes (Jenkins and Smith 1990, p.67). It is also worth noting that the benefit from care by a sibling does not just flow in the direction of the person being cared for. Nurturing may give a child an enhanced

> Siblings
>
> Grandparents
>
> Uncles
>
> Aunts
>
> Friends
>
> Peers
>
> Family of Friends and Peers
>
> Neighbours
>
> Teachers
>
> Adult mentors (for sporting, leisure or cultural pursuits)

Figure 3.1 Possible members of a child's informal social network (other than parents)

sense of competence (Dunn and Kendrick 1982). It is important to acknowledge too, however that the sibling relationship itself may suffer as a result of adversity. Yet, one study has found that, while children in disharmonious homes may have difficulties forming positive relationships with their siblings, if they can do so even with one of their siblings, they have much lower levels of emotional and behavioural problems (Jenkins 1992, p.136). For children in public care, siblings are likely to be of additional importance to each other. This may be especially so in terms of preserving social and family identity (Bilson and Barker 1992–3, p.308). They may also provide for each other a source of solidarity, reassurance and even advocacy. In one British study of young people in residential care siblings topped the list of people the respondents said they would like to see more of (Sinclair and Gibbs 1996, p.9). Children in long-term care risk having thinner social networks when they reach young adulthood and beyond. Sibling relationships may then assume special significance. With few other reliable adults to turn to, siblings may become important sources of social support.

The research evidence suggests that relations with siblings may be valued whether or not there are special stresses in a child's life. Kosonen (1996) undertook a small community study of Scottish children's views of important people in their lives. Majorities of respondents considered siblings as:

- 'important' (83% – ranked third after mothers and fathers)
- a source of 'support' (56% – second after mothers)
- a source of 'help' (63% – second after mothers).

One study of sibling relationships found that a majority of the children reported support from their sibling 'in the face of problems such as difficulties with other children at school, maternal illness, or accidents and illnesses that they themselves had suffered' (Dunn, Slomkowski and Beardsall 1994, p.322). Siblings can offer each other many supports at a practical and emotional level. These may take the form of companionship and emotional support, caretaking of younger siblings, practical help – perhaps to compensate for parental inadequacy – money lending, physical protection, teaching of skills, helping with homework, sharing of friends (Goetting 1986 cited in Cicerelli 1995, p.109). In the normal course of development, a sibling may serve as a significant attachment figure (Dunn 1993, p.46).

In a study of children from disharmonious homes, those children with support from a sibling seemed less adversely affected (Jenkins and Smith 1990). Among 116 young people known to social work services in five local authorities in England and Scotland, siblings were third overall in categories to whom the young people felt 'closest' – 30 per cent nominated siblings compared to 46 per cent for mothers and 42 per cent for friends (Triseliotis *et al.* 1995). Siblings were ranked fourth for being 'best helpers' and second, though a long way behind, to friends for being 'most fun'.

Grandparents and extended family

While parents and peers seem most important, non-parental adults (particularly extended family members) may play a significant role. One US study of a community population of 169 pre-adolescents and young adolescents found relationships with grandparents were generally meaningful, supportive and conflict free, although this was less often true of relations with parental grandfathers. Girls tended to be somewhat closer to their grandparents than boys (Creasey and Kalliher 1994). In the Jenkins and Smith (1990) study of children in disharmonious households, a relationship with a non-parental adult – most typically a grandparent – was found to be a protective factor against poor outcomes. Werner and Smith (1992) report the key role that grandparents frequently played as carers or mentors in the childhoods of youngsters who overcame adversity.

For children in care, grandparents may represent an important potential source of constructive interest and support. Relationships with grandparents may also not be laden with the hazards sometimes associated with parental contact. One study has argued that while contact for children in care with their parents was equivocal in its effects contact with other key figures such as grandparents was not found to pose any difficulties (Rushton, Treseder and Quinton 1995). Unfortunately however the value of grandparental contact may not always be recognised and nurtured in practice. This is illustrated well in one case example cited from research in Northern Ireland where examination of the case records revealed a failure to respond effectively and imaginatively to grandparental interest in two boys in foster care (Horgan and Sinclair 1997, p.61).

Non-related adults

Non-related adults who are important to children and young people are often in a socialising role, as teacher, coach or youth group leader, developing talents and abilities. They can help validate in the adolescent's eyes the young person's efforts, ability and personal qualities. The young person may experience positive feedback as more genuine perhaps than praise from a parent or best friend who the young person may suspect feels obliged to offer such praise (Darling, Hamilton and Niego 1994, pp.229-230).

Relationships with non-kin adults had a positive effect on the educational progress and social behaviour of a sample of 92 sixteen-year-old Norwegian boys. These adults were drawn from four main sources: friends of the family; coaches; teachers and youth workers; family of friends; and neighbours. They helped broaden the boys' horizons teaching, modelled new opportunities and introduced new contacts and resources for later life (Cochran and Bø 1989).

In considering mentoring relationships, it is necessary to distinguish between naturally occurring relationships and created mentoring relationships. A naturally occurring mentoring relationship might be with a grandparent, neighbour or teacher, and the work of Werner and Smith (1992) emphasises the value of this type of relationship for a vulnerable young person. In a contrived mentoring relationship, the young person is matched to an adult volunteer or para-professional. The benefits of this type of mentoring appear positive but modest according to one review of US evidence (Scales and Gibbons 1996). It has been suggested that such a mentoring relationship is most successful where the mentor is keen to teach the young person something through shared activity rather than just spend leisure time with them (Darling, Hamilton and Niego 1994, p.228). Relationships with supportive adults may help a young person find a niche in the world of work or an interest in a hobby. A British study of young people in residential care found that 'those who were involved in work or proud of something they did in their leisure time were happier' (Sinclair and Gibbs 1996, p.10).

Young children too may benefit from a consistent relationship with a committed adult outside the home as in the Swedish Contact Person and Contact Family Programme (Andersson 1993). On the basis of two studies of this programme, Andersson observes that the contact person or family 'provides both support and relief, not only for the parent(s) but also for the children'. She suggests that the 'contact family can be an important "extra family" for the children'.

Big Brothers and Big Sisters of America offer same sex adult volunteer contact with children from single parent households. The volunteer has weekly contact for 3 to 5 hours a week for at least a year and is meant to provide the child with 'friendship, understanding, feedback, and concern for the child's wellbeing' (Turner and Scherman 1996, p.877). In a study of 45 boys (23 'Little Brothers' and 22 boys on a waiting list to become 'Little Brothers'), they found that boys linked with a Big Brother had higher self-concept scores (Piers-Harris Children Self Concept Scale) than boys on the waiting list. In a different study of the Big Brothers and Big Sisters of America, Frecknall and Luks (1992) found that parents considered that their children had benefited from involvement, and the success of contact was correlated with length of involvement and parental contact with the Big Brother/Sister. A British study also found that volunteer befrienders were mostly well regarded by young people and parents (Triseliotis et al. 1995).

Teachers

Teachers may serve many important supportive roles in children's lives in addition to their primary educational function (Gilligan 1998). They may act as an ally and confidant for a child with worries or a guarantor who will ensure that help is accessed when the teacher's threshold of concern is crossed. They may be encouragers who help a child to develop interests and self-esteem through extra-curricular activities by the structure, support and routines they provide. Teachers and schools may also help a child to recover from the trauma of loss or abuse (Robson, Cook and Gilliland 1995; Romans *et al.* 1995).

Friends

Friends may be an important source of support for young people in difficulty. Kochenderfer and Ladd (1997) report from a study of kindergarten children who had experienced relatively high levels of bullying by peers, that for boys support from a friend proved a more effective means of stopping being bullied than fighting back. The same effect was not seen among girls. Boys who relied on help from a friend were less likely to report continuing harrassment by peers 4–6 months later. This difference did not appear to be due to differences in quality of friendships enjoyed by boys who ceased and continued to be bullied. The implication for intervention seems to be to try to help children form friendships with children 'who will offer protection or serve as allies' (p.71). On the other hand, friends may be a negative influence. In Triseliotis *et al.* (1995, p.236) 60 per cent of the young people in the study (all known to social workers) admitted that friends had got them into trouble at some point. This links to a point made in a New Zealand study which highlights the risk to social development posed by association with 'anti-social' peers (Fergusson and Lynskey 1996). It seems that friends are important – they have influence, but this can be positive or negative. Hartup (1996, p.10) states that 'supportive relationships between socially skilled individuals' may be advantageous developmentally. Yet 'coercive and conflict-ridden relationships' are disadvantageous especially among 'anti-social' children.

Pets

It may often be appropriate to include even pets as family or network members according to Byng Hall (1982, p.361) because although 'not blood members of the family, they often fulfil family roles. A dog might comfort a father, protect a mother and be looked after by a child all during the same day'. Van Houtte and Jarvis (1995) found that pet owning pre-adolescents were more autonomous than non-pet owners. This suggests that pet ownership may be a way of encouraging more independence in young people about to enter adolescence.

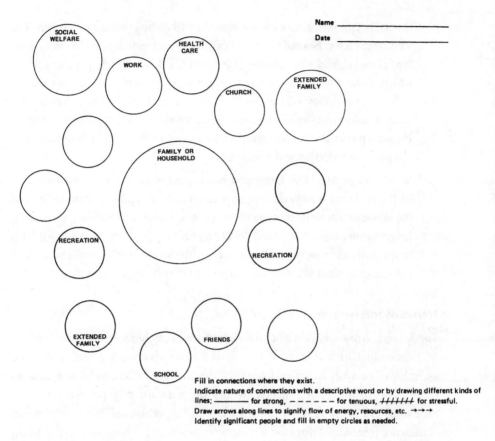

Figure 3.2 Hartman's Eco-Map

Harnessing the network

For professionals to engage effectively with children and their networks, it is necessary to assess carefully the composition, structure and functions of the network.

Assessing and mapping the network

Two instruments may be particularly helpful for the practitioner who is trying to identify network members and assess the quality of relationships the person of concern (anchor person) has with the various network members identified; the eco-map and the social network map.

Eco-Map. This instrument was developed in 1975 by Hartman (see Figure 3.2) who claims it can be used not only as an assessment tool but also for 'interviewing, planning and intervention' (1995, p.113). It is a single page pro forma which allows the service user and worker together to plot key figures and resources in the person's current network, the direction of flows of energy and resources and the quality of the connections, whether strong, tenuous or stressful. It gives a powerful visual summary representation of the client's life situation and can provoke reflection and discussion.

Social Network Map. This instrument is also used to explore in a systematic way with a client the membership of their social network and key characteristics of the relationships with those network members, such as frequency of contact, length of time known, type and direction(s) of support if any (Tracy 1990). This instrument can be used very productively with clients in social work practice and has also been used in research on aspects of clients' social networks.

Network intervention

Speck and Attneave describe the intervention technique of *social network intervention* in which a team of two or three workers work directly with the assembly of network members (including the younger members) 'to stimulate, to reflect, and to focus the potential within the network to solve one another's problems' (1971, p.315). While it carries strong echoes of the family group conference (see below) this model of network intervention is more interventionist in the sense that the intervention 'event' becomes the centre piece rather than a prelude as is more the case in FGCs. Yet in the network intervention approach, the workers according to Speck and Attneave, must avoid casting themselves, or being cast, in the role of therapists who become responsible for 'healing'. The worker's role is to help the network recognise and mobilise its own capacity for healing, whatever the target difficulty is. In a British case example, Beal (1981) gives a very interesting account of how she as a social worker assisted a family in organising a meeting to help sort out a dispute with neighbours who had signed a petition to the Council to have action taken against the family. It underlines how the social network can become hostile as in this case, but also demonstrates that skillful social work can assist in defusing conflict and enhance mutual tolerance, problem solving and relationships within a network. Tracy *et al.* (1995, p.57) however urge some caution in terms of expectations of this overall approach. They believe that while they may show promise network interventions are 'no panacea' and are 'best seen as part of more comprehensive service intervention'.

Kinship care

Kinship care represents another example of the relevance of social network members. In this instance, a relative undertakes the role of a full-time carer for a child who would otherwise have to go into foster care with a stranger carer or into residential care. Kinship care, the placement of children in state care with relatives or the acceptance of children already living with relatives into the state care system, has grown dramatically in many jurisdictions around the world. In the early 1990s in New York state, Illinois and California, kinship placements accounted for 40–50 per cent of all placements in use (George, Wulczyn and Harden 1996).

Kinship care is the subject of much debate. In its favour it has been argued to be a culturally appropriate response to the need for placement out of the home. In the view of US commentators it is a 'resilient, natural system of child rearing' for African American children and families (Scannapieco and Jackson 1996, p.194). At its best it may seem a way of 'squaring the circle' in terms of pursuing sim-ultaneously what are frequently incompatible goals of child protection and family preservation. In this instance the preservation embraces the child's retention within the extended family. Much of the published evidence on kinship care is American and this is reflected in the discussion below. One American study comparing non-relative and kinship carers found that relative care givers were 'more likely to be single women, members of ethnic minority groups less educated and older' than the non-relative foster carers. The relative carers were also found to identify more strongly with the various aspects of the foster parent role than non-relatives (Le Prohn 1994).

Children in kinship care seem to enjoy more stability with much lower risk of moves than those in non-kin placements (Berrick, Barth and Needell 1994). British studies have also found this tendency for kinship placements to be more stable (Milham *et al.* 1986; Berridge and Cleaver 1987). Children placed with kin may also be safer in terms of any risk of child maltreatment compared to children placed with strangers (Zuravin, Benedict and Somerfield 1993). Children in kinship care also tend to have easier and more frequent contact with their parents than those children placed in conventional foster care (Berrick, Barth and Needell

1994). Rowe, Hundleby and Garnett (1989) in a British study found that kinship care tended to be more durable despite often taking on some of the more challenging types of fostering tasks (e.g. long-term care of adolescents). On the other hand, in the US, children in kinship care are less likely to return home quickly. They have been found to be subject to a 30 per cent longer duration of stay than children not placed with relatives (George, Wulczyn and Harden 1994, p.43). Kinship carers tend to be poorer and to get fewer services and less support than mainstream carers (Dubowitz, Feigelman and Zuravin 1993; Gebel 1996). In a study of 214 adults aged 19–31 who had as children formerly been in kinship (40%) and non-kin foster homes (60%), few differences were found in adult functioning in either group 'in terms of education, current employment, physical and mental health, risk-taking behaviours, and the stresses and supports in their lives' (Benedict, Zuravin and Stallings 1996, p.545). This may seem a curious finding when compared to the evidence cited above that those youngsters in kinship care did better than those in mainstream foster care during placement to a statistically significant degree. Perhaps the impact of the more deprived home backgrounds in kinship care begins to tell in adult functioning. These questions really remain to be explored by further research in a complex and fascinating area. At the very least it seems that kinship care does not lead to *worse* outcomes.

Family group conferences

Developed in New Zealand where they have a legally recognised role, Family Group Conferences have become an influential concept internationally where they are seen as introducing a new relationship between state professionals and the extended families of children known to the child protection or juvenile justice systems (Marsh and Crow 1998). Once it has been agreed to convene a family Group Conference, an independent and culturally attuned co-ordinator begins the process of preparation and planning. The first task is to identify who makes up 'family' in the particular instance – this may include significant adults who are not related, for example, family friends or neighbours. Inviting and securing the attendance of the 'family' members is the next issue. At the meeting, the first stage which the co-ordinator chairs, entails information sharing. The relevant professionals 'explain their roles, responsibilities, concerns and local resources' (Morris 1995, p.5). After any clarification, the family is given private time to address the issues and come up with a plan (including contingency and review arrangements). The co-ordinator and professionals then come back in to hear the plan. If the plan is satisfactory from the professionals' perspective, it will be agreed and resources will be negotiated (Morris 1995). Marshall and Crow (1998) report a study in England and Wales in 1995–96 of 80 Family Group Conferences involving 99 children in 69 families. 74 of the 80 conferences produced agreements which were 'fully acceptable to professionals and families as being in the best interests of the children'. Plans developed seemed to be carried out and remained stable in three-quarters of the cases. Families were positive about FGCs and three-quarters said they would choose to be involved in another.

Swain and Ban (1997) report on a study of the view of 128 participants in Family Group Conferences in Victoria, Australia. These were made up of 52 family members and 76 professionals – 37 from statutory services and 39 NGO (non-governmental organisations) representatives. Three-quarters of family members interviewed were content with the plans made for the child(ren) and 80 per cent were satisfied 'in terms of involvement, the process and its outcome'. Eighty-five per cent of professional respondents 'supported the process both in principle and in terms of their actual experience of it' (p.42). The authors concede that effective implementation of FGC plans relies on the availability of resources and agency commitment, which are not easy to guarantee where there is no legal obligation to adhere to the plan. This issue of follow through (for any type of case conference including FGCs) has also been identified by another Australian commentator (Campbell 1997). Campbell however also argues that the FGC 'challenges the professional to relinquish fixed expectations of what a family can or ought to do or be, and to avoid treating family members as quasi-professionals to whom offial functions (such as monitoring, or foster care) are contracted' (p.7).

Burford *et al.* (1996) describe the use of Family Group Conferences in a Newfoundland family reunification project where efforts are made to return children in care to their immediate or extended family. Thirty-two different families attended 37 conferences involving 384 family members and 88 professionals. All but one of the conferences came up with a definite plan. In almost all cases it seemed these were acceptable to the professionals involved and their managers although the release of necessary resources did prove problematic in some instances. Overall the conferences were deemed to have 'increased understanding and respect between families and professionals' (Burford *et al.* 1996, p.51) without putting a vulnerable or abused child at risk.

Parental networks and the welfare of (young) children

Research evidence on the prevention of child abuse and neglect generally stresses the importance of informal social support as a key factor in effective intervention (Thompson 1995). In his review on physical child abuse and neglect Guterman (1997) highlights the importance of links to informal support within family's social networks as one key element in preventive approaches. In a review on neglect, De Panfilis (1996) stresses the importance of 'an examination of the availability and helpfulness of the social network' and 'the development of personal networks' (p.49). Fortin and Chamberland (1995) cite 'insertion into the community network' (p.289) as an important antidote to the risk of psychological maltreatment of children by parents in conditions of poverty.

The Neighbourhood Parenting Support Project is a specific example of a programme aimed at demonstrating the application of the principle of support to vulnerable parents. It was a four-year research and demonstration project (1988–1992) in two inner city, high risk, multi-cultural neighbourhoods in Winnipeg, Canada. The networker in the project worked with target parents, members of the neighbourhood and other professional workers and agencies. The worker had contact with 100 parents and 50 workers and agencies, and tried in each case to identify concerns; map the parent's network; reduce connections to sources of stress; build up supportive links with existing or newly introduced network sources; and mediate in key relationships where necessary. The Project carried out measures at two points in time in the intervention community and in a comparison community (without intervention). The major findings 'are (1) that informal helping and support can be strengthened by social network intervention, (2) the formal systems can be meshed with informal structures, and (3) that risk for child maltreatment can be reduced by social network intervention' (Fuchs 1995, p.121).

How may professionals work in a way that takes account of social networks?

In working with networks and network members, professionals may have a number of roles:

1. Mapping the network: establishing who are the people who make up the network.

2. Validating the network for the focal member, other members and key professionals: reminding all concerned of the significance and potential of the network.

3. Gathering information from relevant members of the network: consulting members individually or collectively, through interviews, participation in case conferences etc.

4. Negotiating and mediating between the focal member and other members with a view to (re-)establishing a flow of help to the focal member: for example helping to re-engage an interested aunt who has previously fallen out with the young person.

5. Mediating between key network members and professionals where necessary.

6. Assembling and/or intervening in the network: for example, calling a meeting to discuss matters relevant to the welfare of the child.

7. Helping reinforce the identity of the network through the encouragement or support of rituals and celebrations: for example, by arranging a party or outing for network members.

8. Seeking to graft on additions to the network where appropriate: for example, by involving a child in youth or sporting organisations.

9. Seeking to buffer the effect of negative forces in the child's social network: for example, helping a child to secure assistance in dealing with bullying by peers.

It is essential that in assessing needs and planning intervention in the lives of children, professionals give sufficient weight to evidence about children's personal networks (and parental networks especially in the case of younger children). This evidence should be used to discern the flow of positive and negative energy through the network to the young person. Networks have influence and can reach out to provide help in ways that other forms of intervention may find hard to match. The risk that some aspects of network involvement may be negative or unhelpful does not mean that networks should be discounted – it means they cannot be ignored. In some instances it may be appropriate to rely primarily on the network as the focus of intervention, in other instances it will of course be necessary to rely mostly on other forms of intervention, but even then it is suggested that the quality and impact of those interventions will be enhanced by keeping the network central in thinking in the assessment and intervention phases.

References

Andersson, G. (1993) 'Support and relief: the Swedish contact person and contact family program.' *Scandinavian Journal of Social Welfare 2*, 54–62.

Banks, S. (1992) 'Remembering and reinterpreting sibling bonds.' In F. Boer and J. Dunn (eds) *Children's Sibling Relationships: Developmental and Clinical Issues.* Hillsdale, NJ: Lawrence Erlbaum Associates.

Beal, A. (1981) 'A family and its neighbours.' In J. Miller and T. Cook (eds) *Direct Work with Families.*

Belle, D. (ed) (1989) *Children's Social Networks and Social Supports.* New York, NY: John Wiley.

Benedict, M., Zuravin, S. and Stallings, R. (1996) 'Adult functioning of children who lived in kin versus nonrelative family foster homes.' *Child Welfare 75*, 529–549.

Bennett, L., Wolin, S. and Reiss, D. (1988) 'Deliberate family process: a strategy for protecting children of alcoholics.' *British Journal of Addictions 8*, 3, 821–829.

Berrick, J., Barth, R. and Needell, B. (1994) 'A comparison of kinship foster homes and foster family homes: implications for kinship foster care as family preservation' *Children and Youth Services Review 16*, 1/2, 33–63.

Berridge, D. and Cleaver, H. (1987) *Foster Home Breakdown.* Oxford: Blackwell.

Bilson, A. and Barker, R. (1992–3) 'Siblings in care or accommodation: a neglected area of practice.' *Practice 6*, 4, 307–318.

Boer, F. and Dunn, J. (eds) (1992) *Children's Sibling Relationships: Developmental and Clinical Issues.* Illsdale, NJ: Lawrence Erlbaum Associates.

Bryant, B. (1985) 'The neighbourhood walk: sources of support in middle childhood.' *Monographs of the Society for Research in Child Development 50*, 3, 1–122.

Burford, G., Pennel, J., MacLeod, S., Campbell, S. and Lyall, G. (1996) 'Reunification as an extended family matter.' *Community Alternatives – International Journal of Family Care 8*, 2, 33–55.

Byng Hall, J. (1982) 'Grandparents, other relatives, friends and pets.' In A. Bentovim, A. Cooklin and G. Gorell Barnes (eds) *Family Therapy: Complementary Frameworks of Theory and Practice. Vol. 2.* London: Academic Press.

Campbell, L. (1997) 'Family involvement in decision making in child protection and care: Four types of case conference.' *Child and Family Social Work 2*, 1, 1–11.

Cicerelli, V. (1995) Sibling Relationships Across the Lifespan. New York, NY: Plenum.

Cleaver, H. (1996) *Focus on Teenagers – Research into Practice.* London: HMSO.

Cochran, M. and Bø, I. (1989) 'The social networks, family involvement and pro- and antisocial behavior of adolescent males in Norway.' *Journal of Youth and Adolescence 8*, 4, 377–398.

Cowen, E., Pedro-Carroll, J. and Alpert-Gillis, L. (1990) 'Relationships between support and adjustment among children of divorce.' *Journal of Child Psycology and Psychiatry 31*, 727–735.

Creasey, G. and Kalliher, G. (1994) 'Age differences in grandchildren's perceptions of relations with grandparents.' *Adolescence 17*, 5, 411–426.

Darling, N., Hamilton, S. and Niego, S. (1994) 'Adolescents' relations with adults outside the family.' In R. Montemayor, G. Adams and T. Gulotta (eds) *Personal Relationships During Adolescence*. Thousand Oaks, CA: Sage.

De Panfilis (1996) 'Social isolation of negectful families: a review of social support assessment and intervention models.' *Child Maltreatment 1*, 1, 37–52.

Dubowitz, H., Feigelman, S. and Zuravin, S. (1993) 'A profile of kinship care.' *Child Welfare 72*, 2, 153–169.

Dunn, J. (1993) *Young Children's Close Relationships – Beyond Attachment*. Newbury Park, CA: Sage.

Dunn, J. and Kendrick, C. (1982) *Siblings: Love, Envy and Understanding*. London: Grant McIntyre.

Dunn, J., Slomkowski, C. and Beardsall, L. (1994) 'Sibling relationships from the preschool period through middle childhood and early adolescence.' *Developmental Psychology 30*, 3, 315–324.

Fergusson, D. and Lynskey, M. (1996) 'Adolescent resiliency to family adversity.' *Journal of Child Psychology and Psychiatry 37*, 3, 281–292.

Fineran, S. and Bennett, L. (1998) 'Teenage peer sexual harassment: implications for social work practice in education.' *Social Work 43*, 1, 55–64.

Fortin, A. and Chamberland, C. (1995) 'Preventing the psychological maltreatment of children.' *Journal of Interpersonal Violence 10*, 3, 275–295.

Frecknall, P. and Luks, A. (1992) 'An evaluation of parental assessment of the Big Brothers/Big Sisters program in New York city.' *Adolescence 27*, 715–718.

Fuchs, D. (1990) *Networking and Social Group Work Practice for Neighbourhood Mutual Aid and Empowerment*. Child and Family Study Series # 10715. Winnipeg, Manitoba: Child Family Services Research Group, School of Social Work, University of Manitoba.

Fuchs, D. (1995) 'Preserving and strengthening families and protecting children: Social network intervention, a balanced approach to the prevention of child maltreatment.' In J. Hudson and B. Galway (eds) *Canadian Child Welfare*. Toronto: Thomson.

Gebel, T. (1996) 'Kinship care and non-relative family foster care: a comparison of caregiver attributes and attitudes.' *Child Welfare 75*, 1, 5–18.

George, R., Wulczyn, F. and Harden, A. (1994) *Foster Care Dynamics 1983–92 California, Illinois, Michigan, New York and Texas – A Report from the Multistate Foster Care Data Archive*. Chicago: The Chapin Hall Centre for Children at the University of Chicago.

George, R., Wulczyn, F. and Harden, A. (1996) 'New comparative insights into States and their foster children.' *Public Welfare*, Summer, 12–25.

Gilligan, R. (1998) 'The Importance of Schools and Teachers in Child Welfare.' *Child and Family Social Work 3*, 1, 13–25.

Guterman, N. (1997) 'Early prevention of physical child abuse and neglect: Existing evidence and future directions.' *Child Maltreatment 2*, 1, 12–34.

Hartman, A. (1995) 'Diagrammatic assessment of family relationship.' *Families in Society: The Journal of Contemporary Human Services, 76*, 3, 111–122.

Hartup, W. (1996) 'The company they keep: Friendships and their developmental significance.' *Child Development 67*, 1, 1–13.

Hill, M. (1989) 'The role of social networks in the care of young children.' *Children and Society 3*, 3, 195–211.

Hill, M., Laybourn, A. and Brown, J. (1996) 'Children whose parents misuse alcohol: a study of services and needs.' *Child and Family Social Work 1*, 3, 159–167.

Holman, B. (1988) *Putting Families First*. Basingstoke: Macmillan Education.

Horgan, G. and Sinclair, R. (1997) *Planning for Children in Care in Northern Ireland.* London: National Children's Bureau.

Hudson, J. and Galway, B. (eds) (1995) *Canadian Child Welfare.* Toronto: Thomson.

Jenkins, J. (1992) 'Sibling relationships in disharmonious homes: Potential difficulties and protective effects.' In F. Boer and J. Dunn (eds) *Children's Sibling Relationships: Developmental and Clinical Issues.* Hillsdale, NJ: Lawrence Erlbaum Associates.

Jenkins, J. and Smith, M. (1990) 'Factors protecting children in disharmonious homes: Maternal reports.' *Journal of the American Academy of Child and Adolescent Psychiatry 29,* 1, 60–69.

Kashani, J., Canfield, L., Borduin, C., Soltys, S. and Reid, J. (1994) 'Perceived family and social support: Impact on children.' *Journal of the American Academy of Child and Adolescent Psychiatry 33,* 6, 819–823.

Kochenderfer, B. and Ladd, G. (1997) 'Victimised children's responses to peers' aggression: Behaviors associated with reduced versus continued victimisation.' *Development and Psychopathology 9,* 59–73.

Kosonen, M. (1996) 'Siblings as providers of support and care during middle childhood: Children's perceptions.' *Children and Society 10,* 4, 267–279.

Le Prohn, N. (1994) 'The role of the kinship foster parent: A comparison of the role conceptions of relative and non-relative foster parents.' *Children and Youth Services Review 16,* 1/2, 65–84.

Lewis, M. (1994) 'Does attachment imply a relationship or multiple relationships?' *Psychological Inquiry 1,* 47–51.

Marris, P. (1996) *The Politics of Uncertainty – Attachment in Private and Public Life.* London: Routledge.

Marsh, P. and Crow, G. (1998) *Family Group Conferences in Child Welfare.* Oxford: Blackwell Science.

Milham, S., Bullock, R., Hosie, K. and Haak, M. (1986) *Lost in Care: The Problem of Maintaining Links Between Children in Care and Their Families.* Aldershot: Gower.

Montemayor, R., Adams, G. and Gulotta, T. (eds) (1994) *Personal Relationships During Adolescence.* Thousand Oaks, CA: Sage.

Morris, K. (1995) *Family Group Conferences – an Introductory Pack.* London: Family Rights Group.

Robson, M., Cook, P. and Gilliland, J. (1995) 'Helping children manage stress.' *British Educational Research Journal 21,* 2, 165–174.

Romans, S., Martin, J., Anderson, J., O'Shea, M. and Mullen, P. (1995) 'Factors that mediate between child sexual abuse and adult psychological outcome.' *Psychological Medicine 25,* 127–142.

Rowe, J., Hundleby, M. and Garnett, L. (1989) *Child Care Now – A Survey of Placement Patterns.* London: British Agencies for Adoption and Fostering.

Runyan, D., Hunter, W., Socolar, R., Amaya-Jackson, D., English, D., Landsverk, J., Dubowitz, H., Browne, D., Bangdiwala, S. and Mathew, R. (1998) 'Children who prosper in unfavourable environments: The relationship to social capital.' *Pediatrics 101,* 1, 12–18.

Rushton, A., Treseder, J. and Quinton, D. (1995) 'An eight year prospective study of older boys in permanent substitute families: A research note.' *Journal of Child Psychology and Psychiatry 36,* 4, 687–695.

Sandler, I., Miller, P., Short, J. and Wolchik, S. (1989) 'Social support as a protective factor for children in stress.' In D. Belle (ed) *Children's Social Networks and Social Supports.* New York, NY: John Wiley.

Scales, P. and Gibbons, J. (1996) 'Extended family members and unrelated adults in the lives of young adolescents: A research agenda.' *Journal of Early Adolescence 16*, 4, 365–389.

Scannapieco, M. and Jackson, S. (1996) 'Kinship care: The African American response to family preservation.' *Social Work 41*, 2, 190–196.

Sinclair, I. and Gibbs, I. (1996) *Quality of Care in Children's Homes – a Short Report and Issues Paper.* York: Social Work Research and Development Unit, University of York.

Speck, R. and Attneave, C. (1971) 'Social Network Intervention' In J. Haley (ed) *Changing Families: A Family Therapy Reader.* New York, NY: Grune & Stratton.

Swain, P. and Ban, P. (1997) 'Participation and partnership–family group conferencing in the Australian context.' *Journal of Social Welfare and Family Law 19*, 1, 35–52.

Thompson, R. (1995) *Preventing Child Maltreatment through Social Support – A Critical Analysis.* Thousand Oaks, CA: Sage.

Tracy, E. (1990) 'Identifying social support resources of at-risk families.' *Social Work, 35*, 3, 252–258.

Tracy, E., Whittaker, J., Boylan, F., Neitman, P. and Overstreet, E. (1995) 'Network interventions with high-risk youth and families throughout the contiuum of care.' In I.M. Schwarz and P. Au Claire (eds) *Home-Based Services for Troubled Youth.* Lincoln: University of Nebraska.

Trinke, S. and Bartholomew, K. (1997) 'Hierarchies of attachment relationships in young adulthood.' *Journal of Social and Personal Relationships 14*, 5, 603–625.

Triseliotis, J., Borland, M., Hill, M. and Lambert, L. (1995) *Teenagers and the Social Work Services.* London: HMSO.

Turner, S. and Scherman, (1996) 'A big brother's impact on little brother's self-concepts and behaviors.' *Adolescence 31*, 124, 875–82.

van Houtte, B. and Jarvis, P. (1995) 'The role of pets in preadolescent psychosocial development.' *Journal of Applied Developmental Psychology, 16*, 463–479.

Werner, E. and Smith, R. (1992) *Overcoming the Odds – High Risk Children from Birth to Adulthood.* Ithaca: Cornell University.

Westcott, H. and Davies, G. (1995) 'Children's help seeking behaviour.' *Child: Care, Health and Development 21*, 4, 255–270.

Zuravin, S., Benedict, M. and Somerfield, M. (1993) 'Child maltreatment in family foster care.' *American Journal of Orthopsychiatry, 63*, 4, 589–596.

CHAPTER 4

Community Work with Children

Paul Henderson

Introduction

Concern about children is in evidence across society. Wherever one turns, it seems, the issue of children's well-being appears to be dominant: children and poverty, children and safety, children and crime, children and the environment. These are some of the parts which make up the complex mosaic of children and society, the 'external' world of children which complements their 'internal' world.

A large proportion of work undertaken on these issues takes place 'in the community' in the sense that it occurs in open, non-institutional and mainly neighbourhood-based settings, and one purpose of this chapter is to indicate the extent to which this work has expanded in recent years. Community work, however, has a much sharper definition than simply work carried out in the community, and the chapter's main purpose is to discuss what is meant by the phrase 'community work with children', to examine the research evidence for this way of working and to explore the implications for research and policy.

It is vitally important for adults to remind themselves that children are affected by a range of factors and forces: commercial pressures on children, particularly as consumers; the culture of a developed society which puts a premium on fashion and popular music; the problems that adults and children have of communicating with each other; the fear and nascent conflicts existing in Britain's most deprived communities.

Children may experience one or a combination of these forces, and statistical data on various aspects of children's lives needs to be understood within this context. Nearly one-third of children in Britain are trapped in poverty. The Joseph Rowntree Foundation's inquiry into income and wealth states that 'we are concerned by the position of children being brought up in low-income families, particularly those in neighbourhoods where most families are poor' (Joseph Rowntree Foundation 1995, p.8). This is a devastating indictment of society, especially given the centrality of poverty to chaildren's life chances: 'The more we learn, the clearer it becomes that, in post-industrial societies at least, poverty is the biggest risk of all' (Leach 1994, p.188). Evidence from research on children in poverty, on lack of safety for children in public places, on blighted environments and depressed communities is giving us critically important messages about the impact on children's lives of unacceptable conditions in the communities in which they live. Research on these and other issues also tends to point to the need for adults to pay more attention to the views of children themselves: 'Children have to be involved, without denying their rights to be children' is the message emphasised by Middleton (1992, p.115) in relation to disabled children, for example.

Community work

The term community work is usually taken to refer to a method: working with a range of groups and organisations on issues identified by participants and members and aligned to a commitment to collective action. Community work connotes the idea of intervention, usually by a community worker, and assumes that there is a distinctive set of skills and techniques available (see Twelvetrees 1982; Henderson and Thomas 1987; ACW 1994). Underpinning many of them is the capacity of community work to make connections between issues. This way of defining community work allows us to understand the term community development as a broad-based process of change taking place in communities. It is a process which can be observed and evaluated with a high degree of rigour. For example, the evaluation model prepared by the Scottish Community Development Centre for the Department of Health and Social Services in Northern Ireland (Barr, Hashagen and Purcell 1996) has received widespread recognition within the statutory, voluntary and community sectors in Northern Ireland as well as across the rest of the UK. Community work is one of a number of possible methods or approaches which can support community development (see Thomas 1983). Community work with children and families is a specialist area which is informed by core community work principles. Broadly speaking one can distinguish between community work carried out with and on behalf of children in co-operation with parents and other adults; and community work which is targeted more directly at young people (usually over approximately 13-years-old) and which overlaps sometimes with youth work (see Chapter 9).

Historically, under the influence of American social work theorists, community work was conceived of as being the third method of social work, i.e. complementary to casework with individuals or families and group work. This tradition remains important in some European countries, notably France and Spain. In Britain, however, over the last 20 years, community work has moved away from its social work origins. Jacobs (1994) argues that in the 1970s community work sought to distance itself from social work, presenting itself as a radical alternative, and from youth work, which was caricatured as being simply a means of keeping young people off the streets. Twelvetrees (1982) acknowledges a common viewpoint in stating that 'the relationship between community work and social work in Britain has never been an easy one' (p.5). Part of this has been to do with differences between social work and community work practice, and these have been exacerbated over the last ten years by the increased emphasis within social services agencies on tight procedures for work undertaken with individuals and families, particularly in the child care context. The effect has been to draw most social workers away from more broad-based concerns of communities to do with housing, the environment and employment. They literally have not had time to become involved in community work. Conversely, those people using community work from within these agencies have felt distanced from the pressures experienced by social workers.

Over the same period, social work qualifying courses have – with one or two exceptions – reduced the time allocated to community work. If community work is there at all it tends to be studied in the context of individual and family problems. Inevitably, this gives a particular slant to community work.

During the 1970s, influenced by the political economy analysis advocated by the Community Development Projects, a neo-Marxist, structuralist ideology had a major influence on community work in Britain. Towards the end of the decade, feminist theories had an increasing impact on community work. During the Thatcher years, community work's theoretical direction was much less evident. In seeking to survive in a political climate which was essentially unsympathetic to community development notions which put a premium on collective action and the mobilisation of poor people, community work tended to react to developments as they arose. It could even be said to have taken on a chameleon quality, changing its language and priorities in response to pressures and opportunities. It certainly moved even further away from social work than before, responding to the economic development imperatives of the Government and playing its part in the formation of inter-sectoral partnerships geared towards regeneration strategies.

The flurry of activity in the 1980s around community social work (McGrath and Hadley 1981; National Institute for Social Work 1982) among a small number of social workers seems, with the benefit of hindsight, to have been merely a temporary deviation from the main routes down which social work was being forced to go: towards closely managed implementation of legislation within a context of rising public expectations and diminishing resources. Yet, as we shall see, community social work initiatives produced important findings for work with children. Almost in parallel with the weakening of community work within the statutory social services sector, a number of voluntary organisations were seeking to open up the community dimension of their work with and on behalf of children. The work of Bob Holman with children, young people and community groups on estates in Bath and Glasgow became particularly well known, but other practitioners in The Children's Society, Barnardo's, Save the Children and NCH Action for Children were also extending this area of work. It should be remembered too that work with children and young people took place within the settings of community education and youth work. Both of these experienced the effects of public expenditure cuts between 1979–97 and yet their commitment to neighbourhood-based work was retained, albeit unevenly, across the country.

Research and practice

There has been virtually no UK research targeted specifically on community work with children. One has to go back to the Harlesden Project to find such an example. The researchers in this case were interested in tracing the connections between community work practice and residential child care and it is worthwhile looking in a little more detail at this unusual project. It took place in Harlesden, in the London borough of Brent, and was funded and managed by the local authority's Social Services Department. It grew out of discussion between two workers about the links between community work and residential care and about the possibility of establishing a service which would:

- provide community work for the residents of the area
- provide, if needed, residential accommodation for young people
- examine whether community work might be able to make any useful contribution to residential care for the young people.

The publication reporting on five years of the Project's work (Harlesden Community Project 1979) contains fascinating details of the support given to children and young people, as well as to neighbourhood groups. It also, however, illustrates some of the difficulties and conflicts of interest between young people in a residential home and local adults, particularly over the question of noise. This, from time to time, put the Project under pressure from the local authority and eventually the Social Services Committee insisted upon the residential unit being closed. The Project was, however, a ground-breaking initiative and 25 years on it might be useful for policymakers to return to it and connect it with developments in child care and community work since that time. It certainly highlighted the core issue of young people's and adults' differing perspectives on rights and social control. It also displayed the tensions, which are perhaps inherent, between the holistic approach of community work and some of the compartmentalisation associated with much outcome research.

While research material on community work with children is meagre, there have been many case studies of community work projects which, to a greater or lesser extent, worked with and on behalf of children (e.g. Edwards 1988; Hulyer 1997). Running through these, as well as the way in which practitioners describe their work, is the belief that this way of working appears to be effective. Hulyer, for example, in writing about work on two estates, assumes that the benefit to children (and their parents) of after-school clubs, summer playschemes and playgroups are self-evident:

> Equally it can be seen that community associations, residents' associations and a community festival can benefit children and families through improving the area generally, or the housing. (Hulyer 1997, p.193)

The writer goes on to argue that there are also less tangible benefits:

> If community members are being empowered in the ways described by Thomas (1983) and Twelvetrees (1982) and some of them are social services clients, then it seems reasonable to assume that their new-found confidence and self-belief

will help them avoid the stressful situations that lead to, for example, physical abuse of their children. (p.193)

Most community workers would share this confidence that, in a myriad of different ways, children are helped as a result of community work. This is one of the most valuable aspects of Bob Holman's writing on neighbourhood work (Holman 1997). There might be anxiety among some community workers at the idea of researching or measuring the actual benefits to children, because trying to separate out one aspect of community work cuts across the defining characteristic of their method of intervention, namely a holistic approach in which deliberate efforts are made to make connections between issues. Community work is also loath to work to 'categories' of people or age groups. The benefits of community involvement include children, and this needs to be more widely recognised, but attempting to isolate this particular outcome might put at risk the enterprise as a whole because of the need for community work to retain a broad agenda: it depends on people getting involved for all sorts of reasons, so that insisting upon a very specific focus might undermine local support and participation.

Community work, therefore, is faced with a choice: to continue to rely on experience and observation of children's participation in community projects, hoping that policymakers and resource holders will come to share this conviction, or to argue for research and evaluation of children and community work which is compatible with the principles and methods of community work. As will be seen, I opt for the second choice because of the need to have more evidence-based data, and because of the emergence in recent years of evaluative tools designed specifically for use in community development projects.

It can also be argued that the existence of a cluster of related research and policy outputs provide supportive evidence that community or neighbourhood approaches are helpful. In addition to the Harlesden Community project and the case study tradition in community work referred to above, there are other sources of knowledge and information.

Related research and policy

There have been a number of policy documents in recent years, some coming from the national voluntary child care organisations (e.g. Save the Children 1997), some from local government (see Willow 1997) and some from the Children's rights movement (Children's Rights Development Unit 1994). Their existence is evidence of the commitment of a range of organisations to the issue of collective participation by children and young people. The organisations are acutely aware of the need to present arguments at policy levels in addition to being able to point to examples of good practice.

Of all the topics which relate to community work with children, that of family centres is the most thoroughly researched. The research by Gibbons, Thorpe and Wilkinson (1990) concluded that family projects had 'strengthened local comm-unity resources, by providing new activities and advice points, by drawing in new volunteers, and by opening up new opportunities for local people' (p.158). Cannan and Warren (1997), commenting on the evidence, state that 'neigh-bourhood-oriented family centres are a recent success story' (p.8). The way in which such centres provide a flexible and accessible resource for children, adults and community groups has been one of the most positive developments to have taken place within social welfare over the last two decades. It is crucial that the neighbourhood model of centres retains a clear identity alongside more client-orientated models focused mainly on children at risk.

With the new government giving clear signals about reviewing the universalist assumptions of the Beveridge Welfare State, one can anticipate the need to repeat, forcefully, why the neighbourhood model of family centres is so important. It is a model which takes seriously the principle that local people – clients and non-clients alike – should have opportunities to define needs and how services are delivered. It also has the potential to open pathways for parents to develop skills, self-esteem and employability. The evidence is that such centres can be key building blocks in the implementation of social cohesion strategies. They reduce the likelihood of children and families feeling stigmatised when using local services and they provide an accessible source of help to families in crisis. Their relevance to community work *per se,* especially to community work with children, is very clear. It is of interest to note how organisations such as Contact a Family, set up to facilitate support from volunteers to families, are seeking to locate their work more substantially in and with communities. This development builds on im-portant evidence contained in some of the community social work practice in the 1980s. For example, the team working on the Canklow estate in Rotherham were convinced of the value of establishing close partnerships with the community. After two years they were also able to record a significant decline of children on the at risk register (Eastham 1990). While there may have been other factors influencing this outcome, it was nevertheless a noteworthy achievement.

There is increasing evidence of the priority being accorded by practitioners to setting up structures and projects which encourage the views of children to be heard. There is a fascinating variety of group activities and workshop methods being tested, and this is reflected too in practitioners' research. An excellent example of the latter is by two practitioners employed by The Children's Society in East Cleveland who had the opportunity to carry out a pilot study with children aged 4–11 years in a rural area. The children were asked particularly about their locality – where they play and places they visit. 'Our experience has shown that given the correct circumstances children enjoy being asked, are enthusiastic and keen to participate if the subject is relevant to their lives' (Callaghan and Dennis 1997, p.44). Children's willingness to be involved is echoed in practitioners' reports from other projects in both the voluntary and statutory sectors. The Local Government Information Unit's guide to promoting children and young people's democratic participation in local government identifies the following key message: 'Children and young people want to be listened to and involved. Whenever children and young people are asked what can be done to improve services, or local communities, they invariably suggest – listen more to what we have to say' (Willow 1997, p.107).

One senses that there now exists a momentum, led by practitioners, to find imaginative ways whereby adults – in agencies and in community groups – can listen to children's voices. We are surely likely to see more examples similar to the Children's Research Group (supported by The Children's Society) in Liverpool 8: 'From the very first meeting of the Liverpool 8 Children's Research Group attention has been given to the importance of research being a foundation for action. Of promoting the positive benefits of children participating in making their community and city a better place' (Liverpool 8 Children's Research Group 1997, p.1). Action against racism and drugs were key priorities identified by the children.

The new sociology of childhood has particular implications for the way adults perceive children and, therefore, also how community work with and on behalf of children is practised. The Economic and Social Research Council (ESRC) is currently running a programme on children aged 5–16 growing into the twenty-first century. A significant number of research institutes and universities are involved, covering a range of topics. Taken together, the programme provides an important research context and one which is directly relevant to community work with children because the programme will 'attempt to illuminate the middle period of childhood and the nature and quality of children's family and social lives, children's sense of belonging and their contributions to society, together with their understandings, expectations and aspirations for the future' (ESRC 1997, p.12). The outcomes and influence of the programme could be as important for community work as the European research on children a few years ago led by Jens Quortrup: 'Childhood is part of society in the sense that children do in fact participate in organised activities, and it constitutes a part of the social structure interacting in many ways with other parts' (Quortrup 1991, p.14).

The wider research and policy context, therefore, for community work with children is relatively vibrant: case studies, policy papers, family centres, children's voices and academic research all provide important signposts for community work. The fact remains, however, that the actual research findings for our topic remain relatively thin. If community work with children is to obtain the recognition and resources it deserves, then it is time for community workers to be more tough-minded about a research agenda. They will be seen to be naïve and irresponsible if they continue to rely solely on observable practice to achieve recognition for their method.

A research agenda

Research on family centres is an example of the cumulative effect of focused research linked to dissemination, and it is important to sustain this line of enquiry to draw out the implications for neighbourhood-based social work. However, a more powerful, broad-based strategy than this is required, one which connects work with children in communities to key issues.

Children and regeneration

I have raised questions elsewhere about some of the assumptions surrounding the funding and programming of urban regeneration projects and the dominance of economic criteria (Henderson 1997). In the important debate about the relationship between economic and social regeneration it is essential for the issue of children's participation to be included: the right of children to be consulted about plans for neighbourhoods; ensuring that their need for play areas, meeting places, safety and security is taken seriously; finding ways whereby children and adults can discuss issues about their neighbourhood and work together on projects:

> A danger in our present time is to have too narrow a focus in the way we view work with children. Projects are easily defined in a way that segments the community. Work is often with this group or that management committee, or organised around a single target. An alternative way of defining the work is in relation to the whole, in this case the neighbourhood. (Hasler 1995, p.177)

These are matters which should be of central importance in regeneration policies, not relegated to the margins, and it is time that we saw evidence of this happening in the plans of Government Regional Offices, local authorities and regeneration agencies.

Children and poverty

The setting up by the Government of the Social Exclusion Unit, led by the Prime Minister, to spearhead plans to combat social exclusion provides an opportunity to address the issue of child poverty *per se* and to specify ways in which community work can be used, alongside other methods, to support children's initiatives and projects. Producing measurable outcomes on the issue of social exclusion is one of the most challenging areas facing the Government and, given the alarming figures of the number of children living in poverty, ensuring that children are an integral part of local strategies is essential.

Community work's experience of working with adults and children in many of Britain's most divided, oppressed and poor communities represents an important resource on which to build. Community work principles, it should be recalled, put a premium on working with the most deprived communities and, by and large, this is where most community work resources have been targeted. Community work has more going for it than merely a wish to support participation in a loose, generalised sense. On the contrary, it is interested in who participates, in identifying blocks to participation among particular groups of people, and in encouraging such people to become involved – many for the first time. It is equipped to work with people – including children and young people – who are alienated from and angry with 'officialdom'. To be at all effective, community work has to put itself alongside such people and to be capable of sustaining its commitments. It must, therefore, be properly planned and resourced in order to deliver results on the issue of children and poverty.

Community work and targeting

The most effective community work often takes place when the process of intervention, moving through identifiable stages, is combined with specific and tangible targeting. A welfare rights campaign taking place alongside skilled support for existing community groups is an example: the campaign benefits from being able to relate to networks of local people, and groups have a concrete agenda item on which to work.

The same idea applies to community-based drugs and alcohol programmes, an increasing number of which are realising the need to target children. Several projects founded and supported by the Home Office Drugs Prevention Teams have grown from generalist community work. In the Gorton area of Manchester, for example, a group of parents were involved in running holiday playschemes and from there went on to establish Gorton Against Drug and Alcohol Abuse. This illustrated how the interweaving of the development process with tangible resources of information, training and workers can be an effective combination (Henderson 1995). Evidence of drugs and alcohol misuse in deprived neighbourhoods is growing. Community work offers a method for reaching and working with a range of people and organisations: concerned local residents; children and young people; users; service providing organisations.

The above three issues are priorities for community work with children. It is being argued that, in addition to expanding work in these areas, it is imperative that the work undertaken is properly evaluated. The handbook summarising the evaluation model produced by the Scottish Community Development Centre can be used with all policies, programmes and projects which are intended to encourage community development and it is based on community development principles: 'This means that the community should be involved fully in agreeing how the evaluation will be done, and what will be measured' (Barr *et al.* 1996, p.11). The handbook is also unusual in the emphasis it places on the need to evaluate how services and policies of organisations change as well as local people in communities. Accordingly, evaluation of community work with children needs to take into account:

- the way people are involved in their community and the changes affecting it
- the way communities are organised
- the way communities relate to the world outside
- the way the world outside relates to communities. (Barr *et al.* 1996, p.9)

This is helpful in suggesting how the topic of community work with children can be put in context: adults and agencies are as much the targets of change and development as children themselves.

Conclusion

A challenge always facing community work is how to respond to changing social, economic and political contexts and to shape a meaningful identity for itself. Work with and on behalf of children at a time when there is mounting concern at the extent of poverty and alienation among children and young people is one such opportunity.

In this chapter, I have sought to argue that a priority must be to expose the practice of community work and children to more rigorous, longitudinal research and evaluation. This, it seems to me, is a serious gap at present, particularly when put alongside the rich material emanating from practitioner research, case studies and conferences. In responding to the changing context of children and young people it is vital for this aspect to be recognised. It is likely to require a co-ordinated effort between children's voluntary organisations, local authorities, research institutes and government. It may also stand more chance of gaining recognition if it is examined in the international context. This applies particularly to the issue of arguing for a safe and sustainable environment for present and future generations of children. There is considerable interest in this area (Hart 1997) as well as a growing realisation that environmental action has to find ways of connecting with the day-to-day concerns of children and adults. The scope for community work to make links between environmental and social welfare issues is considerable.

It is essential for policy makers to realise the extent to which 'community' is of central importance for children, not marginal. Alongside the home and school it is where children learn and develop. This, fundamentally, is why community work with children is of critical significance: 'Community is, alongside family and educational facilities, a Child Development System. It is where children establish associations, gain identity and develop social skills through play, investigation and interaction with peer groups' (Callaghan and Dennis 1997, p.6).

The perspective of child development is as poweful an argument for community work with children as needs and rights-based arguments. It should encourage practitioners, managers and researchers to move the method out of the side eddies of social policy into the mainstream.

References

Association of Community Workers (ACW) (1994) *Community Work Skills Manual.* Newcastle: ACW.

Barr, A., Hashagen, S. and Purcell, R. (1996) *Measuring Community Development in Northern Ireland.* Belfast: DHSS.

Callaghan, J. and Dennis, S. (1997) *'Right Up Our Street.' Research with Children, Their Account of Living in East Cleveland.* London: The Children's Society.

Cannan, C. and Warren, C. (eds) (1997) *Social Action with Children and Families.* London: Routledge.

Children's Rights Development Unit (1994) *UK Agenda for Children.* London: CRDU.

Darvill, G. and Smale, G. (eds) (1990) *Partners in Empowerment: Network of Innovations in Social Work.* London: National Institute for Social Work.

Eastham, D. (1990) 'Plan it or suck it and see.' In G. Darvill and G. Smale (eds) *Partners in Empowerment: Network of Innovations in Social Work.* London: National Institute for Social Work.

Edwards, R. (1988) 'Issues for Community Projects Developing Local Involvement.' In P. Henderson (ed) *Working with Communities.* London: The Children's Society.

Economic and Social Research Council (1997) *Changing Britain. Newsletter for the ESRC Population and Household Change Research Programme,* Oxford: Oxford Brookes University.

Gibbons, J., Thorpe, S. and Wilkinson, P. (1990) *Family Support and Prevention: Studies in Local Areas.* London: NISW/HMSO.

Harlesden Community Project (1979) *Community Work and Caring for Children.* Ilkley: Owen Wells.

Hart, R. (1997) *Children's Participation.* London: Earthscan.

Hasler, J. (1995) 'Belonging and becoming: The child growing up in community.' In P. Henderson (ed) *Children and Communities.* London: Pluto Press.

Henderson, P. (1995) *Drugs Prevention and Community Development.* London: Home Office.

Henderson, P. (1997) 'Community development and children: A contemporary agenda.' In C. Cannan and C. Warren (eds) *Social Action with Children and Families.* London: Routledge.

Henderson, P. and Thomas, D.N. (1987) *Skills in Neighbourhood Work.* London: Unwin.

Henderson, P. (ed) (1988) *Working with Communities.* London: The Children's Society.

Henderson, P. (ed) (1995) *Children and Communities.* London: Pluto Press.

Holman, B. (1997) *FARE Dealing.* London: CDF Publications.

Hulyer, B. (1997) 'Long-term development: Neighbourhood community development work on estates.' In C. Cannan and C. Warren (eds) *Social Action with Children and Families.* London: Routledge.

Jacobs, S. (1994) 'Community work in a changing world.' In S. Jacobs and K. Popple (eds) *Community Work in the 1990s.* Nottingham: Spokesman.

Jacobs, S. and Popple, K. (eds) (1994) *Community Work in the 1990s.* Nottingham: Spokesman.

Joseph Rowntree Foundation (1995) *Inquiry on Income and Wealth.* York: Joseph Rowntree Foundation.

Leach, P. (1994) *Children First.* London: Michael Joseph.

Liverpool 8 Children's Research Group (1997) *Listen to the Children.* Liverpool: Liverpool 8 Children's Research Group.

McGrath, M. and Hadley, R. (eds) (1981) *Going Local: Neighbourhood Social Services.* London: Bedford Square Press.

Middleton, L. (1992) *Children First. Working with Children and Disability.* Birmingham: Venture Press.

National Institute for Social Work (1982) *Social Workers, Their Role and Tasks.* London: Bedford Square Press.

Quortrup, J. (1991) *Childhood as a Social Phenomenon – An Introduction to a Series of National Reports.* Vienna: European Centre for Social Welfare Policy and Research.

Save the Children (1997) *All Together Now. Community Participation for Children and Young People.* London: SCF.

Thomas, D.N. (1983) *The Making of Community Work.* London: George Allen and Unwin.

Twelvetrees, A. (1982) *Community Work.* Basingstoke: Macmillan.

Willow, C. (1997) *Hear! Hear! Promoting Children and Young People's Democratic Participation in Local Government.* London: Local Government Information Unit.

CHAPTER 5

Social Learning and Behavioural Approaches to Work with Children and Families

David Gough

Introduction

Behavioural theory has informed a very large number of therapeutic approaches for child and family problems. Many of the principles derive from the basic theories of classical and operant conditioning and observational learning. These have been further extended by developments in cognitive theory and cognitive behavioural therapies (CBT).

The number of child and family problems to which such therapies have been applied are also very diverse, but this chapter is restricted to examining some of the main applications for which behavioural derived therapies have shown to be successful, particularly externalising problems of conduct disorder and internalising problems of depression and anxiety and phobias. These behavioural and psychological problems are commonly present in children and families presenting with various types of other problems to health and welfare services. The specialist area of behavioural work with children with intellectual disabilities is not considered.

Behavioural, social learning and cognitive theories

Before considering the research evidence for the effectiveness of behavioural and cognitive therapy with children, it is useful to review briefly the range of behavioural theories and techniques (fuller accounts can be found in Payne 1997; Ronnen 1997).

Classical and operant conditioning

Behavioural theories of therapeutic change go back to Pavlov's original research on classical conditioning. He described the way that certain stimuli (such as presentation of food) were automatically followed by specific responses (e.g. salivation). If an unrelated stimulus (such as the sound of a bell) is presented with the initial stimuli then, after some time, this unrelated stimuli could alone produce the conditioned response (e.g. salivation). In this way, new associations between stimuli and responses could be built up. Such learning is crucial in allowing humans and other animals to adapt their patterns of behaviour to the various changing circumstances they experience in the world.

Behaviour change can also occur through operant conditioning where the probability of a particular behaviour occurring is changed due to the reinforcement that follows rather than the stimulus which preceded it. When a behaviour increases in frequency, then the experience following the behaviour is, by definition, reinforcing or rewarding. If the behaviour decreases in frequency, then the experience was either punishing, or had no reinforcing quality and would lead to a weakening or *extinction* of a behavioural association and a reduced probability that the target behaviours will occur. Partial reinforcement where the behaviours are only sometimes followed by reinforcement is more resistant to extinction. Secondary reinforcement is where some non-reinforcing event systematically occurs at the same time as a positive reinforcer and thus develops reinforcing properties. For example, if a child is positively reinforced by parental attention for misbehaviour, then other co-occurring behaviours such as parental raised voice, threats, or physical assault may become rewarding by association. Secondary reinforcers can dramatically increase the number of reinforcers that influence our behaviour in daily life.

Reinforcement changes the frequency of already occurring or spontaneously occurring behaviours but it can also create new behaviours through shaping. For example, a rat can at first be rewarded with a peanut for being at one end of a cage near a lever. Once this has been achieved, then stricter criteria can be applied so that the rat is only rewarded if it is right next to the lever, then actually pressing the lever. In this way new behaviours that are difficult to teach directly can be gradually shaped.

Social and cognitive-based learning

Behavioural change can also arise through observation and imitation. Social learning theory has detailed the way in which people not only react to primary and secondary reinforcers impinging upon themselves, but also change their behaviour after having observed the consequences of certain behaviours on others (Bandura 1977).

Although Bandura's work on observational learning emphasised the social aspect, it also introduced a cognitive dimension because such processes require interpretations of the actions of others and their consequences. Subsequently, there has been a dramatic increase in the study of the influence of cognitive processes on behaviour and, more recently, an emphasis on the active role of interpretation where individuals are influenced by socio-cultural forces yet are still active constructors of their own social reality (Mahoney 1993). Some constructionist explanations involve emotional and unconscious processes and concepts such as self and resistance, so resemble psychodynamic theories which are anathema to traditional behaviourists (Mahoney 1993).

Behavioural treatments increasingly include a cognitive perspective which takes account of the thoughts and feelings which precede behaviour and try to modify these. Cognitive behavioural therapy assumes that behaviour is determined by the way that the individual perceives, codes, and experiences the world. Therapy aims to change cognitive processes in order to change behaviour. Most forms of 'talk' psychotherapy are in a sense cognitive, but overtly cognitive approaches are likely to be more directive than psychodynamic therapies in suggesting methods of change in cognitions and behaviour (Jones and Pulos 1993). They are primarily aimed at teaching new cognitive skills or at rectifying dysfunctional cognitive processes (Kendall 1993) as there is considerable evidence that children with psychological and behavioural problems have cognitive deficits or distortions of some kind (Spence 1994).

Cognitive restructuring methods for children have mostly been adapted from work with adults, particularly the work of Aaron Beck on depression (Beck *et al.* 1979). Therapy has three main constituents. First, the identification by therapist and client of maladaptive modes or templates (cognitive schemata) for processing information (cognitive operations) and the resultant maladaptive thoughts and beliefs (cognitive products). Second, challenging these schemata and products.

Third, development, practice, and reinforcement of more adaptive cognitive processing methods (Spence 1994).

Behavioural research

Research on the effects of psychotherapeutic interventions often lacks precision, uses heterogeneous samples, does not ensure equivalence of therapy across research participants, and measures outcome in non-standardised ways. In contrast, the emphasis of behavioural methods on explicit behaviour rather than hypothesised internal processes has led behaviourists to be very precise in specifying the aims and purposes of any therapeutic intervention and the measurement of any change. They are also more likely to control potentially confounding variables with full experimental research designs (involving random allocation to treatments and ratings of change made 'blind' by people unaware of who belong to which treatment group). Such precision of purpose and outcome has resulted in both better standards of research and a greater measured efficacy of behaviour compared to other therapeutic interventions (Gough 1993). This greater recorded efficacy may simply be due to a greater power to identify statistically significant effects (Shirk and Russell 1992), but a meta analysis of studies suggests that behavioural methods do more reliably produce greater change (Weiss and Weisz 1995).

Besides group comparison, single case studies may be employed, and here again behavioural studies often have an advantage. The specificity of the interventions and their effects allow for ABA designs where intervention (A) is followed by no intervention or a counter acting intervention (B) and then by the original therapy (A) again. If the target behaviours increase, decrease, and then increase in correspondence with the change in therapy, then it is likely that the changes are due to a therapeutic effect and not due to attention or simple time effects.

One criticism of behavioural studies is that they have mainly evaluated treatment at specialist clinics whose clients and methods of working may not be representative or may not be easily transferable to community clinics, health care centres or homes. Research based treatments typically differ from routine practice as they involve researcher recruitment of patients, homogeneity of patients, treatment of one focal problem rather than broad based treatment, and special training and use of protocols and manuals in delivering the research therapy

(Weisz, Weiss and Donnenberg 1992). It is therefore not surprising that clinic-based studies report poorer outcomes than research based treatments (Weisz *et al.* 1995; Shadish *et al.* 1997).

Hoagwood *et al.* (1995) also contrast research based therapy with routine practice. Research interventions are usually highly structured and focused compared to broader unstructured approaches of routine work. The researchers tend to be concerned with the internal logic and validity of the research defined variables rather than with the meaning of the measures to clinicians and others in the outside world (external validity). Also, researchers typically focus on patient symptoms measured on standardised scales, whilst clinicians are also interested in quality of life, consumer satisfaction and costs. Kazdin (1997) argues that the principal issue is whether any statistically significant treatment effects also have clinical significance such as the child being able to function within normative levels.

Treatment and research on child behavioural and psychological problems is often divided into externalising problems where behaviour is expressed outwardly such as in aggression towards other people or things and internalising problems which are directed inwards as in depression and eating disorders. These two areas of work will now be discussed in turn.

Externalising problems

Many children are at times non-compliant, lie, are aggressive or are in some ways difficult to manage. These behaviours may be occasional and reflect temporary difficulties or a particular developmental stage where a child wishes to express his or her independence. At some point, however, severe and prolonged anti-social behaviour is seen as a psychological problem and may be diagnosed under the psychiatric classification system of DSM IV (American Psychiatric Association 1994) as Oppositional Defiant Disorder or Conduct Disorder.

Recent reviews conclude that between 7 and 25 per cent of children have mild to severe conduct problems (Webster-Stratton 1996) and that as many as half of those with moderate to severe problems continue with these until adolescence (Campbell 1995). Such children are described as *Early Starter* or *Early Onset* and often first exhibit impulsivity and inattention, attention deficit hyperactivity disorder (ADHD) and oppositional behaviour before developing full conduct disorder (McMahon 1994). In contrast, *Late Starter* or *Late Onset* children tend to move directly into conduct disorder which is often less serious and less long standing compared to early onset cases (McMahon 1994). Patterson, Capaldi and Bank (1991) argue that late starters are often teenagers from families with inadequate supervision and poor adolescent management skills who become involved in socially deviant peer groups. These late onset children had many prior years of normal social experiences and development of social skills which usually help them to manage better and to desist from their short term anti-social behaviour. Most concerns and needs for effective therapy therefore relate to the early onset group.

Case characteristics

Research has attempted to identify the characteristics of the children with conduct disorder, their parents, and families (McMahon 1994; Campbell 1995).

CHILD FACTORS

Children with behavioural problems are more likely than other children to have exhibited difficult temperaments in infancy and to have poor social understanding and interpersonal problem solving skills, to perceive aggressive intent in others, to be less able to play alone and to engage in aimless activities rather than structured solitary play (Campbell 1995). They are typically more fidgety and restless particularly in structured tasks compared to other children.

There is some evidence that children with callous unemotional personality traits are more at risk of anti-social behaviour and that this risk is independent of the common risk factor of ineffective parenting (Wootton *et al.* 1997). Boys seem slightly more at risk of anti-social behaviour and tend to use more physical aggression than girls, but the differential rate of anti-social behaviour between the sexes disappears in adolescence (Webster-Stratton 1996).

Conduct problems are most likely to persist if they are severe, multiple, and unresponsive to treatment. The nature and extent of the child's behaviour and its effects on later behavioural processes (Fergusson and Horwood 1998) is more predictive of outcome than contextual factors such as socio-economic circumstances (Campbell 1995) or educational achievement (Fergusson and Horwood 1998). For girls, parental negativity and maternal depression predict persistent conduct problems, but for boys pre-treatment problem scores are the best predictor (Webster-Stratton 1996). For boys, anti-social behaviour in childhood, impulsivity and low intelligence or attainment are all risk factors for adult offending (Farrington 1995). It is important to remember, however, that many children with risk factors such as externalising behaviour do not develop conduct disorder and anti-social behaviour (Bennett *et al.* 1998).

PARENT AND FAMILY FACTORS

The main parental factor associated with anti-social behaviour in children entails care and control that is arbitrary, inconsistent, uninvolved, impatient, and assertive leading to increasingly coercive exchanges (Patterson 1982; Browne and Herbert 1997). The parents are more likely to reward negative behaviour and ignore or punish pro-social behaviour. Children may use aggression to prevent themselves being controlled and parents reinforce this by inconsistent punishment, so that parents and children reinforce each others' aggressive patterns of behaviour (Snyder and Patterson 1995). As a consequence, mothers act more negatively to their own rather than other people's sons (Campbell 1995).

In some cases, parents unable to deal with the stresses of their lives and care of their children may become depressed (a risk factor for girls) or resort to extreme methods that can lead to physical and emotional maltreatment and possible removal into local authority care (Gough 1993). All these factors can have long-term consequences for the children's social and psychological adjustment as adults and future parents. For boys, poor child-rearing methods are also a risk factor for later criminality (Farrington 1995).

Although coercive patterns of family interaction can involve all family members, much research on parental factors in child conduct problems reports only on mothers. Hence 'parents' usually means 'mothers' and so implicitly stresses maternal rather than paternal deficiencies, roles and responsibilities. It is not surprising that mothers of anti-social children, for example, are found to have more symptoms of depressed mood and report more stressful events in the last year (Campbell 1995), though socio-economically depressed mothers may over-report child behaviour difficulties (Dumas and Serketich 1994). One of the few studies on gender differences reports that mothers of children with conduct disorders tend to punish boys physically more than girls, whilst the fathers are more negative and less communicative to both male and female children (Webster-Stratton 1996).

Other parent and family factors associated with child conduct problems include adverse social and economic circumstances, single or reconstituted families, relationship problems including marital conflict and dissatisfaction, and parental disagreement over child-rearing. For boys parental disagreement in child-rearing is a greater risk, for girls the greater risk is poor marital adjustment (Shaw *et al.* 1994). The continuance of child behaviour problems is predicted by continuing family adversity, maybe through its disruptive effects on parenting. Poverty and history of family criminality are also risk factors for later offending in males (Farrington 1995).

Treatment approaches and efficacy

Child, parent, and family characteristics have all been found to be correlated with and to predict future child conduct problems and have led to the development of behavioural therapeutic interventions at each of these levels.

CHILD SKILLS

The two main child focused approaches are social skills training and cognitive behavioural training. Most of the research has been concerned with older children and has relied on parental and professional reports rather than direct observational measures of outcome. The results in terms of therapeutic efficacy have been mixed, particularly for younger children (Webster-Stratton and Herbert 1994).

Despite the mixed results, some interventions have demonstrated significant effects that have been maintained at one year follow up. One of the best known is Problem Solving and Social Skills Training (PSST), which uses cognitive instructional and problem solving training plus behavioural modelling, role play, and reinforcement techniques (Kazdin 1995; 1997). Treatment involves approximately six sessions per month for three or four months consisting of (a) a step by step approach with self statements about key aspects of the problems or tasks necessary to solve interpersonal problems; (b) modelling and reinforcement of positive behaviours for problem solving; and (c) structured tasks and games that are then increasingly applied to real life situations. The therapist provides modelling, cues, feedback, positive reinforcement and mild punishment such as loss of tokens (Kazdin 1997). The treatment has been shown to be effective with samples from both the general population and clinics. It is unclear which families and children benefit most, though children with multiple problems, low academic attainment, and who come from families with multiple difficulties in their relationships and general functioning, improve the least (Kazdin 1995).

One difficulty in achieving change with older children with severe conduct problems is the length of time that they have been using negative behaviours and relationships and the extent of their social exclusion. Earlier intervention would therefore be preferred but until recently there has been less evidence of effective intervention with younger children. This may have been because the younger children lack the cognitive abilities to understand and benefit from cognitive interventions or the interventions have not been developmentally appropriate for other reasons. Webster-Stratton and Hammond (1997) have shown that younger children can show significant improvements in observed management of interpersonal conflict when the intervention focuses on the specific behaviours that children need help with and uses more non-verbal cognitive methods. They used a performance-based approach with four- to eight-year-old children involving videotape modelling of one hundred ways of solving interpersonal difficulties plus fantasy play with giant puppets (including the interpersonal problems of dinosaurs).

For older children, group treatment has sometimes been advocated as a cost efficient and effective method of intervention, but there are also dangers (Kazdin 1997). Dishion and Andrews (1995) found that adolescent groups had positive short-term effects on family functioning and attitudes to such things as tobacco use. At one year follow up, however, the positive effects had faded. The adolescents had more behaviour problems at school and positive attitudes towards tobacco use.

PARENT AND FAMILY INTERVENTIONS

The discussion of parent causal factors referred to poor child care management techniques that lead to worsening child behaviour with increasing but ineffective parental punishments. Parent management training (PMT) aims to alter the coercive pattern of antecedents and consequences that are eliciting and maintaining the child's negative behaviours by training the parents in behavioural management techniques. Parents are taught to give positive reinforcement of their children's pro-social behaviours by means of praise, token reward systems, or contracts of reward negotiated with the child (contingency contracting). Parents learn to respond to the child's negative behaviour with time out, loss of tokens, and loss of privileges. Training parents involves teaching of techniques, parental practice in the clinic and in the home, and a progression from tackling simpler to more complex behavioural problems and interventions. This process has to be tailored to each child and family, as it requires careful specification of each of the problem behaviours, the pre-existing reinforcement contingencies that maintain them, and the substitute responses (Browne and Herbert 1997).

PMT has been shown to be effective in reducing conduct problems in children aged from three- to twelve years-old with effects maintained for at least a year, though treatment effects do not always generalise, for example from home to school settings (Webster-Stratton and Herbert 1994). Research suggests that treatment is more effective when it lasts longer than ten hours, when parents are taught about the bases of behavioural therapy, and the therapists are fully trained in the methods (Kazdin 1997). Parents with more social and family adversity improve the least. Rates of successful treatment are, for example, significantly lower for parents who are both socially disadvantaged and socially isolated, than just socially disadvantaged (Dumas and Wahler 1983). Improvement after PMT is also much worse for families where the mothers had unresolved loss or trauma or insecure relationships with their own parents when they were children (Routh *et al.* 1995).

Parent training for adolescents has not produced such consistent research results. Most programmes have been developed primarily for pre-adolescents. Also, early onset children at adolescence have a longer history of social conduct problems, and there is a greater drop out of parents during therapy (Kazdin 1997). However, some studies have shown positive effects. Dishion and Andrews (1995), for example, found that parent training improved older children's immediate behaviour at school, though this effect had faded at one year follow up.

Intervention strategies such as PMT cannot solve all the problems faced by families with multiple difficulties, but if successful, they can alleviate some stresses of child care, the extra stresses caused by coercive patterns of family interactions, and help avoid precipitating events that lead to individual instances of abuse. Research has found PMT and similar behavioural training to be effective at improving parent and child behaviour in physically maltreating families though many studies suffered from high rates of participant drop out (Gough 1993). Drop out may be due to parental avoidance of social work intervention in their lives, parental misunderstanding of their need for or the effectiveness of the help that they are being offered, or simply that the other problems in their lives are too pressing for them to be able to engage in the treatment programmes.

PMT is usually taught to individual families, but a Canadian study by Cunningham, Bremner and Boyle (1995) reported that a large 12-week parent training group produced greater improvements in child behaviour than the same number of clinic sessions with individual families. The group structure allowed parents to discuss the solution of their individual and common child management problems and to provide supportive feedback to each other. The group may also have provided parents with a broader perspective of child management problems, put more responsibility on parents to explain and to solve the particular problems in their family, and encouraged more commitment to the therapy (Cunningham *et al.* 1995). In addition, parents who were immigrants to Canada or for whom English was a second language were more likely to prefer the group to individual clinic based treatment.

Another variant of parent training uses videotape modelling as used with children (Webster-Stratton and Herbert 1994). The programme encourages parents to feel positive about the people acting as models in the videotapes who are chosen to be similar to the parents in sex, age, socio-economic and cultural group, and temperament. Each programme contains brief vignettes concerned with parental communication strategies and problem solving with their children, use of differential attention to the children's behaviour and careful use of commands (McMahon 1994; Webster-Stratton and Herbert 1994). An assessment of the intervention, not experimentally controlled, showed that child behaviour improved for at least two-thirds of cases (Webster-Stratton and Herbert 1994). The authors stress the importance of working in partnership with rather than 'doing to' families.

Functional Family Therapy (FTT) is another treatment strategy used for child conduct problems that has some similarities to PMT. The therapist helps the family members to identify and negotiate change in maladaptive communication and behaviour patterns, but also intervenes directly by positively reinforcing adaptive family interactions and providing other feedback during family treatment sessions. The technique has been shown to be effective in changing behaviour and lowering recidivism rates in adolescents guilty of minor crimes (McMahon 1994; Kazdin 1997).

Other studies have also found positive effects of providing help with adults' own issues. Benefits included significant reductions in parental drop out from treatment, particularly for high adversity families, and less expressed dissatisfaction with the programme if they did drop out, compared with provision of PMT only (Prinz and Milner 1994). Programme drop out is important because families with the most severe and extensive problems are the least likely to participate or to complete the training (Kazdin 1997).

COMBINED CHILD AND PARENT INTERVENTIONS

Child skills and parent management training are both proven successful treatment strategies, and several researchers have reported that combined treatments are even more successful (Tremblay *et al.* 1995; Webster-Stratton and Hammond 1997). A recent study found that the individual and combined training packages all produced significant improvements compared to controls but the combined treatment had a greater impact on the observed interaction patterns of the children with friends (Webster-Stratton and Hammond 1997). At one year post treatment, the combined intervention group also had significantly fewer behavioural problems at home (independently measured) compared to the other treatments.

Internalising problems

Case characteristics

Anxiety, depression, and other internalising problems in children have only recently gained much clinical or research attention. This is despite the high rate of attempted suicide amongst adolescents (1–3% per annum) and the high correlation of such attempts with depression, hostility, impulsivity and aggression (Brent 1997). A recent review by Ollendick and King (1994) concluded that New Zealand data was typical of most studies in reporting clinical anxiety/phobia rates of 7.4 per cent at age 11 rising to 10.7 per cent at age 15. The proportion experiencing depression was 1.8 per cent at age 11 rising to 4.1 per cent at age 15. Anxiety over separation from loved ones and simple phobias are more common for younger children, whilst high levels of anxiety, fear of social situations, and depression are more common in older children.

Many studies have found evidence of persistence over time in internalising problems, though the continuity is not as strong as for externalising problems in children (Ollendick and King 1994). One study in the United States found that children who were anxious depressed were 9.3 times more likely than non anxious depressed children to suffer from anxious depression three years later, whilst the probability of persistence of aggressive behaviour was 16.4 times (Stanger, McConaughy and Achenbach 1992).

It is not clear why some children are more anxious than others, but one factor may be a low threshold for arousal that makes some children easily distressed and overwhelmed by external stimuli (King and Ollendick 1997). Children's specific fears can arise from genetic factors, experiencing frightening conditioning events, modelling from someone else's fearful experience or behaviour, or instruction. For example, parents' reports indicate that fear of dogs arises in their children mostly from modelling, but fear of water seemed not to be related to any prior experiences (King and Ollendick 1997).

Treatment approaches and efficacy
DEPRESSION

The cognitive model of depression developed by Beck *et al.* (1979) posited that depressed individuals develop a predisposition to negative interpretations of events which leads to depression. Cognitive behaviour therapy (CBT) aims to change these, first by examining and changing distorted thoughts related to overt behaviour, and then examining more fundamental distorted cognitive schemata. Research with adults has found that CBT is approximately as effective as antidepressant drugs or interpersonal psychotherapy (Hollon, Shelton and Loosen 1991; Harrington 1992; see also Chapter 10).

There is less research on the effects of CBT on children with depression, but studies have shown that CBT is effective with adolescents (Recneke, Ryan and Dubois 1998) and can have a significant impact on depressive symptoms over a two-year period (Lewinsohn *et al.* 1990). Among factors associated with positive outcome were lower levels of depression at baseline and parental involvement in treatment (Clarke *et al.* 1992).

CBT plus additional intervention components was shown to be more effective than relaxation control condition in reducing anxiety (Wood, Harrington and Moore 1996). One additional component of the programme was to teach children social problem solving, by agreeing goals, generating alternative strategies, self monitoring and evaluation. Another component was aimed at symptoms of depression, such as sleep problems and activity scheduling. Although the intervention was successful in reducing depression it had no observable effect on symptoms of anxiety or conduct disorders. At six month follow up the treatment effects were reduced due to relapses in the treatment group and improvements in the relaxation control group. Relaxation training is mostly used to treat anxiety but seems to have some positive effect also on depressive symptoms (Ollendick and King 1994).

CBT is also advocated for the prevention of suicide attempts. Brent (1997) argues for the importance of CBT in treating feelings of hopelessness which are correlated with suicide behaviour. He proposes a causal model of (a) precipitant events leading to (b) three intervening variables of cognitive distortion, lack of assertiveness, and inability to influence others, interacting with (c) intense affect with poor affect regulation to (d) impulsive decision making and inability to generate alternative strategies leading to (e) a suicide attempt (Brent 1997). Cognitive and behavioural treatments could intervene in several stages of this causal process including the avoidance of precipitants such as interpersonal conflict, social skills training to influence others, affect regulation, and impulsivity. The efficacy of CBT in reducing suicide attempts has been shown by several studies on young adults (Linehan *et al.* 1991).

ANXIETY

CBT is a commonly used form of treatment in childhood anxiety because it attempts to change thought patterns that are distressing for the individual and that leads to avoidance of the anxiety provoking situations and hence help to maintain and continue the anxiety. CBT teaches individuals to recognise their cognitive and somatic reactions to anxiety provoking situations and to restructure the cognitions and develop more effective coping strategies. Modelling, role play and real life exposure to the feared stimuli are behavioural methods used in conjunction with the CBT.

For adults there is clear evidence of effectiveness of CBT and relaxation training on generalised anxiety (Chambless and Gillis 1993). The effectiveness of this approach for children is less well documented, but has been illustrated by two related studies on 9- to 13-year-old children referred to a clinic for anxiety disorder (Kendall 1994; Kendall *et al.* 1997). The CBT treatment consisted of two parts of eight sessions each. Part one concerned cognitive education training. Topics included constructing a hierarchy of anxiety-provoking situations, relaxation training with an audio cassette, enabling the child to self-assess and self-reward. Part two focused on graduated exposure to the feared stimulus. This included practice of new skills in relation to progressively higher levels of anxiety-provoking situations, therapist modelling, the child creating an anxiety-coping advertisement and review of programme and its application to daily life. The advertisement is an audio or video tape presentation created by the child to inform others about how to cope with anxiety.

The studies found that anxiety decreased significantly for the treatment groups compared to the waiting list control groups. Over half of children no longer had a diagnosis of anxiety disorder at post treatment. These treatment effects were maintained at one year follow up and at three to five year follow up for children in the first study (Kendall and Southam-Gerow 1996).

Another study (Barrett, Dadds and Rapee 1996) compared weekly 70-minute sessions of CBT with a combined package of 30 minutes CBT plus 40 minutes of a family management programme (FAM). The FAM training had three main components each taught for 4 sessions each:

1. Training parents through instruction and role play in how to encourage courageous behaviour and reduce excessive anxiety in the child.

2. Helping parents with their awareness of their own anxieties and responses to anxiety provoking situations.

3. Developing family communication, listening and problem-solving skills.

The study reported rates of no continuing anxiety disorder of 84 per cent at the end of treatment rising to 95 per cent at one year follow up. The treatment outcomes were significantly higher than use of CBT only for younger children (7 to 10 years), but not older children (11 to 14 years).

The importance of the child's parents to the effectiveness of treatment is shown by the finding by Cobham and colleagues (1998) that, as with childhood depression, CBT was less effective when the parents suffered from anxiety. Treating the parental anxiety improved the efficacy of the CBT in treating the childhood anxiety.

SPECIFIC PHOBIAS

Behavioural treatment of child phobias is mostly based on imagined or actual exposure to the fear provoking stimuli using classical, operant, or social learning methods. The efficacy of each of these is considered in turn using the conclusions of the recent research review by King and Ollendick (1997).

Systematic desensitisation is based on classical conditioning by counter-conditioning new non-fearful responses to conditioned feared stimuli such as dogs, snakes or embarrassing social situations. This is achieved by eliciting responses that are incompatible with fear. For example, the child is trained to be relaxed then presented with an imagined or real low level feared stimulus. Relaxation can be maintained because of the low level of fear produced, but then more frightening versions of the stimulus are progressively introduced until the child can be relaxed with the previously feared object. This method has been shown to be highly effective at treating specific phobias.

In contrast to the hierarchy of feared stimuli in systematic desensitisation, flooding uses the most feared stimuli from the start. The experience of the feared stimuli in the absence of any traumatic experience should lead to a reduction in fear. A few case studies have reported success with this approach but there have been no controlled studies and many therapists and parents do not consider the treatment humane.

Observational learning or modelling involves demonstrating both non-fearful behaviour in the situation that the child finds fearful and coping strategies for any anxiety that is aroused. Research on children with mild levels of phobia show modelling to be a highly effective treatment. Effectiveness varies depending on the form of modelling with participant modelling being most effective followed by live modelling followed by film modelling.

Contingency management is an operant conditioning method. It does not rely on relaxation as in classical conditioning methods but examines the reinforcement contingencies of positive and negative reinforcement that are maintaining the phobic behaviour. Through reinforcement of less and less fearful responses the child's behaviour can be shaped to not react fearfully to the phobic stimulus. Case studies and a few controlled studies provide some evidence of the effects of this approach but it seems to be less effective than modelling or systematic desensitisation.

Cognitive approaches have also been adapted for child phobias with some success, though in a meta analysis of studies Feske and Chambless (1995) found CBT no more effective than exposure based treatment for social phobia.

Conclusions

Externalising problems

For externalising problems of child conduct disorder, there is good research evidence for the efficacy of child- and parent-focused cognitive and behavioural interventions, which are even stronger when the child and parent programmes are combined. This argues for developing more strategies for encouraging active participation of parents in programmes by involving them in a collaborative partnership, providing them with their own services and benefits, and reaching out to them in the community. Community-based group programmes have the added benefit of being more cost effective so that more families can receive help for the same money.

The persistence of problems for early onset conduct problems suggests that preventive work should start as early as possible. Overactivity and inattentiveness occur together and may pre-date anti-social behaviour so should be a possible focus for preventive treatment and monitoring for the possible development of conduct problems. The intervention programmes for conduct problems can be adapted to be effective for different age groups but this requires the selection of age appropriate materials and methods. Younger children may respond better to modelling rather than verbal cognitive approaches. Groups have the risk that older children may learn deviant behaviour from other participants (Dishion and Andrews 1995).

A continuing problem is the minority of cases that do not seem to respond to the interventions. A better understanding of process variables may enable the development of more effective strategies for this subgroup. In addition, greater knowledge is needed as regards gender, racial, and cultural factors in the development of conduct disorder and in effective treatment.

Internalising problems

There has been relatively little research on the associated characteristics and causal processes in child anxiety and depression, but they seem to be susceptible to treatment by behavioural and cognitive behavioural methods with an important role for CBT and relaxation training and with phobic behaviour being particularly responsive to exposure based behavioural treatments. Many of the conclusions are the same as for externalising problems in that early identification and intervention are to be preferred.

Implications for policy and practice

The most important conclusion for policy and practice is that behavioural and cognitive behavioural methods have been proven to be effective in a number of specific child psychological and behavioural problems. These problems often aggravate other social and psychological adversities faced by children and families that are likely to be in need of extra attention and provision by health, welfare, education and law enforcement services. Behavioural interventions are therefore indicated as one form of assistance to these children and families.

The conceptual and practical background of these behavioural approaches requires therapists to be highly specific about the focus of their intervention, their assessment of the problem, their method of intervention, how this should impact on the problem, and how such possible change is assessed and tested. This clarity of purpose and specification encourages good research and evidence-based practice, a precision that is sometimes lost when broad-based terms such as social support, casework, counselling, working with the child and psychotherapy are used.

Many of the research studies found that the inclusion of extra treatment or supportive components added to the efficacy of the interventions. The danger is that the use of too many extra components can lead to a loss of focus and provide a cocktail of different interventions in the hope that they will all provide added value or that at least some of the components of the cocktail may have a beneficial effect (Kazdin 1997). Each individual therapy becomes weakened through less time allocated and lack of conceptual clarity for therapists and for those receiving the treatment (Chambless and Gillis 1993). In addition, the cocktail treatment strategy reduces the possibility of identifying which components are effective and informing the development and improvement of treatment services.

On the other hand, behavioural-based interventions can be criticised for being too narrow, concentrating on behavioural symptoms, and ignoring more basic underlying psychological or social adversities. Is it, for example, relevant to provide parent management training to a mother in extreme economic and social stress who is being physically assaulted by her partner and under threat of having her children removed into care by the local authority social services department? This is obviously a question of balance. If very basic needs and stresses are not addressed, then a parent is unlikely to be able to properly participate and benefit as shown by the high drop out rates and lack of success from PMT in families with high social adversity. On the other hand, behavioural therapies can be an extremely important method of providing parents with skills to manage some of the worst symptoms of their predicaments and to develop their own feelings of self-efficacy. Similarly, children who are difficult to manage may appreciate the benefits of decreased family coercion, if they can be weaned off the reinforcement contingencies that rewards their aggression and anti-social behaviour.

A final issue is the provision of these services. Many children and families with multiple difficulties plus child internalising and externalising problems are not offered these effective behavioural services. A parent unable to control and at risk of physically maltreating their child may be offered no service or only advice about financial management and non-specific emotional support and advice. The lack of referral to more specialist services is partly due to lack of awareness of its efficacy, partly due to the tendency for agencies to use services within their control (Gough 1993), and partly due to simple lack of available provision. One solution is to train other professionals such as health visitors and social workers in the use of these techniques, but this has hitherto not been very successful (Association of Child Psychology and Psychiatry 1990), perhaps because of the high levels of training necessary to use such methods effectively (Kazdin 1997). A better solution is probably to develop the use of group-based interventions as long as deviant peer group influences are controlled. The challenge is not only for researchers and practitioners to develop such evidence-based interventions but to ensure that these are adopted by service providers, and made appealing to parents, whilst maintaining the fidelity of the programmes and their effectiveness.

References

American Psychiatric Association (1994) *Diagnostic and Statistical Manual of Mental Disorders (DSM IV)*. Washington: APA.

Association of Child Psychology and Psychiatry (1990) *Health Visitor Based Services for Preschool Children with Behaviour Problems. London: ACPP.*

Bandura, A. (1977) *Social Learning Theory.* Englewood Cliffs, NJ: Prentice Hall.

Barrett, P.M., Dadds, M.R. and Rapee, R.M. (1996) 'Family treatment of childhood anxiety: A controlled trial.' *Journal of Consulting and Clinical Psychology 64,* 2, 333–342.

Beck, A.T., Rush, A.J., Shaw, B.F. and Emery, J. (1979) *Cognitive Therapy of Depression.* New York: John Wiley and Sons.

Bennett, K.J., Lipman, E.L., Racine, Y. and Offord, D.R. (1998) 'Annotation: Do measures of externalizing behaviour in normal populations predict later outcome?: Implications for targeting interventions to prevent conduct disorder.' *Journal of Child Psychology, 66,* 6, 893–905.

Brent, D.A. (1997) 'Practitioner review: The aftercare of adolescents with deliberate self harm.' *Journal of Child Psychology and Psychiatry 38,* 3, 277–286.

Browne, K. and Herbert, M. (1997) *Preventing Family Violence.* Chichester: John Wiley and Sons.

Campbell, S.B. (1995) 'Behaviour problems in preschool children: A review of recent research.' *Journal of Child Psychology and Psychiatry 36,* 1, 113–149.

Chambless, D.L. and Gillis, M.M. (1993) 'Cognitive therapy of anxiety disorders.' *Journal of Consulting and Clinical Psychology, 61,* 2, 248–260.

Clarke, G.N., Hops, H., Lewinsohn, P.M., Andrews, J., Seeley, J.R. and Williams, J. (1992) 'Cognitive behavioral treatment of adolescent depression: Prediction of outcome.' *Behavior Therapy 23,* 3, 341–354.

Cobham, V.E., Dadds, M.R. and Spence, S.H. (1998) 'The role of parental anxiety in the treatment of childhood anxiety.' *Journal of Consulting and Clinical Psychology 66,* 6, 893–905.

Cunningham, C.E., Bremner, R. and Boyle, M. (1995) 'Large group community parenting programs for families of preschoolers at risk for disruptive behaviour disorders: Utilization, cost effectiveness, outcome.' *Journal of Child Psychology and Psychiatry 36,* 7, 1141–1159.

Davies, M. (ed) (1997) *The Blackwell Companion to Social Work.* Oxford: Blackwell.

Dishion, T.J. and Andrews, D.W. (1995) 'Preventing escalation in problem behaviours with high-risk young adolescents: Immediate and 1-year outcomes.' *Journal of Consulting and Clinical Psychology 63,* 4, 538–548.

Dumas, J.E. and Serketich, W.J. (1994) 'Maternal depressive symptamology and child maladjustment: A comparison of 3 process models.' *Behavior Therapy 25,* 2, 161–181.

Dumas, J.E. and Wahler, R.G. (1983) 'Predictors of treatment outcome in parent training: Mother insularity and socioeconomic disadvantage.' *Behavioral Assessment 5,* 4, 301–313.

Farrington, D.P. (1995) 'The development of offending and anti-social behaviour from childhood: Key findings from the Cambridge study in delinquent development.' *Journal of Child Psychology and Psychiatry 36,* 6, 929–964.

Ferguson, D.M. and Horwood, L.J. (1998) 'Early conduct problems and later life opportunities.' *Journal of Child Psychology and Psychiatry 39,* 8, 1097–1108.

Feske, U. and Chambless, D.L. (1995) 'Cognitive behavior versus exposure only treatments for social phobia: A meta analysis.' *Behavior Therapy 26, 4,* 695–720.

Gough, D.A. (1993) *Child Abuse Interventions: A Review of the Research Literature.* London: HMSO.

Harrington, R. (1992) 'Annotation: The natural history and treatment of child and adolescent and affective disorders.' *Journal of Child Psychology and Psychiatry, 33,* 8, 1287–1302.

Hoagwood, K., Hibbs, E., Brent, D. and Jensen, P. (1995) 'Introduction to the special section: Efficacy and effectiveness in studies of child and adolescent psychotherapy.' *Journal of Consulting and Clinical Psychology 65,* 5, 683–687.

Hollon, S.D., Shelton, R.C. and Loosen, P.T. (1991) 'Cognitive therapy and pharmacology for depression.' *Journal of Consulting and Clinical Psychology 59,* 1 88–99.

Jones, E.E. and Pulos, S.M. (1993) 'Comparing the process in psychodynamic and cognitive-behavioral therapies.' *Journal of Consulting and Clinical Psychology 61,* 2, 306–316.

Kazdin, A.E. (1995) 'Child, parent, and family dysfunction as predictors of outcomes in cognitive behavioral treatments of anti social children.' *Behavior Research and Therapy 33,* 3, 271–282.

Kazdin, A.E. (1997) 'Practitioner review: Psychosocial treatments for conduct disorder in children.' *Journal of Child Psychology and Psychiatry 38*, 2, 161–178.

Kendall, P.C. (1993) 'Cognitive behavioral therapies with youth: Guiding theory, current status and emerging developments.' *Journal of Consulting and Clinical Psychology 61*, 2, 235–247.

Kendall, P.C. (1994) 'Treating anxiety disorders in children: Results of a randomized clinical trial.' *Journal of Consulting and Clinical Psychology 62*, 1, 100–110.

Kendall, P.C., Flannery-Schroeder, E., Panichelli-Mindel, S.M., Southam-Gerow, M., Henin, A. and Warman, M. (1997) 'Therapy for youths with anxiety disorders: A second randomized clinical trial.' *Journal of Consulting and Clinical Psychology 65*, 5, 366–380.

Kendall, P.C. and Southam-Gerow, M.A. (1996) 'Long-term follow-up of a cognitive-behavioral therapy for anxiety-disordered youth.' *Journal of Consulting and Clinical Psychology 64*, 4, 724–730.

King, N.J. and Ollendick, T.H. (1997) 'Annotation: Treatment of child phobias.' *Journal of Child Psychology and Psychiatry 38*, 4, 389–400.

Lewinsohn, P.M., Clarke, G.N., Hops, H. and Andrews, J. (1990) 'Cognitive behavioral treatment for depressed adolescents.' *Behavior Therapy 21*, 385–401.

Linehan, M.M., Armstrong, H.E., Suarez, A., Allmon, D. and Heard, L. (1991) 'Cognitive behavioral treatment of chronically parasuicidal borderline patients.' *Archives of General Psychiatry 48*, 1060–1064.

Mahoney, M.J. (1993) 'Introduction to special section: Theoretical developments in the cognitive psychotherapies.' *Journal of Consulting and Clinical Psychology 61*, 2, 187–193.

McMahon, R.J. (1994) 'Diagnosis, assessment, and treatment of externalizing problems in children: The role of longitudinal data.' *Journal of Consulting and Clinical Psychology 62*, 5, 901–917.

Ollendick, T.H. and King, N.J. (1994) 'Diagnosis, assessment, and treatment of internalizing problems in children: The role of longitudinal data.' *Journal of Consulting and Clinical Psychology 62*, 5, 918–927.

Patterson, G.R. (1982) *Coercive Family Process.* Eugene, OR: Castalia.

Patterson, G.R., Capaldi, D. and Bank, L. (1991) 'An early starter model for predicting delinquency.' In D.J. Pepler and K.H. Rubin (eds) *The Development and Treatment of Childhood Aggression.* Hillsdale, NJ: Lawrence Erlbaum Associates.

Payne, M. (1997) *Modern Social Work Theory.* 2nd Edition. Basingstoke: MacMillan Press.

Pepler, D.J. and Rubin, K.H. (eds) (1991) *The Development and Treatment of Childhood Aggression.* Hillsdale, NJ: Lawrence Erlbaum Associates.

Prinz, R.J. and Milner, G.E. (1994) 'Family-based treatment for childhood anti-social behavior: Experimental influences on dropout and engagement.' *Journal of Consulting and Clinical Psychology 63*, 3, 645–650.

Recneke, M.A., Ryan, N.E. and Dubois, D. (1998) 'Cognitive behavioural therapy of depression and depressive symptoms during adolescence: a review and meta analysis.' *Child and Adolescent Psychiatry 37*, 1, 26–34.

Ronnen, T. (1997) 'Cognitive behavioural therapy.' In M. Davies (ed) *The Blackwell Companion to Social Work.* Oxford: Blackwell.

Routh, C.P., Hill, J.W., Steelee, H., Elliott, C.E. and Dewey, M.E. (1995) 'Maternal attachment status, psychosocial stressors and problem behaviour: Follow up after parent training courses for parenting disorder.' *Journal of Child Psychology and Psychiatry 36*, 7, 1179–1198.

Shadish, W.R., Matt, G.E., Navarro, A.M., Siegle, G., Crits-Christoph, P., Hazelrigg, M.D., Jorm, A.F., Lyons, L.C., Nietzel, M.T., Prout, H.T., Robinson, L., Smith, M.L., Svartberg, M. and Weiss, B. (1997) 'Evidence that therapy works in clinically representative conditions.' *Journal of Consulting and Clinical Psychology 65*, 3, 355–365.

Shaw, D.S., Vondra, J.I., Dowdell-Hommerding, K., Keenan, K. and Dunn, M. (1994) 'Chronic family adversity and early child behaviour problems: A longitudinal study of low income families.' *Journal of Child Psychology and Psychiatry 35*, 6, 1109–1122.

Shirk, S.R. and Russell, R.L. (1992) 'A reevaluation of estimates of child therapy effectiveness.' Child and Adolescent Psychiatry 31, 4, 703–709.

Snyder, J.J. and Patterson, G.R. (1995) 'Individual differences in social aggression. A test of reinforcement model in the natural environment.' *Behavior Therapy 26*, 2, 371–391.

Spence, S. (1994) 'Practitioner review: Cognitive therapy with children and adolescents: From theory to practice.' *Journal of Child Psychology and Psychiatry 35*, 7, 1191–1228.

Stanger, C., McConaughy, S.H., and Achenbach, T.M. (1992) 'Three year course of behavioral/emotional problems in a national sample of 4 to 16 year olds: II. Predictors of syndromes.' Child and Adolescent Psychiatry 31, 5, 941–950.

Tremblay, R.E., Pagani-Kurtz, L., Masse, L.C., Vitaro, F. and Pihl, R.O. (1995) 'A bimodal preventive intervention for disruptive kindergarten boys: Its impact through mid adolescence.' *Journal of Consulting and Clinical Psychology 63*, 4, 560–568.

Webster-Stratton, C. (1996) 'Early-onset conduct problems: Does gender make a difference?' *Journal of Consulting and Clinical Psychology 64*, 3, 540–541.

Webster-Stratton, C. and Hammond, M. (1997) 'Treating children with early-onset conduct problems: A comparison of child and parent training intervention.' *Journal of Consulting and Clinical Psychology 65*, 1, 93–109.

Webster-Stratton, C. and Herbert, M. (1994) *Troubled Families, Problem Children. Working with Parents: A Collaborative Process.* Chichester: John Wiley and Sons.

Weiss, B. and Weisz, J.R. (1995) 'Relative effectiveness of behavioral versus nonbehavioral child psychotherapy.' *Journal of Consulting and Clinical Psychology 63*, 2, 317–320.

Weisz, J.R., Donnenberg, G.R., Han, S.S. and Weiss, J.B. (1995) 'Bridging the gap between laboratory and clinic in child and adolescent psychotherapy.' *Journal of Consulting and Clinical Psychology 63*, 5, 688–701.

Weisz, J.R., Weiss, J.B., and Donnenberg, G.R. (1992) 'The lab versus the clinic: Effects of child and adolescent psychotherapy.' *American Psychologist 47*, 12, 1578–1585.

Wood, A., Harrington, R. and Moore, A. (1996) 'Controlled trial of a brief cognitive-behavioural intervention in adolescent patients with depressive disorders.' *Journal of Child Psychology and Psychiatry 37*, 6, 737–746.

Wootton, J.M., Frick, P.J., Shelton, K.K. and Silverthorn, P. (1997) 'Ineffective parenting and childhood conduct problems: The moderating role of callous-unemotional traits.' *Journal of Consulting and Clinical Psychology 65*, 2, 301–308.

CHAPTER 6

Family Mediation Involving Children

Margaret Robinson

Introduction

The parents of approximately 150,000 children are divorced each year in England and Wales, and it is estimated that between 50 and 60 per cent of the children attending Child and Family Guidance Clinics have divorce-related problems, yet there has been little research in the UK on the *practice* of working with children of separating and divorcing parents. As far as I am aware there is almost none on working directly with children whose parents are involved in mediation. There *is* research on practice in North America (predominantly Canada and California) and also a good deal of clinical experience among mediators and counsellors. However, this empirical omission is likely to be remedied during the next few years as a result of the implementation of the Family Law Act 1996 together with the general concern about the effects of divorce on children.

Family law: the context for family mediation in England and Wales

The practice of mediation is on the boundaries of law and counselling/psychotherapy, so it is helpful to start by considering the legal context within which mediation is carried out. The Finer Committee (HMSO 1974) laid the foundations for family mediation by distinguishing between re-conciliation (seeking to keep couples together) and conciliation, which was defined as:

> assisting the parties to deal with the consequence of the established breakdown of their marriage, whether resulting in a divorce or a separation, by reaching agreements or giving consents or reducing the area of conflict... in every other matter arising from the breakdown which requires a decision on future arrangements. (HMSO 1974, p.176)

While this method of intervention was initially known as 'conciliation' it was officially changed in 1993 to 'mediation', as it appeared that many potential clients were hesitant because they confused conciliation with reconciliation.

The divorce law for England and Wales at that time was (and still is, until the full implementation of the Family Law Act 1996) the Matrimonial Proceedings Act of 1969 (implemented in 1971). This requires one partner, the petitioner, to prove (a) that the marriage has irretrievably broken down and (b) one of several 'facts':

- unreasonable behaviour

- adultery

- two years separation (with the agreement of respondent)

- desertion (of at least two years)

- five years separation.

In 1994 the most common facts cited by clients were unreasonable behaviour, adultery and two years separation.

The Children Act 1989 introduced the concept of parental responsibility towards children under the age of 18. This is shared by both parents unless specifically removed by a court. Parental divorce does not obviate joint parental responsibility, unless again the court makes a definite decision to give it to one parent only. One of the basic principles of the Children Act is that the court should treat the welfare of the child as paramount. The Matrimonial Causes Act (1973) had earlier incorporated a number of factors which the court should take into account when deciding whether or not to exercise its powers under the Act. These include taking into account the wishes and feelings of the child according to age and understanding; and the presumption that in general the welfare of the child is best served by having regular contact with those who have responsibility for him, unless there is evidence of risk to that child.

In 1982 the Lord Chancellor established an interdepartmental committee (known as the Robinson Committee) which proposed a research review of the costs and effectiveness of the independent conciliation schemes. The researchers distinguished four different types of service depending on the degree of judicial control, and whether or not they were under the control of the probation service or not (Ogus, Walker and Jones-Lee 1989). They concluded that in general services which were most independent were the most successful. It was suggested that conciliation should not be mandatory, nor focus exclusively on child issues, nor overlap with other legal and welfare processes. The researchers made various recommendations as to the future of conciliation, including the establishment of a National Conciliation Service in 1989.

By the early 1990s dissatisfaction with the adversarial nature of the divorce law, concern at the rising divorce rate, the growing interest in and experience of mediation and the costs of legally aided proceedings intensified the pressure for a new divorce law. The Family Law Act was eventually passed in 1996 with implementation planned for 1998, subject to certain pilot projects which would be researched. This excluded the concept of fault and allowed divorce to be granted after a period of reflection. The Lord Chancellor also prevailed upon the Treasury to make funds available for grants to be made to various marriage organisations to develop and extend their services.

The Act was based on the principle that a marriage which has broken down should be brought to an end with minimum distress to the parties and to the children affected. Post-divorce arrangements should be designed to promote as good a continuing relationship between the parties and any children affected as possible, with risks of violence minimised.

The statutory period of reflection will begin three months after the statement that one partner or both believe the marriage has broken down, prior to which either one or both partners must have attended an Information Meeting. Here they will be provided with relevant information including details of support and legal services. The importance of considering the welfare, wishes and feelings of the children is emphasised.

Under the Family Law Act 1996, legal divorce will usually be effected nine months after the Information Meeting, provided that the couple have concluded arrangements for their children and financial matters, and subject to certain protection when violence is involved. If there are children under the age of 16 and one or both parties request it, this period can be extended by a further six months, although only if the court considers that a delay would not be detrimental to the welfare of any child of the family.

In any proceedings for a divorce or separation order, the court shall consider whether there are any children of the family who are likely to require the court to exercise its powers under the Children Act 1989 or that there are exceptional circumstances which make it desirable in the interests of the child that the court should give a direction (Sec. 11). In making a decision the court shall have particular regard to the wishes and feelings of the child, the conduct of the parties as regards the child's upbringing, the general principle that the welfare of the child will be best served by regular contact with those who have parental responsibility for him and with other members of the family; and any risk to the child.

According to Bird and Cretney (1996) the Family Law Act (1996) places great importance on mediation as a means of implementing its principles. The following definition was offered by the Policy and Standards Committee of the UK College of Family Mediators in 1995:

> Mediation is a process in which an impartial third person, the mediator, assists those involved in family breakdown, and in particular separating or divorcing couples, to communicate better with one another and to reach their own agreed and informed decisions about some or all of the issues relating to, or arising from the separation, divorce, children, finance or property.

The development of family mediation

For much of its history family mediation has involved only adults, though often the children were objects of concern or dispute. Initially known as conciliation, mediation at first focused exclusively on assisting separating or divorcing parents who could not agree between themselves to make arrangements relating to custody and access for their children. This is now known as child centred mediation. Assisting couples to come to agreement on both arrangements for their children and financial matters is known as all issues mediation (AIM) and is now practised by many mediation services where the mediators have had additional training.

Mediation developed as a confidential service, which is not reportable in any court proceedings. Only if the couple reached agreement would this be conveyed to their family lawyers (also with their consent) either direct from the service or by themselves. Couples in conflict about their matrimonial home and or financial arrangements would instruct their lawyers who would usually negotiate these at 'arms length'. If such agreements proved impossible then decisions would ultimately be made by the court. The voluntariness of attending mediation has been universally agreed and stressed in the UK, although in some of the states of the US, notably California, where much of the research into the effects of divorce has been conducted, couples who remain in disagreement and are about to reach the divorce courts are *required* to enter mediation.

The first independent mediation service in the UK was established in Bristol in 1978 and the second under the auspices of the Court Welfare Service in Bromley. Both of these services were reviewed in four studies, most of which primarily considered the relationship between the personal experience of the parties involved and the legal process of divorce (Murch 1980; Davis and Murch 1988). In a later book Davis (1988) argued that because each marital relationship has its own history and norms, it is more favourable to resolve disputes through individualised negotiated settlements, rather than in terms of standard legal precedents. Davis and Roberts (1988) also studied the records of 118 parties who attended for joint mediation appointments over six months at the South East London Conciliation Bureau in Bromley (then under the auspices of the probation service). Forty-five per cent of the couples reached agreement and 29 per cent made some progress. This research was later used in a practice handbook which sets out the Bromley Model of family mediation (Roberts 1988; 1997).

In the last 20 years or so many mediation services have been established all over the UK. Some are independent services or operate under the auspices of existing charitable bodies. Others are supported at least in part by the probation and after care service. This led to the establishment of National Family Mediation (NFM) and Family Mediation Scotland. These organisations provide training for mediators and give recognition to affiliated services which meet the required standards. The extension of mediation to include negotiation over finance and the matrimonial home inevitably presented a threat to the lawyers' hitherto exclusive territory. Many lawyers began to train as mediators, either with NFM or with the newly established Family Mediators Association. A College of Family Mediators was established in 1996 and is now working towards agreed standards for all mediators.

In 1990 the Comprehensive Mediation Project was initiated with the aim to develop comprehensive mediation (later renamed all issues mediation) based in five family mediation services and available to families on low or moderate incomes. This was carried out by the same Newcastle University unit which had conducted the original research on family mediation and is now the Relate Centre for Family Studies. The research distinguished three different models of comprehensive mediation:

- lawyers were included as co-mediators throughout the whole process
- lawyers joined the mediator(s) at times during the mediation
- lawyers provided legal advice to the mediators outside the mediation.

The final report of the research clarified what were by then generally recognised stages of the mediation process (Walker *et al.* 1994; see also Haynes with Fisher 1993). These were summarised by Robinson (1997) as follows:

- *Establishing the arena:* explaining the task and aims of mediation
- *Clarifying* the issues on which the couple agree or disagree and outlining an agenda
- *Exploring the issues:* the mediator takes charge of the process, carefully maintaining impartiality, and does not recommend solutions but uses various techniques to promote positive discussion, e.g. reframing, power balancing
- *Developing options:* this is the process of negotiation in which the couple are helped to float and test out ideas within the confidential safety of the mediation process rather than the legal process of the divorce
- *Securing agreement:* the mediator(s), with the agreement of the couple, draw up a memorandum of agreement to take to their respective lawyers for legal advice. (pp.52–3)

Outside the UK, perhaps the most significant comprehensive review of research into mediation and its practice was carried out by Irving and Benjamin (1995) in Canada. The model they devised and recommend is one based on a family systems approach to family therapy. Based on their evaluation and experience they advise an initial assessment process, which may include a period of therapy to enable the couple to participate in mediation. While all the research and most practitioners agree that not all couples are suitable for mediation, Irving and Benjamin suggest that there are certain key attributes which predict outcome failure. Among these are intense stress, often experienced as overwhelming; extreme rigidity in expectations and plans; current and ongoing family violence (whether child or spouse abuse); obsessive preoccupation with the rejecting spouse.

Children and divorce

The main reason why family mediation is considered so important in relation to children is that experience and research has shown that many children suffer considerably in the aftermath of unmediated divorce (Mitchell 1985). In the USA there has been a great deal of research into the effects of divorce upon children, the most well known being the Wallerstein and Kelly study (1980) of 60 families with 161 children who were referred to a mental health centre in California. They were subsequently followed up by Wallerstein at four and ten years subsequent to the separation (Wallerstein and Blakeslee 1989). They highlighted how the impact varied according to the child's age. Not all children are negatively affected by divorce. Both Emery (1988) and Hetherington *et al.* (1985) found that many children can and do cope well enough with the separation and divorce of their parents. It appears that 'evidence suggests that when children begin the divorce experience in good enough shape with close and loving relationships with both parents their adjustment will be maintained by continuing those relationships with both parents on a meaningful basis' (Kelly 1993, p.45). Both the American and British research suggest that it is parental conflict and the manner in which it is expressed which affects children's adjustment (Elliott and Richards 1991). An examination of the behaviour of a group of children from the National Child Development Survey before and after divorce found pre-divorce conflict was a significant predictor of poor outcome (Elliott and Richards 1991).

Johnston and Campbell (1998) interviewed children of parents referred for mediation to a Californian court because of their high conflict and inability to agree and found that most children respond to parental separation (as distinct from the legal divorce) according to their age and understanding of the process. Building on this research and my own clinical experience I have devised a diagram of children's understanding of parental disputes, which has proved a useful guide to parental understanding and interventions by mediators, court welfare officers and others, although individual children may diverge from this pattern:

Children's cognitive understanding of parental disputes

Young children (2–4)	Their capacity to comprehend others' perspective on social relations is limited to recognition of concrete and observable distinctions between people. Young children often assume they themselves caused their parents to have problems. They find it hard to understand their parents' motives and actions.

Late pre-school and early school (4–7)	They have a budding capacity to take another person's viewpoint. They usually can take on only one parent's perspective at a time, though not both simultaneously. Ambivalent feelings are difficult for them to comprehend. They can become easily confused and can unwittingly cause concern and conflict by telling different stories to each parent.
Early latency (7–9)	They have begun to develop the capacity for self-reflective thinking. They can now simultaneously understand the viewpoint of both parents and they may make judgements about parental behaviour. They can begin to imagine how their parents might view them; and this may account for the considerable pain, sadness and powerlessness, typically seen in their reactions to the quarrels of their parents.
Late latency (9–13)	Loyalty conflicts typically cannot be maintained, probably because they are too painful, and so children often make alignments with one or other parent. These may waver between mild and often secret preferences and wishes not to hurt the rejected parent or represent the child's attempt to maintain a distance and not get involved in parental battles. However, a significant proportion of children make strong alliances, and sometimes overtly reject or refuse to visit the other parent.
Early–middle (13–15)	These alliances (if they occur) typically continue into adolescence. The teenager develops a capacity for third person perspective taking. This greater objectivity can allow them to withdraw strategically from parental fights.
Late adolescence	Many become concerned about their own sexuality and capacity for marriage. Resentment grows at being requested to 'parent or partner' one parent. Loyalty conflicts are sometimes accompanied by deep anger.

Interventions with children during parental divorce

Since the implementation of the Children Act 1989, in 1991 what used to be known as 'custody' and 'access' are now called 'residence' and 'contact', the latter including letters and telephone calls. The parent with whom the children primarily reside is usually referred to as the 'residential parent' (usually the mother) and the other (usually the father) known as the 'non-residential' or 'absent parent' (as described in the Child Support Act 1991). Although there is now a legal presumption in favour of continuing contact with both parents, recent research indicates that sometimes contact with the non-residential parent is inadvisable and should not be enforced (Smart and Neale 1997).

At the present time in cases where parents arrive at the divorce court still in conflict about arrangements as regards residence, parents are either referred to the local family mediation service, if available and they are willing, or to the Court Welfare Service (probation officers). The research of James and Hay (1993) provided an overview of the practice of six areas of the court welfare service. The precise arrangements vary depending on local agreements between individual courts and the local probation service. However, couples are usually given conciliation appointments for interviews which enable the judge to scrutinise the arrangements made for their children. Some judges and court welfare officers carry out joint interviews; in other instances, the judge interviews the parents while the court welfare officer interviews children. James and Hay concluded that there appears to be disagreement about the main unit of need being addressed: the individual child whose needs must be protected or the family which must be helped through the difficult process of breakdown and reorganisation, thereby reducing the disruption to the individual child. The practice of the court welfare officers seemed to range along a continuum. At one extreme they saw their role primarily as officers of the court, essentially investigative, making recommendations about the children of the families referred to them. In contrast others took on more therapeutic work with the family. Since this research the Court Welfare Service has recently been reviewed by the inspectorate of the Home Office who have laid down National Standards of Practice. These state that 'all children should be seen by the Court Welfare Officer unless there are strong grounds for not doing so.' Boldero and Swan (1997) have edited a practitioners' resource pack for Court Welfare Officers on Working with Children, which includes exercises for ascertaining their wishes and feelings and trigger drawings which encourage them to reveal their feelings.

Consultation with children in mediation

From the outset the mediation service had always encouraged parents to take a child-centred view about separation and/or divorce and to make decisions about their future parental care. Frequently an important part of the mediation sessions were taken up by the parents struggling to agree on what and how to tell their children. This process is now known as indirect consultation with children.

By the late 1980s many of the Family Mediation services were beginning to involve children directly in the process of mediation. In some cases this was because parents or the children themselves had asked to be seen. Some services, particularly in the US, have a session with the children, either with or without their parents, after the parents have made their decision. This is intended to allow the children to comment on the proposed future arrangements. Garwood (1989) monitored the children who were directly involved in the conciliation process of their parents from April 1986 to May 1988 at the Lothian Conciliation Service. The decision whether or not to see the children was made in half the cases by the parents, while the conciliators decided whether or not to do so in most of the other cases. The children themselves initiated involvement in only two cases, while two further cases were seen as the result of a decision from a judicial or legal source. Of the 36 children who were seen, more than half were consulted in order to give their views, while in seven cases this was to give their parents a focus or response. Almost all the children appreciated having the opportunity to talk to the conciliator and most discussed similar topics, such as access, family relationships, custody, and the children's own feelings and needs. In seven cases the children's interview was followed by a family session. Some of the conciliators offered complete confidentiality to the children, while others did not do so, as they wished to avoid learning secrets which could not be shared with their parents. The majority of children, parents and conciliators were positive about the outcome of the sessions involving the children. The researcher made various recommendations as to the variety of occasions when conciliators might involve children, the main ones being:

- to reinforce the parents' roles and open up communication with their children
- to establish or re-establish access.

There is some recent evidence that involving the children in mediation may reduce their anxiety level, although it is also considered to be inappropriate for children to choose with which parent they primarily reside as this would involve them in a conflict of loyalties as well as giving them a sense of 'unrealistic omnipotence' (Lansky *et al.* 1996). Practice across the UK now encompasses varied ways of involving children – through indirect consultation, in separate sessions, in family discussion meetings and/or in family systems sessions (Fisher 1990).

National Family Mediation set up a working party in 1993 to 'review and where necessary improve the practice of incorporating the children's perspective more effectively into parental decision-making in mediation and to train mediators to see children directly in ways that will advance parental agreement and reduce conflict' (p.8). Questionnaires were sent out to all services (at that time 56) of whom just over half responded. Few services had a clear policy about how mediators were to proceed if children were to be seen, while 18 had a policy on confidentiality, 14 a child protection policy which took account of abuse disclosures, and 16 a policy about feedback to parents. Some services offered counselling for children. The majority left it to the invididual mediator to decide when to see children. The working party made specific recommendations about working with children, notably about the context, the need for supervision, advocating children's rights, emphasising parental responsibility and ways in which to introduce special forms of communication into mediation, such as encouraging parents to put themselves imaginatively into the child's place. The report specified the conditions under which children should be directly included in an agreed plan with the parents and the necessity to clarify the extent of the confidentiality with the parents and the children beforehand. It concluded with recommendations to develop training. Trainers have been appointed who between them cover the various models of mediation, which range from those whose theoretical base is largely based on negotiation theory to those whose base is family systems (see Robinson 1991; 1997; also Chapter 7). NFM trained mediators now learn about indirect and direct consultation with children.

It is important for the mediator to remember that the intervention can only be a brief one and that it is the parents who will make the decisions regarding residence and contact for the child. In carrying out interventions as part of family mediation, experience and research suggest that it is necessary to set out the ground rules carefully. I have devised the following principles which the mediation team of the family mediation service at the Institute of Family Therapy have found helpful:

- The parents are voluntarily engaged in mediation and have made some progress towards agreement.

- Children are only seen if both parents concur and also agree to prepare them for their visit which entails:

  explaining why they themselves are in mediation and explaining the role of the mediator in seeing the children and the areas in which this might be helpful to them; for example they may be able to share their worries and ask questions about the impending separation/divorce which they do not like to ask parents.

- Children may be seen alone, or with one or both parents, and this is agreed beforehand with both parents.

- Parents understand that the children are guaranteed confidentiality in their interviews (unless the mediator thinks they are at risk).

- Children may be offered one further appointment or a follow up and this possibility is agreed beforehand with their parents.

- This is brief intervention and not child therapy or counselling.

- At the end of the session with the children, the mediator reviews what has been discussed, and they are asked whether parents should be told their views and if so what they would like their parents to be told. Most agree that they should be told and the session is used as a rehearsal or bridge to communicating with their parents.

- The parents agree to return for at least one further feedback session.

- If the mediator considers that a child needs long-term help, whether counselling or therapy, then a referral is made to the appropriate agency.

Many mediation services (such as those run by Relate in Northern Ireland) now provide counselling groups for children of divorcing parents.

Skills used in direct consultation with children

The NFM working party stressed the need to have a suitable room with appropriate equipment such as paper, crayons and toys which are age appropriate. Many children can only demonstrate what they feel indirectly either through drawing or play. It can be useful to have a play 'road map' and cars on which the children can act out the journey from the parental home to the other (usually referred to as Mum's house and Dad's house). It is also possible to get 'dolls' houses which can be divided into two homes.

The skills which are most useful are those commonly used in communicating with children many of which are indirect and involve play. The mediator should try to match the child's own language and check that he or she has understood correctly what the child is trying to communicate. It is not part of his or her task to translate this into direct speech unless the child indicates that he or she would like it conveyed to the parents.

Shared parenting

Many post-separated or divorced couples seek ways of sharing the parenting of their children and indeed this is one of the major tasks of child-centred mediation. Irving and Benjamin (1995) in their comprehensive review of contemporary issues in family mediation give a full and comparative analysis of shared parenting and sole custody in which they stress the complexities of the factors involved. Their own research in Toronto was based on a sample of 201 shared parenting and 194 maternal sole custody arrangements. The findings indicated that in the majority of cases shared parenting worked well and improved through time, but it did not always work out well. It was especially indicated for couples who:

- have low to moderate levels of pre-separation conflict
- have a child-centred orientation to parenting
- mutually agree to end their marital relationship and choose shared parenting
- have the motivation to accept and overcome the day-to-day exigencies and complications invariably associated with shared parenting.

In recent years there has been some research which stresses the importance of focusing on resilience in response to family crises and adversity (Rutter 1985). The research most relevant to children of divorcing parents is that of Gately and Schwebel (1991) who criticised the models which emphasise negative responses to divorce and ignore favourable post-divorce outcomes. They suggest that children at risk may be or become resilient if they have:

- positive personality dispositions such as affection and autonomy
- good intelligence
- a family environment which supports and encourages coping
- a wide social environment that provides positive role models and reinforces coping efforts.

Their 'challenge model' incorporates attention to these factors, which help children adjust positively after divorce.

Conclusion

Although little formal evaluation exists, children are increasingly involved in family mediation and this appears to be mainly beneficial. Hence the possibility that the children might be directly involved in mediation is something which should be discussed with parents (for example at information meetings). Many mediators consider that it is better for children if their parents consult and inform them about future arrangements for their residence and contact, but both their involvement and the making of agreed plans are most difficult when the children are caught up in extreme parental conflict. It is therefore critical to their well-being that both parents agree about any direct interventions for the children, lest their plight become exacerbated. Providing that there is parental agreement and that both parents understand everyone's right to confidentiality, then involving children directly in mediation can be helpful to them. Sadly, for those children whose parents remain in conflict it is likely that they will need long-term counselling or therapy.

It also seems to be important at what stage in the mediation process the children might become involved. Some mediation services involve children either on their own or in family interviews after their parents have come to some agreement, while others involve the children earlier in the process. Some research has recommended that this should happen only after the parents are well engaged in the process. The availability of brief counselling for children either individually or in small groups has also been found to be useful, as it can be supportive for children to realise that there are others who share this process. All the research stresses the importance that those who see children of parents who are engaged in the mediation process should have specialised further training before they undertake such intervention. Should direct involvement of the children reveal that they need further specialised therapeutic intervention then this can be suggested to the parents but, unless the children are found to be 'at risk', this cannot be compulsory.

More systematic evaluation is needed, but there does seem to be evidence that brief intervention involving children, given at a strategic time in the divorce process, can assist in the adaptation process as well as achieving a positive outcome for them.

References

Bernstein, B. and Brannen, J. (eds) (1996) *Children Research and Policy.* London: Taylor and Francis.

Bird, R. and Cretney, S. (1996) *Divorce The New Law: The Family Law Act 1996.* Bristol: Family Law Publishing.

Boldero, J. and Swan, J. (1997) *Working with Children: A Practitioners' and Trainers' Resource Pack.* London: Association of Chief Officers of Probation.

Davis, G. (1988) *Partisans and Mediators.* Oxford: Clarendon Press.

Davis. G. and Murch, M. (1988) *Grounds for Divorce.* Oxford: Clarendon Press.

Davis, G. and Roberts, M. (1988) *Access to Agreement.* Milton Keynes: Open University Press.

Elliott, J. and Richards, M. (1991) *Children of Divorce.* Unpublished paper.

Emery, R. (1988) *Marriage, Divorce and Children's Adjustment.* London: Sage.

Finer Committee (1974) *Report of the Finer Committee on One Parent Families.* London: HMSO.

Fisher, T. (1977) *National Family Mediation Guide to Separation and Divorce.* London: Vermilion.

Fisher, T. (ed) (1990) *Family Conciliation within the UK: Policy and Practice.* Bristol: Jordans.

Garwood, F. (1989) *Children in Conciliation: A Study of the Involvement of Children in Conciliation by the Lothian Family Conciliation Service.* Edinburgh: Scottish Association of Family Mediation Services.

Gately, D. and Schwebel, A. (1991) 'The Challenge Model of children's adjustment to parental divorce: Explaining favourable postdivorce outcomes.' *Children Journal of Family Psychology 5,* 1, 61–81.

Haynes, J. with Fisher, T. (1993) *Alternative Dispute Resolution: The Fundamentals of Family Mediation.* London: Old Bailey Press.

Irving, H. and Benjamin, M. (1995) *Family Mediation: Contemporary Issues.* London: Sage.

James, A. and Hay, I. (1993) *Court Welfare Action.* Hemel Hempstead: Harvester Wheatsheaf.

Johnston, J. (1993) 'Children of divorce who refuse visitation in Nonresidential Parenting.' In C. Depner and J. Bray (eds) London: Sage.

Johnston, J. and Campbell, L. (1993) 'Parent–child relationships in domestic violence families disputing custody.' *Family and Conciliation Courts Review 31,* 3, July, 283–298.

Lansky, D., Swift, L., Manley, E., Elmore, A. and Gerety, C. (1996) 'The role of children in mediation.' *Mediation Quarterly 14,* 2, 147–153.

Mitchell, A. (1985) *Children in the Middle.* London: Tavistock.

Murch, M. (1980) *Justice and Welfare in Divorce.* London: Sweet and Maxwell.

National Family Mediation Annual Report 1996.

National Family Mediation (1994) 'Giving children a voice in NFM mediation' in *A Study of Mediation Practice.* London: NFM.

Ogus, A., Walker, J. and Jones-Lee, M. (1989) *Costs and Effectiveness of Conciliation in England and Wales* (1989). Summary of the Report of the Conciliation Project Unit. Newcastle: University of Newcastle upon Tyne.

Richards, M. (1996a) 'Divorce numbers and divorce legislation.' *Family Law,* 151–153.

Richards, M. (1996b) 'The sociolegal support for parents and their children.' In B. Bernstein and J. Brannen (eds) *Children, Research and Policy.* London: Taylor and Francis.

Roberts, M. (1988) *Mediation in Family Disputes.* Aldershot: Wildwood House.

Roberts, M. (1997) *Mediation in Family Disputes: Principles and Practice.* 2nd edn. Aldershot: Arena.

Robinson, M. (1991) *Family Transformation Through Divorce and Remarriage. A Systemic Approach.* London: Routledge.

Robinson, M. (1997) *Divorce as Family Transition: When Private Sorrow Becomes a Public Matter.* London: Karnac.

Rutter, M. (1985) 'Resilience in the face of adversity: Protective factors and resistance in psychiatric disorder.' *British Journal of Psychiatry 147,* 598–611.

Smart, C. and Neale, B. (1997) 'Arguments against virtue – must contact be enforced?' *Family Law 27,* 332–336.

Walker, J. (1994) *An Evaluation of Comprehensive Mediation Services for Divorcing Couples.* Newcastle: Newcastle University and Joseph Rowntree Foundation.

Wallerstein, J. and Blakesee, S. (1989) *Second Chances.* London: Bantam.

Wallerstein, J. and Kelly, J. (1980) *Surviving the Breakup.* London: Grant McIntyre.

CHAPTER 7

Family Therapy

Arlene Vetere

What is family therapy?

Family therapy has been defined as 'any psychotherapeutic endeavour that explicitly focuses on altering the interactions between or among family members; and seeks to improve the functioning of the family as a unit, or its subsystems, and/or the functioning of individual members of the family' (Gurman, Kniskern and Pinsof 1986, p.565). This is a broad definition of psychotherapeutic work with families, which includes approaches that draw on different theoretical models as well as those that attempt to integrate more than one model. The above definition reflects the broad orientation taken to family therapy and family intervention in this chapter.

There are many different schools of family therapy, most of which are informed by family systems theory, although some incorporate other theoretical approaches, such as behavioural and social learning principles or psychodynamic principles. Examples include structural family therapy, behavioural family therapy, psychodynamic family therapy, Milan family therapy, strategic family therapy and parent management training. All the theoretical bases for family therapy seek to describe and explain the organised complexity of family relationships in household groups and extended family systems. In addition, later developments look more carefully at relationships between family groups, health care systems and other social agencies, as well as the relationship between the family therapist and the family group in treatment. Family therapists are interested in patterns of interaction and communication among family members and how these patterns are reciprocally influenced by beliefs, held by individuals alone and together, which may be handed down between the generations. These affect family functioning across the domains of parenting, affectional exchange and emotional support, coping and adaptation, and so on. Family therapists assume that in households with children, carers have executive power and responsibilities for supervision and guidance of the children, which adapts to the biological and social maturation of the children over time. Thus the focus for thinking and practice is the dynamic relationship between (a) the connectedness among family members and their individual autonomy and (b) the changing balance in family relationships according to the evolving needs of family members.

There is sufficient empirical evidence to indicate that family therapy is a promising treatment approach for many child and adolescent psychological problems (Estrada and Pinsof 1995), although there is not enough evidence accumulated at present to allow us to choose with confidence between the different approaches to working with families.

The rationale for family therapy

Family therapy as a treatment for child and adolescent psychological problems arose during the 1950s and 1960s partly as a result of therapist frustration with individual child therapies to bring about and sustain changes in child behaviour, and partly with a growing recognition of the importance of the child's physical and emotional context in the development and maintenance of child problem behaviours. Family therapists view the family as

- both the cradle and web of family members' emotional development
- a significant source of attitudes and beliefs about self, others and relationships, including gendered beliefs about appropriate relational and communicative behaviours for men and women, and beliefs about conflict identification and resolution
- providing opportunities for role modelling and other forms of learning about relationships and attachments in a developmental context that often spans three or four generations at any one time.

Thus, the cognitive, emotional and behavioural interdependence of family members is seen as the context that supported the development and maintenance of children's behavioural and emotional problems and hence as the appropriate context for intervention aimed at restoring adaptive functioning of both the identified child, i.e. the one referred with the problem, and other family members.

For example, family interaction patterns that are characterised by anxiety, aggression and depression appear to foster the development of corresponding cognitive and behavioural styles in children. In particular, marital discord has been shown to be a risk factor for a range of behavioural disturbances in children (Dadds 1995).

Some recent developments

Vetere (1993) has written of the usefulness of family therapy thinking and practice for families with children with learning disabilities, yet pointed out the slow uptake of a systemic approach within existing services for these families. Until now traditional interventions have been child focused with little consideration of the systemic impact of interventions. For example, a Portage home teaching approach organised around the mother–child relationship might intensify what might already be a close relationship, possibly creating distance between the mother and her other children or between the father and the child.

Family therapy approaches focus on coping and competence in families with children with learning disabilities and provide planned support for managing day-to-day difficulties as well as transition and change. Surveys have identified such problems as wakefulness, difficulty settling at night and behavioural problems as of most concern to parents and most likely to persist (Quine and Pahl 1989). Serious behavioural problems could disqualify a child from using respite facilities, play groups, and similar services. Some authors suggest that parents might change their child rearing practices with their child who has learning disabilities. All of these difficulties are understandable, rather than indicating the presence of deep-seated psychiatric problems. Family therapy approaches are strongly parent-oriented and contractual with their emphasis on teamwork, practical problem solving and the minimun necessary intervention. They are well suited to an open and direct style of service which can adapt to the changing needs, tasks and resources of family members across the life cycle.

The recent development of narrative therapy and social constructionist approaches within the family system therapies has begun to have an impact on thinking and practice, in advance of outcome evidence (Freedman and Combs 1996). These innovative developments have been applied to work with children in families to treat some of the traditional problems for children, such as temper control, encopresis, fears and phobias. Narrative approaches use a linguistic practice called externalisation, which separates problems from people. An externalising conversation about the problem permits the young person to think about their relationship with the problem, in such a way that allows the use of play and other strategies to combat the problem. Family members join forces with the young person to help them 'grow up and shrink the problem down' (p.228), 'get the better of trouble' (p.234), or 'catch Sneaky Poo before it sneaks out' (p.99) (Freeman, Epston and Lobovits 1997). Engaging children in problem solving which pays attention to children's preferred communication styles, uses play and is both serious and lightweight in its approach appears to have captured the imagination of family systems therapists who work with children. Practitioners believe that these approaches are attractive and effective, but we await outcome data.

Needs and services

In the UK, family therapy approaches for child and adolescent psychological problems are delivered most commonly within community-based child and family mental health services, but also in certain child protection teams within social services departments, some education departments and certain residential adolescent psychiatry units. Family therapy can be offered as a separate treatment or as part of an intervention package tailored to meet the child's particular circumstances. The family can be seen as the context for a child-based intervention where the family members are involved in the treatment, or as the focus of intervention itself.

An example of a child-based intervention from my clinical practice concerned a young adolescent girl referred for help with obsessive compulsive problems. She performed washing rituals early in the morning for over four hours, whilst closeted in the bathroom, and tidying up rituals late at night whilst preparing for bed, again for over four hours. Her parents were increasingly worried by the lack of spontaneous improvement in her ritualised behaviours, her lack of attendance at school, her depression, and the disruption to family routines caused by the rituals. They had started to take over some of the ritualised behaviours in the hope of reducing the time she needed to take performing these herself, thereby hoping to make school re-attendance possible. In fact, the parents themselves started being late for work because of the time devoted to 'helping' with the rituals and the associated lack of sleep. The daughter's time spent performing the rituals only decreased slightly, and to make it worse, when the parents tried to stop their 'helpful' behaviour, their daughter increased her expressions of distress within the family and increased the time she spent on her performance of these behaviours.

An example of a family-based intervention which focused on relationship issues, would be a lone parent mother and adolescent daughter referring themselves for help with negotiation and conflict-resolution skills within their relationship. They faced escalating discord between them, including threats of expulsion from home by the mother and suicidal threats by the daughter.

Community-based epidemiological studies estimate the prevalence of child and adolescent psychological disorders to be about 20 per cent, yet referrals to community-based child and adolescent mental health services are estimated to be 2–3 per cent of the population within this age range, although there is some variation according to age and gender (Anderson *et al.* 1987; Offord, Boyle and Racine 1989). How might we account for these differences?

There is little evidence to suggest that those children who are referred are more severely impaired. Rather they seem to come from families where adult and especially parental perceptions and anxieties about the child's behaviour are heightened, since children with disruptive and anti-social behaviour are more likely to be referred than children with anxiety and other emotional problems (Cohen *et al.* 1991). Kolko and Kazdin (1993) review evidence which suggests in addition that children are more likely to be perceived as more disturbed by their parents at times of marital and family stress. Children with emotional difficulties seem less likely to come to the attention of community mental health practitioners than children with disruptive and anti-social behaviour. Perhaps parents and other adults do not think these children merit action because of the persistence of the myth that children will 'grow out' of their difficulties, despite an increasing body of evidence that indicates the continuity of some childhood emotional disorders, such as depression, into adulthood. Most family therapists recognise that children are dependent upon responsible adults to make the referral, that young children might be limited in their ability to articulate their distress and confusion or may be unable to talk about abusive experiences for fear of the consequences. We know that there continue to be reported discrepancies between parents', teachers' and adolescents' views of adolescent distress, with these discrepancies between the informants' perspectives leading to some emotional difficulties remaining hidden for a time (Kolko and Kazdin 1993).

So, what might be the implications, both of the above differences in perceptions of distress and the young person's reliance on adults for an appropriate referral, for the family therapy approaches? Family therapy is one amongst a number of treatment interventions for children and adolescents. An audit conducted recently of referrals to a community child clinical psychology department found that one-fifth of all families referred for treatment during the audit period actually chose to participate in family therapy. The other four-fifths wanted advice about their child's perceived difficulties, reassurance that their child was not mentally ill, and/or individual psychological treatment for their child's difficulty (Street, Downey and Brazier 1991). Although we have limited evidence as to knowledge of family therapy approaches amongst the public, there seems to be a gap between the family systems theoretical rationale for the development and maintenance of some childhood emotional and behavioural problems and family members' beliefs about children's difficulties, alongside a general reluctance to seek professional assistance.

Recently family therapy practitioners have paid attention to issues of convening and engaging family members in treatment with the development of user-friendly approaches and a preparedness to critique those procedures and strategies that mystify the process of family therapy (Reimers and Treacher 1995). The client–therapist alliance is often referred to as the common factor under-pinning therapeutic effectiveness across a number of different therapy modalities, including the family therapies (Roth and Fonagy 1996). This alliance includes opportunities for problem solving, the ventilation of emotion and the formulation of plans for change, common to the contractual nature of many of the family therapy approaches.

Assessment and treatment

Assessment in family therapy focuses on the family's organisational structure; its subsystems, interpersonal boundaries and relationships, and family functions. This organisation is explored to identify:

- areas of strength, competence and coping
- possible flexibility for change, such as sensitivity to members' needs, behaviours and attitudes
- evidence of previous changes in alliances in response to changing circumstances.

The context of family life is considered with specific reference to sources of support and sources of stress both within and outwith the family. Both the family and the family members' developmental stage and the stage-appropriate performance of family tasks are considered within the particular socio-cultural context. The symptomatic behaviour is assessed in terms of functional significance, such as whether the symptomatic behaviour helps maintain preferred transactional patterns or whether it can be considered the ironic consequence of attempted solutions to family problems, where the response to the problem becomes part of the problem (see example on p.148).

Treacher and Carpenter (1984) describe three stages of family therapy: joining, middle therapy and termination. Family therapists believe that therapy can be effective when the therapist forms a new system with the family. The therapist relies heavily on techniques of joining and accommodation, such as planned support of the existing family structure, tracking the process and content of family members' communication and accommodating to the range and style of family emotional expression. Middle therapy interventions confront and challenge family members in the attempt to create therapeutic change. The locus of change is at the level of family relationships, so that individual changes in experience are contingent on change at the level of the family's organisational structure. Interventions can include the enactment and re-enactment of interactional patterns, the development of negotiation and problem solving skills, reinforcing parental authority, reframing interpersonal dilemmas, creating opportunities for empathic appreciation of others' perspectives and needs, providing support for change, and negotiating tasks within and between sessions. The therapy contract is terminated when the family members have had the opportunity to solve earlier problems and have rehearsed their ability to solve new or anticipated problems.

Outcome studies of clinical effectiveness: methodological issues

The research on the effectiveness of all therapies for children has lagged behind that of adults. It is important to assess separately the impact of therapies for children and adolescents without assuming a straightforward translation from the adult literature. Researchers have tried both to assess the differential effectiveness of specific family therapy approaches and to compare family therapy with other forms of intervention for children and families. However, the available meta-analytic reviews (Hazelrigg, Cooper and Borduin 1987; Markus, Lange and Pettigrew 1990) lead to broad conclusions only, that is, that family therapy treatments, broadly defined, obtain somewhat better effect sizes than individual psychodynamic interventions for children, and that three-quarters of children are improved after treatment compared to untreated controls.

Family therapy effectiveness for child and adolescent disorders is assessed using both single case designs and group comparison designs. The quality of family therapy outcome studies is improving, although most studies have some methodological problems. Space does not permit extended discussion, so the main issues will be listed here:

- In the past, studies have overly relied on single measures of outcome, often either the therapist's or the mother's view. Increasingly multiple perspectives on outcome are being included, such as the child's, therapist's, parents' and teacher's views. However multi-perspective outcome data do not solve the problem of validity when, as often happens, different views are found between the different informants.

- Early studies usually relied on single measures of symptom change and adjustment, but now outcome studies are beginning to assess child behaviour across a number of symptom domains, such as behavioural, cognitive, and interpersonal.

- Studies of outcome effectiveness need to assess child functioning across a range of settings, such as family, school, and peer group, given the acknowledged reactivity of children's behaviour to the context in which it occurs.

- The follow-up period employed needs to reflect the time span within which relapse might occur, but of course the longer the follow-up period the more possibility there is that other positive life events might account for continuing positive change in a child's or adolescent's behaviour.

- Attrition and drop out from outcome studies presents a problem not only of engaging families in treatment and retaining them in treatment, but of ensuring representativeness across comparison groups.

- There are peculiar ethical difficulties attached to group comparison designs when children are the identified clients. Waiting list controls, however ethically managed, raise problems of the impact on a child's development given delays in the offer of treatment. Treatment is offered to people in waiting list control groups on demand, which means that some of these control groups might be made up of people with less severe difficulties.

- The assessment of outcome must be made in the context of the natural history of the psychological disorder, particularly where symptom patterns change with the course of the child's development. This challenges researchers to be more specific about whether their outcome findings are relevant to early or later stages of a problem, and younger and older children.

- Outcome studies need to show clear evidence of clinical significance beyond statistical significance. The available meta-analytic reviews referred to earlier, lead to broad conclusions only.

- Process checks on the therapy are often missing from studies, so it is unclear to what extent the therapists are following the particular school or approach that is being researched. This makes it difficult to disentangle the possible effects of therapist experience and therapist allegiance to the particular approach under scrutiny.

Kazdin (1997) has identified criteria for the most promising treatments for childhood problems to be:

- a theoretical rationale for the development of the problem and how the treatment redresses the problem
- basic research evidence to support the theoretical rationale, such as Patterson's (1982) 'coercion model' of the development of childhood conduct disorders
- outcome evidence that treatment can effect change

- evidence for a relation between the processes hypothesised to be critical to therapeutic change and actual change.

No single family therapy treatment meets all these criteria, though some family-based treatments have been identified in the literature as having positive outcomes for conduct disorders and eating disorders in children and adolescents. Some studies of the effectiveness of family therapy treatment approaches have used samples of children with mixed disorders, thus making it very difficult to disentangle the suitability of different forms of family intervention for a particular group of children with a particular problem.

Outcome studies of clinical effectiveness: conduct disorders

Disruptive behavioural problems in children are the most frequent reason for the referral of children for all forms of treatment (Robins and Rutter 1990); they are persistent through childhood into adolescence (White *et al.* 1990); and they extend into anti-social behaviour in adulthood (Offord and Bennett 1994). Family therapy approaches offer early intervention which addresses the interpersonal context in which the behaviour is occurring. The most commonly used and evaluated family based intervention approaches are Parent Management Training (Patterson, Dishion and Chamberlain 1993), Functional Family Therapy (Alexander and Parsons 1982) and Multisystematic Therapy (Henggeler 1994). These approaches include both children and parents and attend to their interactions. Typically parents are trained to modify children's behaviour at home, using social learning principles, and focusing on replacing negative interaction sequences with more positive interactions. It is not often recognised that many other family therapy approaches use behavioural principles to strengthen parent–child relationships and to develop parental teamworking, such as the structural and strategic family therapies (Minuchin 1974).

For example, in the Patterson studies, (Patterson, Dishion and Chamberlain 1993) which span four decades of research, the child is usually pre-adolescent, referred for outpatient treatment for aggressive behaviour at home and/or in the class, and for stealing, lying, truancy or fire setting. Treatment lasts several sessions to several months. Outcomes are based on parent and teacher ratings and observations of parent–child behaviour in the home. In 1997 Kazdin noted that no other intervention for children with anti-social behaviour and their parents had been researched so thoroughly, nor shown such favourable results. The main findings can be summarised as follows:

1. Parent Management Training is superior to no treatment (i.e. spontaneous recovery).

2. The treatment effects are maintained at eighteen months follow-up.

3. Improvements in behaviour at home extend to changes in behaviour in school.

4. The treatment effects are observed to generalise to other problematic behaviour.

5. The problematic behaviour of siblings at risk for conduct disorder have been observed to reduce as a result of Parent Management Training.

6. Mothers have reported reductions in depression and increases in their self-esteem.

Parent Management Training involves teaching parents teamwork, which lies at the heart of structural family therapy (Minuchin 1974). Structural therapists work with individuals and smaller groups of family members, such as the parents, a parent and a child, as appropriate. Structural therapy involves setting consistent limits for children's behaviour, teaching problem solving skills, developing a family forum for some negotiation and decision making, such as a family council, and challenging unhelpful expectations and beliefs held by the parents and adolescents. This work is supported by Baumrind's (1971) research which suggests that parental warmth, democratic control and psychological autonomy produces competent youngsters.

However, not all outcome studies report such favourable results as these; generalisation and maintenance of treatment effects continue to be a problem. Parent–child interaction is influenced by other contextual factors, such as discord in the marital relationship, depression in parents, poverty, social support for the family members, and so on (Dadds 1995). Additional interventions are needed to help with these contextual factors; a systemic approach to prevent piecemeal delivery.

Therapies that combine multiple levels of assessment and intervention are emerging as the most successful, such as family systems interventions combined with behavioural ones (Dishion, Reid and Patterson 1988). Estrada and Pinsof (1995), in their review of variants of Parent Management Training for childhood conduct disorder, found that additional packages, which also included marital therapy and child therapy, were superior to the basic package. In fact most family therapists work with household and extended family groups, smaller groups within the household, such as sibling relationships, parent–child relationships and so on, as well as with individuals. Kuehl, Newfield and Joanning's (1990) study of their clients' views of therapy for substance abuse in adolescence, found that higher satisfaction and better outcomes were reported by young people when they were offered individual meetings as part of the family treatment process.

Chamberlain and Rosicky (1995) in their review of family intervention studies for adolescent conduct disorder and delinquency, found that the family therapy approaches appeared to decrease adolescent conduct problems and delinquent behaviour when compared to individual therapy, treatment as usual and no therapy. Treatment failure in the studies reviewed occurred more often with poor and/or isolated families. It is interesting to note that structural family therapy (Minuchin 1974) developed in part through working with lone parent mothers and their sons, who lived in poverty, and where the sons had been referred to a special school because of their delinquent behaviour.

The Florida Network Study of high risk families found that families who had more than five treatment sessions were twice as likely to stay together as families who had fewer than five sessions, and that those families who received family therapy were four times as likely to stay together as those families who did not receive family intervention (Nugent, Carpenter and Parks 1993). Family therapy approaches clearly have a role to play in providing a service to high risk family groups.

However, providing a mix of interventions places a huge demand on the resources of most child and family mental health teams, and in particular to liaise well with colleagues in other agencies providing services to the same child and family. Clearly family therapy approaches with their emphasis on networking and thinking about relationships between systems are well placed to help in this endeavour.

Outcome studies of clinical effectiveness: eating disorders

During their critical review of psychotherapy research, Roth and Fonagy (1996) consider eating disorders, including anorexia. They concluded that the available outcome evidence for younger anorexic patients is that they may respond better to family therapy than to individual therapy. The research on the effectiveness of family therapy for bulimia nervosa is limited and as yet not very promising (Dodge *et al.* 1995), thus only family therapy as an outpatient treatment for anorexia nervosa will be considered here.

Hsu (1990) describes eating disorders as an excessive concern with the control of body weight and shape, accompanied by grossly inadequate, irregular or chaotic food intake. Estimates of prevalence vary according to the methodology used, along with age, gender, ethnicity and socio-economic grouping, but are accepted as between 0.5 per cent and 1.0 per cent, with a 9:1 female to male ratio. The mean age of onset is 17 years with two bimodal peaks at age 14 and 18. The long-term outlook is believed to be poor, with bulimia nervosa the most common diagnosis at follow-up, and a mortality rate of 4.4 per cent (Hsu 1990).

Vandereycken and Vanderlinden (1989) have developed an eclectic family therapy approach to outpatient treatment, which includes behavioural principles. The goals of their approach are as follows:

1. Emphasise the responsibility of the young person for their own health and recovery

2. Provide ways for parents to decrease their anxiety and feelings of helplessness, such as performing concrete tasks at home

3. Avoid the escalation of power struggles by reducing conflict around food refusal and threats to lose weight

4. Normalise interactions and behaviours regarding food issues at home.

The therapist is both supportive and challenging of the family members' efforts to cope. The approach uses behavioural contracting with agreed targets for weight and calorific intake, places responsibility with the young person for weight gain and encourages family members to stop unhelpful power struggles.

Their approach is similar to that developed by Dare *et al.* (1995) in over 12 years of family therapy practice and research at the Maudsley Hospital. The team is sceptical of family process as the cause of eating problems in young people, preferring a multifactorial approach to causation. This recognises the important role family members may have in maintaining the problem whilst trying to cope effectively with the young person's often life-threatening disorder. Their studies have all taken the form of randomised clinical trials with appropriate comparison groups and other checks on internal validity.

Their conclusions are interesting for the field of family therapy as a whole because through the interweaving of clinical and research derived insights, they have contributed to a more fine-grained understanding of the efficacy of family therapy approaches with eating disorders. First, the greater effectiveness of family therapy in the outpatient treatment of anorexia nervosa in young women under the age of 18 years compared to individual psychotherapy has been established (Dare *et al.* 1990). Second, the Maudsley team can now tailor the approach according to the age of onset and duration of the eating problems. In addition, they have shown that in families where criticism and self-blame are high, family members respond better to a supportive family counselling approach rather than the more confrontational and actively restructuring approaches typical of some family therapy. The family counselling approach ensures in addition that these families are less likely to drop out of treatment. Follow-up data from the family members two years after the completion of treatment indicated that both highlighting the seriousness of the problem and the emphasis on putting the parents 'in charge' was helpful.

Outcome studies of clinical effectiveness: depression and school refusal

Family therapy approaches have been used in the treatment of childhood and adolescent depression and refusal to attend school. Not surprisingly, depression and refusal to attend school often occur together. So far, few of these interventions have been formally evaluated. Evidence is accumulating to suggest that problems of depression in childhood are associated with significantly greater risk of affective disorders in adulthood. There are a number of descriptions of family interventions when working with depressed young people, such as those by Oster and Caro (1990) and Matson (1989). They consist of the application of more traditional behavioural methods for the treatment of childhood depression within the family unit. The maintenance of the child's problems within family interaction patterns is addressed, along with support for the parental hierarchy and efforts to improve family communication. Early clinical accounts show good progress with these interventions, but there are no systematic controlled outcome data.

In the case of school refusal though, there has been some research on short-term family oriented treatment which is worthy of note. Estrada and Pinsof (1995) report one large uncontrolled study where all 50 children resumed attending school after receiving family-based treatment. In another controlled study with a smaller sample where families received Parent Management Training plus training for the teacher, this led to virtually all children returning to school. The children in these studies have an early age of onset of refusal to attend school, which has been demonstrated to respond well to behavioural intervention (Blagg and Yule 1984). Bryce and Baird (1986) report an uncontrolled study of family therapy for ten adolescents who were refusing to attend school and their families. All ten adolescents returned to school. These early studies hold some promise for the amelioration of problems, which if they become entrenched clearly have worrying implications for the psychosocial development of the young people involved.

Conclusion

The meta-analytic study of family therapy outcome reported by Shadish *et al.* (1993) is the most thorough meta analysis to date and provides strong support for family therapy in the treatment of general child conduct disorder, child aggression, global family problems, family communication and problem solving difficulties. Yet most family therapy outcome studies do not include data on cost effectiveness, which is a serious shortcoming in these days of managed health care, professional accountability and limited resources. The short- and long-term financial and psychological costs of maintaining children in residential and other forms of substitute care are known to be high compared to the costs of family therapy in outpatient settings.

There appears to be little consensus on what variables might be included in a cost-benefit analysis. We might speculate that the embeddedness of childhood problem behaviours in their social and emotional context and the power of those contexts to maintain those problem behaviours might indicate that spontaneous remission rates for childhood problems would be lower than for adults. Thus the significance of prevention and early intervention using family-based treatment approaches would seem to be of paramount importance. The review of clinical effectiveness presented in this chapter has drawn broadly on family therapies and family interventions that seek to change parent–child and family-wide interactional patterns. Such interventions do not need to rely on expensive technology. The use of teams of therapists and technical support such as video monitoring and one-way screens is most often used in the training of family therapists. As long as the family therapy is supervised, it need not be accompanied by the more costly attributes with which it has become associated and can be conducted in people's homes and other settings outside of the therapist's office (Vetere 1993).

Lack of available outcome evidence does not mean that family therapy is not efficacious. Parent–child behaviour patterns are more than the reciprocal antecedent and consequent behaviours, they are influenced in addition by nested layers of context that include the parent's well-being and their confiding relationship with an adult partner, the quality of social support for the family, economic and political conditions, and so on, as conceptualised within family therapy thinking. Such acknowledgement of the complexity of the multiple layers of context leads to a recognition that for the effective treatment of the more serious manifestations of child and adolescent disorders a multidisciplinary approach with the potential for tailoring an intervention package across multiple treatment modalities is likely to be most helpful. Clearly such a conclusion is costly, but until we can show that these approaches are both helpful and cheaper in the longer term, residential treatment for seriously disturbed adolescents will continue to be the treatment of choice.

References

Alexander, J.F. and Parsons, B.V. (1982) *Functional Family Therapy*. Monterey, CA: Brooks Cole.

Anderson, J.C., Williams, S., McGee, R. and Silva, P.A. (1987) 'DSM-III disorders in preadolescent children: Prevalence in a large sample from the general population.' *Archives of General Psychiatry 44*, 1, 69–76.

Baumrind, D. (1971) 'Current patterns of parental authority.' *Developmental Psychology Monograph 4*, 1, 1–103.

Bergin, A. and Garfield, S. (eds) (1986) *The Handbook of Psychotherapy and Behaviour Change, 3rd edition*. New York, NY: Wiley.

Blagg, N.R. and Yule, W. (1984) 'The behavioural treatment of school phobia: A comparative study.' *Behaviour Research and Therapy 22*, 1, 119–127.

Bryce, G. and Baird, D. (1986) 'Precipitating a crisis: Family therapy and adolescent school refusers.' *Journal of Adolescence 9*, 2, 199–213.

Carpenter, J. and Treacher, A. (eds) (1993) *Using Family Therapy in the 90s*. Oxford: Blackwell.

Chamberlain, P. and Rosicky, J.G. (1995) 'The effectiveness of family therapy in the treatment of adolescents with conduct disorders and delinquency.' *Journal of Marital and Family Therapy 21*, 4, 441–459.

Cohen, P., Kasen, S., Brook, J.S. and Struening, E.L. (1991) 'Diagnostic predictors of treatment patterns in a cohort of adolescents.' *Journal of the American Academy of Child and Adolescent Psychiatry 30*, 3, 989–993.

Coombs, R.H. (ed) (1988) *The Family Context of Adolescent Drug Use*. New York, NY: Haworth.

Dadds, M.R. (1995) *Families, Children, and the Development of Dysfunction*. London: Sage.

Dare, C., Eisler, I., Colahan, C., Crowther, C., Senior, R. and Asen, E. (1995) 'The listening heart and the chi-square: Clinical and empirical perceptions in the family therapy of anorexia nervosa.' *Journal of Family Therapy 17*, 1, 31–57.

Dare, C., Eisler, I., Russell, G.F.M. and Szmukler, G. (1990) 'The clinical and theoretical impact of a controlled trial of family therapy in anorexia nervosa.' *Journal of Marital and Family Therapy 16*, 1, 39–57.

Dishion, T.J., Reid, J.B. and Patterson, G.R. (1988) 'Empirical guidelines for a family intervention for adolescent drug abuse.' In R.H. Coombs (ed) *The Family Context of Adolescent Drug Use*. New York, NY: Haworth.

Dodge, E., Hodes, M., Eisler, I. and Dare, C. (1995) 'Family therapy for bulimia nervosa in adolescents: An exploratory study.' *Journal of Family Therapy 17*, 1, 59–77.

Estrada, A.U. and Pinsof, W.M. (1995) 'The effectiveness of family therapies for selected behavioural disorders of childhood.' *Journal of Marital and Family Therapy 21*, 4, 403–440.

Freedman, J. and Combs, G. (1996) *Narrative Therapy: The Social Construction of Preferred Realities*. New York, NY: Norton.

Freeman, J., Epston, D. and Lobovits, D. (1997) *Playful Approaches to Serious Problems: Narrative Therapy with Children and their Families*. New York, NY: Norton.

Giles, T.R. (ed) (1993) *Handbook of Effective Psychotherapy*. New York, NY: Plenum.

Gurman, A.S., Kniskern, D.P. and Pinsof, W.M. (1986) 'Research on the process and outcome of marital and family therapy.' In A. Bergin and S. Garfield (eds) *The Handbook of Psychotherapy and Behavior Change. 3rd edition*. New York, NY: Wiley.

Hazelrigg, M.D., Cooper, H.M. and Borduin, C.M. (1987) 'Evaluating the effectiveness of family therapies: An integrative review and analysis.' *Psychological Bulletin 101*, 3, 428–442.

Henggeler, S.W. (1994) *Treatment Manual for Family Preservation Using Multisystemic Therapy*. Charleston, SC: Medical University of South Carolina.

Hsu, L.K.G. (1990) *Eating Disorders*. New York, NY: Guilford Press.

Kazdin, A.E. (1997) 'Psychological treatments for conduct disorder in children.' *Journal of Child Psychology and Psychiatry 38*, 2, 161–178.

Kolko, D.J. and Kazdin, A.E. (1993) 'Emotional/behavioural problems in clinic and nonclinic children: Correspondence among child, parent and teacher reports.' *Journal of Child Psychology and Psychiatry 34*, 6, 991–1006.

Kuehl, B.P., Newfield, N.A. and Joanning, H. (1990) 'A client-based description of family therapy.' *Journal of Family Psychology 3*, 3, 310–321.

Markus, E., Lange, A. and Pettigrew, T.F. (1990) 'Effectiveness of family therapy: A meta-analysis.' *Journal of Family Therapy 12*, 3, 205–221.

Matson, J.L. (1989) *Treating Depression in Children and Adolescents.* New York, NY: Pergamon.

Minuchin, S. (1974) *Families and Family Therapy.* London: Tavistock.

Nugent, W.R., Carpenter, D. and Parks, J. (1993) 'A statewide evaluation of family preservation and family reunification services.' *Research on Social Work Practice 3*, 1, 40–65.

Offord, D.R. and Bennett, K.J. (1994) 'Conduct disorder: Long term outcomes and intervention effectiveness.' *Journal of the American Academy of Child and Adolescent Psychiatry 33*, 4, 1069–1078.

Offord, D.R., Boyle, M.H. and Racine, Y. (1989) 'Ontario child health study: Correlates of disorder.' *Journal of the American Academy of Child and Adolescent Psychiatry 28*, 3, 856–860.

Oster, G.D. and Caro, J.E. (1990) *Understanding and Treating Depressed Adolescents and Their Families.* Chichester: John Wiley and sons.

Patterson, G.R. (1982) *Coercive Family Processes.* Aegean, OR: Castilia Publishing.

Patterson, G.R., Dishion, T.J. and Chamberlain, P. (1993) 'Outcomes and methodological issues relating to treatment of anti-social children.' In T.R. Giles (ed) *Handbook of Effective Psychotherapy.* New York, NY: Plenum.

Quine, L. and Pahl, J. (1989) *Stress and Coping in Families Caring for a Child with Severe Mental Handicap: A Longitudinal Study.* Canterbury: University of Kent.

Reimers, S. and Treacher, A. (1995) *Introducing User-friendly Family Therapy.* London: Routledge.

Robins, L.N. and Rutter, M. (eds) (1990) *Straight and Devious Pathways from Childhood to Adulthood.* London: Oxford University Press.

Roth, A. and Fonagy, P. (1996) *What Works for Whom? A Critical Review of Psychotherapy Research.* New York, NY: Guilford Press.

Shadish, W.R., Ragsdale, K., Glaser, R.R. and Montgomery, L.M. (1993) 'The efficacy and effectiveness of marital and family therapy: A perspective from meta-analysis.' *Journal of Marital and Family Therapy 21*, 4, 345–360.

Street, E., Downey, J. and Brazier, A. (1991) 'The development of therapeutic consultations in child-focused family work.' *Journal of Family Therapy 13*, 3, 311–334.

Treacher, A. and Carpenter, J. (eds) (1984) *Using Family Therapy.* Oxford: Blackwell.

Vandereycken, W. and Vanderlinden, J. (1989) 'A family-oriented strategy in outpatient treatment.' In W. Vandereycken, E. Kog and J. Vanderlinden (eds) *The Family Approach to Eating Disorders.* New York, NY: PMA Publishing.

Vandereycken, W. and Vanderlinden, J. (eds) (1989) *The Family Approach to Eating Disorders.* New York, NY: PMA Publishing.

Vetere, A. (1993) 'Using family therapy in services for people with learning disabilities.' In J. Carpenter and A. Treacher (eds) *Using Family Therapy in the 90s.* Oxford: Blackwell.

White, J., Moffitt, T.E., Earls, F. Robins, L. and Silva, P. (1990) 'How early can we tell? Pre-school predictors of boys' conduct disorder and delinquency.' *Criminology 28*, 3, 507–533.

CHAPTER 8

Educational Services for Children with Social, Emotional or Behavioural Difficulties

Gwynedd Lloyd and Pamela Munn

Introduction

Our understanding of the causes of and the 'cures' for troublesome behaviour has grown over the years. In the past, most explanations were rooted in the individual child who was seen as either 'mad' or 'bad' and so requiring either sustained medical or psychiatrically-based intervention or punishment (Bridgeland 1971). Often the best that could be done was to provide some form of containment. As Sandow (1994) makes clear, 'The implication of such a view is that education for the affected child is impossible and may be almost sacrilegious: "flying in the face of nature"' (p.2). Contemporary explanations include the neo-biological, used for example to explain the behaviour of children who show an apparently abnormal incapacity for sustained attention. Labels like attention deficit and hyperactivity disorder are increasingly used by teachers and psychologists to explain problem behaviour (Armstrong and Galloway 1994; Ferguson, Lloyd and Reid 1997). This chapter concentrates on two other sets of explanations for troublesome behaviour, the psychological and the sociological. These can be seen as underpinning most of the educational services currently provided to children perceived as having social, emotional and behavioural difficulties.

We begin by setting the context in terms of what counts as social, emotional and behavioural difficulties before going on to consider services at three levels – whole school, class and individual. We describe a range of specific strategies and consider the research evidence underpinning them. We conclude that a good deal of innovative and imaginative work is taking place in providing for pupils with social, emotional and behavioural difficulties but that more needs to be done to disseminate this work and to evaluate its effectiveness. Indeed a great deal of work done in schools to provide for children with social, emotional and behavioural difficulties has not been systematically researched in terms of effectiveness.

Furthermore, the concept of effectiveness is itself problematic since short- and long-term effects need to be considered separately as do criteria relating to such diverse concerns with effectiveness as cost effectiveness, pupil attainment in public examinations, pupil behaviour in school, classroom and home and juvenile offending. Conventional research on school effectiveness defines effectiveness in terms of pupils' attainments in public examination results at ages 16, 17 and 18. Researchers working in this area stress the need for large sample sizes in order to make generalisations; measures over time so that 'blips' in effectiveness can be taken into account; connections between whole school effects and departmental and teacher effects; good baseline attainment measures; and value added measures which can accurately measure the 'boost' given by the school to pupils' attainments over and above what might have been expected. These features are generally conspicuous by their absence when one reviews the literature on service provision for pupils with social, emotional and behavioural difficulties. The norm is for small scale 'one-off' studies, which are interesting and revealing enough in themselves but do not provide the statistically robust accounts on outcomes which one might expect. This is a substantial and serious gap in the research literature.

What counts as a social, emotional and behavioural difficulty?

It is easy to assume that challenging behaviour is self-evident and that we would all recognise such behaviour when we saw it. Yet a number of studies indicate the context specific nature of such behaviour and whether it is regarded by teachers as a 'problem' (Galloway and Goodwin 1987; Graham 1998; Munn, Johnstone and Chalmers 1992; Sanders and Hendry 1997). Key influences include the teacher's knowledge and expectations of the pupil, the ethos or culture of the school (particularly its rules, rewards and sanctions) and the extent to which pupils participate in decision making about these matters. The assessment of and the prognosis for pupils deemed to have social, emotional and behavioural difficulties is likewise value laden (McPhee 1992). Experts can tend to assume a deficit model of the child rather than considering the social and organisational circumstances in which problem behaviour manifests itself.

Closs (1997) reports that there are 1150 children in mainstream schools in Scotland recorded as having social, emotional and behavioural difficulties and that these are only the tip of the iceberg. This is because of the well known widespread variation in policy and practice of opening a Record of Need for pupils (the equivalent of a Statement of Need in England and Wales). Other indicators suggest that behavioural problems may be on the increase. For example the number of pupils permanently excluded from school in England and Wales is growing at an alarming rate. Over 11,000 pupils were excluded from secondary schools and 1800 from primary schools in 1995–1996 and this represents a 45 per cent increase since 1993–1994 for primary schools and an 18 per cent increase for secondary schools (Lawrence and Hayden 1997). Equivalent figures for Scotland are not available since the legislative position is different and not all local authorities permit permanent exclusion. Nevertheless there has been sufficient concern in Scotland for the Scottish Office to commission research on the issue and for funding of around three million pounds to be made available to support in-school alternatives to exclusion.

Research on exclusion and on school discipline in general suggests that in most instances it is the drip, drip effect of seemingly trivial pupil behaviour which teachers find most wearisome. Thus talking out of turn, eating in class, work avoidance by pupils and pupils hindering each other from work are the typical behaviours which teachers encounter daily (Elton Committee, DES 1989; Johnstone and Munn 1992, 1997). The following response from a teacher sums up the situation:

> Major incidents of indiscipline, I find, are usually the easiest to deal with… It is the continuous minor infringements during the normal day-to-day running of the class which probably cause the most disruption and take the most time… Almost any methods of trying to deal with and improve poor behaviour over a long period of time takes a significant amount of time and adds to the workload. (Johnstone and Munn 1997, p.10)

Few pupils with social, emotional and behavioural difficulties exhibit distinctively different behaviour from the generality of pupils. Thus school responses to improving discipline in general are likely to have a positive effect on many pupils seen as having these difficulties.

Whole school responses

A wide range of research studies have pointed to the importance of school ethos in influencing pupils' behaviour. Such studies include the large-scale and statistically robust research on school effectiveness (e.g. Rutter *et al.* 1979; Sammons, Thomas and Mortimore 1997) as well as case studies of individual schools (e.g. Hargreaves 1967; Lacey 1970; Ball 1981). These studies show that schools make a difference. Schools with pupils from similar backgrounds can vary in their effectiveness in terms of pupils' behaviour, achievement and much else besides. It is less easy to specify which elements of schooling make the difference, as many are interlinked. Nevertheless, the term 'ethos' has emerged as encapsulating a variety of elements which taken together make up a school's culture or climate. These elements include a welcoming and comfortable physical environment; pupils' work displayed with displays regularly updated; positive teacher–pupil relationships incorporating high teacher expectations of academic and other achievements such as in sports, music or drama; personal and social developments given a high priority; homework set and marked regularly; active leadership from the headteacher; and pupil participation in decision making about school life. Schools have recognised the importance of ethos in a number of different ways although the research evidence on the effectiveness of promoting particular aspects of a positive ethos tends to be anecdotal. Different kinds of approaches are described below.

Perhaps the most common approach to promoting positive behaviour is for such behaviour to be recognised and rewarded. Most schools have well-developed systems of sanctions and punishments in the case of unacceptable behaviour but until recently, fewer positively encouraged good behaviour. Such approaches typically involve a postcard, badge, or some other form of recognition for pupils. Sometimes these are added up and a merit certificate awarded at a public occasion such as a school assembly. This kind of approach has been used in both primary and secondary schools and, much to the surprise of teachers, teenage boys and girls as well as younger children welcome the explicit recognition which the certificates or their equivalent bring. These anecdotal accounts of success from individual schools underline the more generally accepted and systematically researched connection between self-esteem, achievement and behaviour (Lawrence 1996).

A different approach is the setting up of a review base or behaviour support unit within the mainstream school for pupils with social, emotional and behavioural difficulties. Although involving distinctive provision, such approaches can be termed whole school when the expertise staff employ is shared with the generality of staff to enhance their skills in classroom management and broaden their range of teaching strategies. Most units are seen as offering temporary respite for staff and pupils rather than full-time provision for pupils exhibiting challenging behaviour.

Such units can vary in purpose from the old style 'sin bin' which brought its own kind of rewards in terms of reputations to the pupils referred, to a system designed to analyse the reasons for troublesome behaviour and to propose solutions. Many of these forward looking units incorporate learning support as well as behavioural support staff in recognition of the link between behaviour problems and learning difficulties. Underpinning these units are specialist staff, designated behaviour support staff, who often come from rather different educational backgrounds, some from mainstream schools, others from residential special schools for pupils with social, emotional and behavioural difficulties. Behaviour support teachers also operate in schools with no units, sometimes as part of a pupil support team which includes learning support, providing consultancy to class and subject teachers (Fleming 1997). The training and professional development of these staff is an issue we take up in the Conclusion.

Equally, training and development is a major issue in relation to another group of support staff, that is, classroom assistants or teacher auxiliaries, who are increasingly used to provide in-class support to pupils considered to have social, emotional or behavioural difficulties in mainstream schools. There are clear questions over the role of such staff in relation to the class teacher. For example, what is the role of support staff in the behaviour management of identified pupils? Is curriculum planning and diagnostic assessment part of their work? Are such staff a resource only for identified pupils or can they help more generally in the classroom? Concerns have been voiced that some children may be receiving some key teaching from unqualified staff.

Often linked to the integration of learning and behaviour support is a pastoral care system which is geared to interagency working. Schools collaborate with social workers, health professionals, educational psychologists and others in a joint assessment of the troublesome behaviour and try to co-ordinate a joint response. Such evidence that we have on interagency working notes the difficulties inherent in successful operation (Armstrong and Galloway 1994; Kendrick 1995; Lloyd

1997). These include the different beliefs among professions about the likely causes of and cures for troublesome behaviour; the battles for resources which face all concerned and hence the need to protect budgets; and the rather different legislative frameworks which impact on professionals. The Children Acts of 1989 and 1995 in England and Scotland respectively, for instance, explicitly adopt a children's rights philosophy which is markedly absent in education legislation in both countries.

Many schools emphasise the importance of working with parents. When Scottish headteachers were asked about strategies commonly used to support pupils on the verge of exclusion, they most frequently cited involving and working with parents (Cullen *et al.* 1996a). This took different forms in different schools. Sometimes parents were involved in monitoring their child's behaviour in school or in developing common strategies to be used both at home and school, perhaps involving some reward or punishment system. Often they were invited to meetings with school staff, sometimes, but not always, to formal inter-professional meetings. Some schools had parent support groups and others offered parent education classes.

Whole class responses

As we have argued earlier, responses to difficult or disturbing behaviour in schools derive at least in part from the conceptualisation of the origins or 'causes' of the behaviour. In the 1980s and early 1990s there was an emphasis on effective classroom practice deriving in part from research on effective schools mentioned above and in part from a reconceptualisation by educational psychologists of their role. Many moved from individualist perspectives to a more systems-based approach. 'The traditional child-centred approach taken by psychologists... focuses on children's personality and family background. The relevance of this approach has increasingly been questioned because it concentrates on elements which schools are least able to influence' (McLean 1992).

A number of teacher packages have been developed, drawing attention to the whole school factors mentioned earlier and offering models of effective classroom prevention and intervention with disruptive behaviour. In Scotland, the most widely used were the packages on Promoting Positive Behaviour developed by the psychological services of Strathclyde Region (McLean 1992). They were pragmatically based on the notion of observed good practice by teachers, that is on craft knowledge, rather than on any particular theoretical model, although drawing on the work of Kounin (1970) and Kyriacou (1986). These writers emphasised the importance of teachers being proactive in terms of high quality advance preparation and lesson planning to minimise the opportunities for disruptive behaviour and suggested a range of strategies for reacting to disruptive behaviour. These included the seemingly straightforward correct identification of the pupil(s) causing disruption, moving pupils away from disruptive peers, the use of threats and warnings which teachers were prepared to carry out and the development of teacher alertness – a kind of constant scanning and checking on pupils' behaviour so that trouble could be nipped in the bud. They shared some features with the English package Preventive Approaches to Disruption – PAD (Chisholm *et al.* 1986). Other packages used in Scotland we well as in England were those based on clear behavioural principles such as *The Behavioural Approach to Teaching Packages* – Batpack and Batsac (Wheldall 1987).

All of these packs assumed that teachers could be more effective in preventing and responding to indiscipline in the classroom and that they had a professional obligation to review and improve their skills. It is by no means clear that this assumption was, or is, accepted by all teachers who may resist what they see as a 'blame the teacher' approach (Armstrong and Galloway 1994). Such views may explain the recent embracing by a number of schools of an approach, developed by the Canters, which has been used for some years in certain US schools. Assertive Discipline (Moss and Rumbold 1992) restates the right of the teacher to be in charge of the classroom. This is also more evident in some recently developed whole school approaches, as discussed earlier, like Positive Discipline or Discipline for Learning which combine an emphasis on assertive teaching with reinforcement of 'good behaviour' by pupils. These differ from the behavioural packages mentioned above because of their emphasis on clear rules, rewards and sanctions without reassessing the teachers' behaviour management skills in any thorough way or by advocating extended pupil participation in decision making in schools and classrooms.

Other methods which are used with whole classes include those derived from more humanistic theoretical perspectives emphasising self-concept and aiming to enhance self-esteem. Sometimes these involve teaching packs like Skills for Adolescence, often used in social education in the secondary school or Skills for the Primary School Child (TACADE 1990). Circle time is increasingly used in the primary class as a way of promoting positive group relationships and addressing problems. Circle time is based on the thinking of social group work and uses many of the methods developed for use in youth work and intermediate treatment in the 1970s and 1980s (Button 1982; Moseley 1995). Campbell and Dominy (1997) describe how the use of Circle Time as a central feature of their personal and social development programme in a Glasgow primary school has reduced the level of behavioural difficulties. They do not cite statistical evidence, reporting rather on the perceptions of staff and parents and on the willingness of all staff to endorse the approach as it seems to work.

Responding to individuals

Here in particular it can be argued that the strategies adopted reflect how staff conceptualise the problem. In a study of exclusion in Scottish schools, teachers cited different support strategies depending on their view of the origin of the pupil's difficulties (see Table 8.1).

Thus the response will vary, for example, according to whether the teacher sees the child as disaffected with school or as having individual psychologically-based problems. Responses to disaffection in the later years of the secondary school are likely to be largely curricular, involving flexible timetabling, alternative curricula, extended work experience and links with community education or further education colleges. Responses to pupils viewed as having individual difficulties may be more varied according to the age and stage of the child, the theoretical interests of the educational psychologist involved, the confidence or competence of the teacher or resource availability (Lane 1994). One important factor in determining the selection of intervention or support strategies may be the gendered nature of schooling. Boys and girls are identified as having social, emotional or behavioural difficulties in a ratio of 4:1. They are excluded from schools in a similar proportion. Thinking about appropriate responses will therefore inevitably be dominated by a conception of the needs of boys (Crozier and Anstiss 1995).

One approach to responding to young pupils whose behaviour is challenging in the classroom is outlined by Russell (1997). She describes initial liaison with nursery school staff, followed by the provision of auxiliary support, close working with parents, a programme with small specific observable steps and the use of commercially produced curriculum development materials such as Tacade (1990)

Table 8.1 Some support strategies cited by interviewees for pupils evincing behavioural difficulties

	Teachers' perceptions of underlying reasons for behavioural difficulties				
	domestic background	*learning difficulties*	*individual psychological problems*	*broad context of socio-economic deprivation*	*disaffected with school (S3/S4)*
Favoured support strategies	• being more tolerant • offering time out of class as a 'haven' • contact with parents; putting parents in touch with sources of help and advice	• differentiated curriculum • smaller classes • co-operative teaching (more time with pupils having difficulty) • use of interactive computer packages • time in or out of class with learning support teacher • (primary school) focus on early literacy	• offering strategies for coping e.g. with anger, confrontations • counselling • groupwork • support in class • educational psychologist	• headteacher joining with health professionals to propose a local initiative to the council • linking with existing projects of e.g. Family Support Centre • senior staff acting as role models of the benefits of success • work experience organised	• talking over problems; being open to pupils' views • part-time schooling for S4 plus imput from college, work experience, community education • linking with Social Work's youth work • clubs and leisure activities based in school • individually tailored programmes for achieving academic and/or vocational qualifications • links with Community Education staff to offer a more flexible curriculum • school leavers (S4) support group

Source: Cullen *et al.* 1996b

to build personal and social skills. These materials combine features from behavioural and humanistic psychological perspectives. This is probably typical of many approaches in British schools which tend not to rely on one theoretical model but to select eclectically.

Many schools use individual counselling-type interviews to support children thought to be in difficulty. Most often these are informal interviews, usually conducted by pastoral care or guidance staff, who apply basic listening and reflecting skills. A few schools have fully trained school counsellors. There are issues about whether teaching staff could ever undertake a formal counselling role and about the appropriateness of this in school (Lane 1996). Professional counsellors tend to see their work as part of a formal process undertaken by clients voluntarily and with clear understanding of the nature and of the boundaries of the process. Such conditions for counselling are typically not applicable in schools. Sometimes pupils are seen not to have the verbal skills necessary to engage in formal counselling. Guidance teachers in schools also have other kinds of relationship with their pupils, which often conflict with a counselling role especially those involving the exercise of power (Bond 1992). These include subject teaching and pupil preparation for public examination. The literature on the use of counselling in education tends to suggest that it is possible and preferable for teachers to use a more general counselling approach. Indeed training for guidance staff in counselling skills is recommended (Bovair and McLaughlin 1993). One important characteristic of such training should be an awareness of when teachers should refer on to more skilled professionals if available.

The Elton report on Discipline in Schools in England and Wales recommended that training in basic counselling skills should be introduced into initial teacher training (DES 1989). Training, even for guidance teachers, is not mandatory in Scotland. There may however be many circumstances when guidance staff may find themselves conducting interviews on highly sensitive topics. All of the Scottish education authorities have guidelines on procedures in child protection but children may choose to disclose abuse to staff who have had no training in counselling skills. There is no formal structure for either support or supervision of staff undertaking counselling interviews. A guidance teacher described recently, to one of the authors of this paper, an interview with a parent whose child had just been killed in an accident. She said she had 20 minutes with the parent immediately followed by two periods teaching social dance. She had no support in addressing her own feelings in such circumstances.

One form of interview used in some schools is the Life-space interview. This was originally developed by Fritz Redl in the USA, is psychodynamically-based but provides a supportive structure and direction for both pupil and teacher to work through difficulties and develop a plan (Charlton and David 1989). Other methods, especially with younger or less articulate pupils, use strategies involving drawing, drama or games, sometimes derived from play therapy. Many schools offer a programme of small group work where young people can focus on shared difficulties, often aimed at confidence building or improved self-concept. Improved relationships with peers or with adults in school may have an effect on behaviour in classrooms. These often use games and exercises (Brandes and Phillips 1977; Dearling and Armstrong 1979; Dwivedi 1993). The programmes are often offered in the social group work tradition (Button 1982) but sometimes have a more structured cognitive behavioural problem solving flavour, focused on themes like anger management. This perspective is also seen in some individual work with pupils on setting individual targets and self-monitoring of behaviour (Verduyn, Lord and Forrest 1990). There are issues of possible role conflict too for teachers involved in group work. The style of group facilitator is different from that expected of most teachers. There may be issues of confidentiality. Occasionally group work may be offered in collaboration with other professional colleagues (for example youth workers). These may require careful negotiation of issues of boundaries and confidentiality (Wilford 1992).

Recently popular with educational psychologists and in some schools has been brief therapy, sometimes also called solution-focused (de Shazer 1991; Quick 1996). This developed in reaction to the tendency in some problem solving approaches to children's difficulties to dwell excessively on what might appear to be the reasons for the difficulties rather than to focus on the potential solutions. Brief therapy attempts to enable children to picture their lives in a better condition and identify the steps to achieving this. This approach appeals to teachers and others working in schools as it emphasises the potential for change in a relatively short time. The ecosystemic approach, initially written about in the US literature (Molnar and Lindquist 1989), recognises the interactions of difficult behaviour and a range of social contextual factors. It emphasises the importance of intervention involving all aspects of the dynamically interacting system (Cooper and Upton 1990). This approach has not been formally adopted in Scottish schools but the idea of a joint systems approach influences the thinking behind the work of some educational psychologists.

This chapter has concentrated on responses to social, emotional or behavioural problems which are based on assumptions about the social and psychological origins of the pupil's actions. It may be important to refer briefly here to the increasing move, as indicated earlier, toward the development of more medicalised models of explanation and intervention, exemplified in the increasing use of the prescription of controlled drugs like Ritalin (methylphenidate) to manage over-active behaviour in children and increasingly also adolescents (Ferguson *et al.* 1997). Equally there seems to be a trend towards describing disruptive or delinquent behaviour in terms of the psychiatric model of conduct disorder with prescription of behaviour controlling drugs, sometimes those developed for use with adult psychosis or schizophrenia (see also Chapter 10). Such prescriptions may often be made by private medical clinics responding to parents desperately looking for help. Medical diagnoses and drug therapy offer a way of responding to their children's behaviour, which relieves parents and teachers equally of blame and responsibility. In the USA there is concern over the very widespread use of drug therapy in schools (Reid and Maag 1997). Similar concerns are being expressed now in Britain by educational psychologists and teachers.

Conclusion

We have argued that there is a considerable range of strategies used in primary and secondary schools to support pupils considered to have social, emotional and behavioural difficulties. The choice of strategies will vary according to local factors such as local authority and school policies, resource availability and the experience and knowledge of school staff and associated professional colleagues. This diversity of approaches reflects a range of professional understandings on the origins of difficult behaviour in school. Sometimes work may be carried out within one particular theoretical perspective but is more likely to be eclectic in its origin and implementation.

There is little recent research or evaluation into the effectiveness of these methods. The Scottish research into exclusion and alternatives provided very little evidence of systematic evaluation of effectiveness, either of overall support strategies or of individual interventions (Cullen *et al.* 1996b). Nor are there clear definitions of what we mean by effectiveness in this context. This lack of clarity is also apparent in the literature on out of school alternative provision for SEBD (social, emotional and behavioural difficulties), which we have not discussed here (Cullen and Lloyd 1997). However it is clear that the quality of mainstream support for children has implications for the kind of out of school provision needed. Effectiveness may also be different for different groups; its definition needs to take account of gender and cultural differences in school populations. It may be differently constructed by the range of professionals working in and with schools. For classroom teachers, effective intervention may focus on the reduction of visible disruptiveness. Guidance staff and social work colleagues may have concerns over the effectiveness of school support for pupils whose difficulties may not necessarily confront the discipline system. Such difficulties may be expressed in withdrawn behaviour in classrooms and playgrounds or in absence from school.

Much of the above raises issues about the purposes of schooling, relevant in the current climate of emphasis on educational attainment. Schools are publicly accountable for the attainments of their pupils. In secondary schools this is largely expressed via the so-called 'league tables' of performance where schools are compared against local and national averages. In primary schools we are about to see the setting of performance targets in literacy and numeracy. Schools might therefore be tempted not to admit children whose performance is likely to affect adversely the school's place in the league table. This response is likely to be exaggerated if performance targets in attendance and exclusion rates are set. At the time pressure on other services or closing down of specialist services to children may lead to greater pressure on schools to widen their role. The Scottish exclusions research suggests schools can be broadly characterised as either exclusive or inclusive. Inclusive schools had a broad view of educational responsibilities characterised by a notion of extended professionalism for teachers who saw it as their job to teach a wide range of pupils not just those who were well motivated, well behaved and likely to succeed. These teachers valued personal and social development goals as well as academic attainment. It would be a pity if a government committed to tackling social exclusion unwittingly encouraged the rejection of pupils with social, emotional and behavioural difficulties by emphasising the primacy of academic attainment and set unrealistic targets for schools in terms of attendance and discipline.

We have also argued that there are clear training issues for different groups in supporting pupils in difficulty in school. Training for behaviour support staff, guidance teachers and classroom assistants might include counselling skills for teachers, interprofessional working, knowledge of systems, the range of possible strategies and the evidence of their effectiveness.

Existing research and literature support the view that 'some things do work, sometimes (Lane 1994). There are many different 'answers', some of which we have discussed in this chapter, each of which have worked in different situations. Thus, for instance, target setting, social group work, anger control strategies can all be beneficial. It would be naïve, however, to expect there to be one universally effective response to pupils experiencing social, emotional and behavioural difficulties. There is a need for careful evaluation and the use of research, both qualitative and quantitative, which acknowledges the complexity of the issues, not the least being what counts as effective, and includes the views of not only professionals but of pupils and their families.

References

Armstrong, D. and Galloway, D. (1994) 'Special educational needs and problem behaviour: Making policy in the classroom.' In S. Riddell and S. Brown (eds) *Special Educational Needs Policy in the 90's.* London: Routledge.

Ball, S.J. (1981) *Beechside Comprehensive.* Cambridge: Cambridge University Press.

Bond, T. (1992) 'Ethical issues in counselling in education.' *British Journal of Guidance and Counselling 20,* 1, 54–57.

Bovair, K. and McLaughlin, C. (1993) *Counselling in Schools – A Reader.* London: David Fulton.

Brandes, D. and Phillips, H. (1977) *Gamester's Handbook.* London: Hutchinson.

Bridgeland, M. (1971) *Pioneer Work with Maladjusted Children.* London: Staples.

Button, L. (1982) *Developmental Groupwork with Adolescents.* London: Hodder and Stoughton.

Campbell, J. and Dominy, J. (1997) 'Circle time.' In G. Lloyd and P. Munn (eds) *Sharing Good Practice.* Edinburgh: Moray House Publications.

Charlton, T. and David, K. (1989) 'Reflections and implications.' In T. Charlton and K. David (eds) *Managing Misbehaviour.* London: Macmillan.

Charlton, T. and David, K. (eds) (1989) *Managing Misbehaviour.* London: Macmillan.

Chisholm, B., Kearney, D., Knight, H., Little, H., Morris, S. and Tweddle, D. (1986) *Preventive Approaches to Disruption.* Basingstoke: Macmillan.

Clark, M.M. and Munn, P. (eds) (1997) *Education in Scotland.* London: Routledge.

Closs, A. (1997) 'Special education provision.' In M.M. Clark and P. Munn (eds) *Education in Scotland.* London: Routledge.

Cooper, P. and Upton, G. (1990) 'An ecosystemic approach to emotional and behavioural difficulties in schools.' *Educational Psychology 10,* 4, 301–321.

Crozier, J. and Anstiss, J. (1995) 'Out of the spotlight: Girls' experience of disruption.' In M. Lloyd-Smith and J. Dwyfor Davies (eds) *On the Margins: The Educational Experience of 'Problem' Pupils.* Stoke-on-Trent: Trentham.

Cullen, M.A., Johnstone, M., Lloyd, G. and Munn, P. (1996a) *Exclusions from School and Alternatives: The Headteachers' Perspective.* A Report to the Scottish Office Education and Industry Department. Edinburgh: Moray House.

Cullen, M.A., Johnstone, M., Lloyd, G. and Munn, P. (1996b) *Exclusions from School and Alternatives: The Case Studies.* A Report to the SOEID. Edinburgh: Moray House.

Cullen, M.A. and Lloyd, G. (1997) *Alternative Education Provision for Excluded Pupils.* A Literature Review for the SOEID. Edinburgh: Moray House.

Dearling, A. and Armstrong, H. (1979) *The Youth Games Book.* Bridge of Weir: Scottish Intermediate Treatment Resource Centre.

de Shazer (1991) *Putting Difference to Work.* New York, NY: Norton.

DES (1989) *Discipline in Schools.* Report of the Committee of Enquiry chaired by Lord Elton. London: HMSO.

Dwivedi, K.N. (1993) *Groupwork with Children and Adolescents.* London: Jessica Kingsley Publishers.

Ferguson, R., Lloyd, G. and Reid, G. (1997) *Attention Deficit Hyperactivity Disorder.* A Literature Review for the SOEID. Edinburgh: Moray House.

Fleming, M. (1997) 'Developing a whole school policy for behaviour support.' In G. Lloyd and P. Munn (eds) *Sharing Good Practice.* Edinburgh: Moray House Publications.

Galloway, D. and Goodwin, C. (1987) *The Education of Disturbing Children.* London: Longman.

Graham, J. (1988) *Schools, Disruptive Behaviour and Delinquency.* London: HMSO.

Gray, P., Miller, A. and Noakes, J. (eds) (1994) *Challenging Behaviour in Schools. Teacher Support, Practical Techniques and Policy Development.* London: Routledge.

Hargreaves, D.H. (1967) *Social Relations in a Secondary School.* London: Routledge & Kegan Paul.

Johnstone, M. and Munn, P. (1992) *Discipline in Scottish Schools.* Edinburgh: Scottish Council for Research in Education.

Johnstone, M. and Munn, P. (1997) *Primary and Secondary Teachers' Perceptions of Indiscipline.* Confidential research report to the Educational Institute of Scotland.

Kendrick, A. (1995) 'The integration of child care services in Scotland.' *Children and Youth Services Review 17,* 5–6, 619–635.

Kounin, J. (1970) *Discipline and Group Management in the Classroom.* New York, NY: Holt, Rinehart and Winston.

Kyriacou, C. (1986) *Effective Teaching in Schools.* Oxford: Blackwell.

Lacey, C. (1970) *Hightown Grammar.* Manchester: Manchester University Press.

Lane, D. (1994) 'Supporting effective responses to challenging behaviour: From theory to practice.' In P. Gray, A. Miller and J. Noakes (eds) *Challenging Behaviour in Schools. Teacher Support, Practical Techniques and Policy Development.* London: Routledge.

Lane, J. (1996) 'Counselling issues in mainstream schools.' *Emotional and Behavioural Difficulties 1,* 2, 46–51.

Lawrence, D. (1996) *Enhancing Self-Esteem in the Classroom.* London: Routledge.

Lawrence, B. and Hayden, C. (1997) 'Primary school exclusions.' *Educational Research and Evaluation 3,* 1, 54–77.

Lloyd, G. (ed) (1992) *Chosen with Care? Responses to Disturbing and Disruptive Behaviour.* Edinburgh: Moray House Publications.

Lloyd, G. (1997) 'Can the law support children's rights in school in Scotland and prevent the development of a climate of blame?' *Pastoral Care, 15,* 13–16.

Lloyd, G. and Munn, P. (eds) (1997) *Sharing Good Practice.* Edinburgh: Moray House Publications.

Lloyd-Smith, M. and Dwyfor Davies (eds) (1995) *On the Margins: The Educational Experience of 'Problem' Pupils.* Stoke-on-Trent: Trentham.

McLean, A. (1992) 'A staff development approach to improving behaviour in schools.' In G. Lloyd (ed) *Chosen with Care? Responses to Disturbing and Disruptive Behaviour.* Edinburgh: Moray House Publications.

McPhee, H. (1992) 'Assessment – what is the problem?' In G. Lloyd (ed) *Chosen with Care? Responses to Disturbing and Disruptive Behaviour.* Edinburgh: Moray House Publications.

Molnar, A. and Lindquist, B. (1989) *Changing Problem Behaviour in Schools.* San Francisco: Jossey Bass.

Moseley, J. (1995) *Turn Your School Around.* Cambridge: Cambridge Learning Development Aids.

Moss, G. and Rumbold, E. (1992) 'The right to teach.' *Special Children,* June/July.

Munn, P., Johnstone, M. and Chalmers, V. (1992) *Effective Discipline in Secondary Schools and Classrooms.* London: Paul Chapman.

Quick, E. (1996) *Doing What Works in Brief Therapy.* London: Academic Press.

Reid, R. and Maag, J. (1997) 'Attention Deficit Hyperactivity Disorder: Over here and over there.' *Educational and Child Psychology 14,* 1, 10–20.

Riddell, S. and Brown, S. (eds) (1994) *Special Educational Needs Policy in the 90s.* London: Routledge.

Russell, R. (1997) 'Classroom management strategies in a primary school class.' In G. Lloyd and P. Munn (eds) *Sharing Good Practice.* Edinburgh: Moray House Publications.

Rutter, M., Maugham, B., Mortimore, P. and Ouston, J. (1979) *Fifteen Thousand Hours: Secondary Schools and Their Effects on Children.* London: Paul Chapman.

Sammons, P., Thomas, S. and Mortimore, P. (1997) *Forging Links: Effective Schools and Effective Departments.* London: Paul Chapman.

Sanders, D. and Hendry, L. (1997) *New Perspectives on Disaffection.* London: Cassell.

Sandow, S. (1994) 'More ways than one: Models of special needs.' In S. Sandow (ed) *Whose Special Need?* London: Paul Chapman.

Sandow, S. (ed) (1994) *Whose Special Need?* London: Paul Chapman.

TACADE (1990) *Skills for the Primary School Child.* Salford: Quest International.

Verduyn, C.M., Lord, W. and Forrest, A.C. (1990) 'Social skills training in schools: An evaluation study.' *Journal of Adolescence 113,* 3–16.

Wheldall, K. (1987) *The Behaviourist in the Classroom.* London: Allen and Unwin.

Wilford, B. (1992) 'Neighbourhood projects and the school.' In G. Lloyd (ed) *Chosen with Care? Responses to Disturbing and Disruptive Behaviour.* Edinburgh: Moray House Publications.

CHAPTER 9

Youth Work: Young People and Transitions to Adulthood

Simon Bradford

Introduction

Throughout its history, youth work has retained an underlying ethos of introducing informal 'educational experiences' into young people's leisure lives. These are designed to enable them to achieve personal and social development, to support them in taking a responsible and positive role in their communities and to help them in the processes of transition to adulthood. Following World War II, youth work (like similar occupations) went through a process of 'professionalisation', and has achieved some recognition as one of the 'caring professions'. Now comprising a partnership between the 'voluntary sector' and the 'statutory sector' (local authorities), youth work is institutionally located in the wider education service, and in Britain has around 5000 full-time staff, 50,000 part-time staff, and 500,000 voluntary workers. Youth work has become one of a range of expert interventions which have increasingly sought to manage and shape – to *govern* – the social world (Foucault 1991), and as such it contributes to resolving the 'problem of young people and young people's problems.

During the last two or three decades youth work has expanded and is delivered through a complex network of organisations and groups, deploying a multiplicity of approaches and methods. Youth workers have demonstrated a capacity to work in diverse settings, and to shift youth work's identity in response to varying conceptions of 'youth need', whether defined by youth workers and youth services, by young people themselves, or increasingly by managers and funding bodies. Research by Maychell, Pathak and Cato (1996) provides some examples of the diversity of British youth work practice. In one situation youth workers operated from a mobile bus project in a rural area, offering a range of activities to young people in village communities where little other provision existed for them. In another setting, youth workers offered a safe place for young Asian women to meet and to participate in activities and discussion groups. In a drop-in cafe in a town centre youth workers offered young people a place to meet their friends, participate in creative activities, and gain access to information on benefits, youth training and employment opportunities (Maychell *et al.* 1996). Elsewhere, youth workers touch on the therapeutic domain through their work in counselling and advice services, or assume an explicitly 'educational' role helping young people to understand matters connected with health, sexuality, personal and social relationshps, race or gender. This work may be organised and delivered in activity programmes in youth centres and clubs, through 'personal and social education' curricula in schools, in tutorial activity in further education colleges or by supporting young people doing voluntary community service. Other youth workers operate in a 'detached' context, offering services to young people on the streets and in places where they meet. They work with young people who other services often regard as being hard to reach and youth work skills are being increasingly used in work with young people considered to be 'at risk'. Youth work initiatives of the kinds described above are often established in partnership with other agencies, organisations and local authority departments, and youth workers often work alongside teachers, social workers and health professionals. Underlying all this work is a professional commitment to *voluntary* and *participatory* relationships between youth workers and young people.

Youth work as 'social education': values and contexts for practice

The term 'social education' has provided youth work with a discursive but shifting identity since the early 1960s when it was conceived in 'liberal' and humanist terms, and focused largely on individual self-actualisation. Concentrating on the cultivation and development of an abstract and 'universal' young person, liberal social education sought to enable the individual to achieve self-understanding, and more clearly appreciate relationships with others. This type of social education (which continues to inform much youth work practice) is primarily concerned with the development of an ordered, reflexive and active self, able to appraise and transform its own constitutive feelings, attitudes or opinions. Typically, liberal social education has sought to create an equilibrium between individual needs or desires and the social responsibilities which accompany membership of a modern society (Davies and Gibson 1967). It encourages the cultivation of a 'social' sensitivity whilst simultaneously trying to extend young people's capacities to develop their own individual potential. Youth work's essentially *participative* and *experiential* approach to young people provides this form of social education with a natural 'person-centred' curriculum through which to intervene and influence.

During the 1970s and 1980s, social education was 'radicalised' as discourses of gender, race and disability impacted on youth work and youth workers. Radical social education transformed prevailing representations of young people, defining them in terms of their *collective* identities – 'young women', 'young black people' or 'young disabled people' for example – as well as their *individual* personae. It was argued that the 'issues' attending young people's membership of these social categories also mapped out their lives, and youth workers were enjoined to help young people develop the social and political competence necessary to influence their own circumstances, rather than be controlled by them. Radical social education construed its activities as the practice of 'empowerment'. A number of commentators have shown how this ambiguous notion is deployed as a motif in New Right and managerialist discourses of 'individual responsibility', as well as having currency in practices like youth work (Clarke, Cochrane and McLaughlin 1994; Morley 1995). In the latter, the idea of empowerment appears to signal youth workers' attempts to encourage and enable young people to become increasingly autonomous agents (either individually or collectively) through their acquisition of knowledge, dispositions or social and political skills. A discourse of 'rights' and 'social justice' (Karsh 1984) completed the radicalisation of social education, highlighting young people against a political backcloth but sim-ultaneously preserving an individual focus in youth work practice. Although heir to the different liberal and radical traditions (Butters and Newell 1978; Smith 1988; Jeffs and Smith 1990), social education maintains some clear and common ground: a focus on the problematic nature of young people's transitions to adulthood, a claim that experience provides the best vehicle for learning, a concern to balance individual need and social responsibility and the aim of cultivating the autonomous and self-reglating individual. A national Statement of Purpose adopted in the early 1990s (and currently under review) defined the apparently expanding boundaries of youth work and seemed to accommodate elements of both genres of social education. According to this somewhat vague statement, youth work's principal purpose is 'to redress all forms of inequality and to ensure equality of opportunity for all young people to fulfil their potential as empowered individuals and members of groups and communities and to support young people in their transition to adulthood' (National Youth Agency 1992). Although the statement acknowledges that youth work is undertaken with young people between the ages of 11 and 25 ('the transition to adulthood'), the 13 to 19 age range is defined as a priority. Other than specifying this priority age group, the youth service notionally operates as a 'universal' rather than a 'targeted' service.

Youth workers have recognised that youth – construed as a 'process' rather than a chronological state – is constituted by the various status transitions, which young people negotiate in order to achieve adulthood or 'citizenship'. The transition from education to work, the establishment of an independent home and family and the competence and behaviours necessary for these are particularly important (Coles 1995). They form part of the conceptual and material ground on which youth workers operate in helping young people to recognise and negotiate the rights and responsibilities which attend transition. Class, race, gender and other structural factors shape experience of transition and the ways in which different transitions 'mesh'. Most young people negotiate transition relatively successfully despite central government legislation of the last two decades having progressively eroded their access to employment opportunities, welfare benefits and entitlement to housing (Jones and Wallace 1992). However, a substantial minority of young people experience 'marginalisation, impoverishment and exclusion' at this time as a consequence of their social and material circumstances (Williamson *et al.* 1997, p.9).

The effectiveness of youth work

Systematic external research evaluating the effectiveness of 'mainstream' youth work has been extremely limited. Youth work's rather vague objectives, its diverse and somewhat diffuse nature seem to have eluded evaluation based on formal outcome measures. 'Hard' evaluation has no doubt appeared to be incompatible with youth work's holistic emphasis on informal relationships and 'person-centred' activities. The populations with whom youth workers operate are often changing, and the voluntary and informal nature of their contact may not have been thought amenable to research entailing systematic follow-up. However, the wider managerialist climate has forced providers in both the voluntary and statutory sectors to evaluate the effectiveness of their provision and show that tangible outcomes are identified and achieved in their work. Much of this kind of evaluation is inevitably cast in managerialist terms, and may differ significantly from young people's perceptions of youth work's relevance or effectiveness, or indeed from 'professional' definitions and discourses (see for example Office for Standards in Education 1997). Some research effort (undoubtedly reflecting broader social and political preoccupations) has been invested in examining youth work's contribution to young people considered to be 'at risk' and we return to this later. This section of the chapter draws on research providing some evidence of the relevance and effectiveness of youth work generally. Some of the discussion is based on two substantial quantitative studies of young people's involvement in youth work. Other studies referred to are smaller in scale and have adopted qualitative methods, exploring with young people their perceptions of the value and effectiveness of either general or targeted youth work.

One indicator of youth work's effectiveness is the number of young people using its provisions. This is particularly important in the context of a service in which there is no compulsion on young people to participate. Arguably, if users do not see the service provided as relevant they will not use it. Research on young people's participation in youth service facilities (defined in terms of voluntary and statutory *youth service* provision) was conducted recently by the Office of Population Censuses and Surveys (OPCS) for the Department of Education (DfE). A sample of about three and a half thousand young people in England and Wales aged between 11 and 25 took part (Department for Education 1995). The survey suggested that 63 per cent of young people aged 13 to 19 are involved in youth service activities at some time in their lives and that 11 to 15 year olds have the highest levels of participation. However, at any one time, only a minority are involved. At the time of the survey 20 per cent of 13 to 19 year olds were actively participating in youth service activities. Despite these apparently impressive general figures, the survey also indicated that overall participation is skewed towards young people whose parental occupations are categorised as 'professional' (a participation rate of 21% for this group compared with 11% for young people whose parental occupation is classified as 'unskilled'), towards young men (a consistently higher participation rate in all age groups), and towards white young people (an overall participation rate of 14% compared with a non-white rate of

10%). Clearly these findings are at variance with the inclusive ideals of youth work's Statement of Purpose.

Although young people's participation in the youth service varies socially and geographically, there appear to be three principal aspects of youth work which bear on its acknowledged relevance to young people, and which youth workers also identify as indicating the effectiveness of their work. These three aspects of the work are briefly discussed.

Safe space and relationships: constructing the 'social'

A substantial number of young people have only limited access to safe space in which they can meet with their friends in an informal and sympathetic context during their leisure time. Recent research in the West Midlands showed that young people living on urban estates constantly complained of having nowhere to go. Often they would not stay at home because of pressures that their families were already experiencing: overcrowding, tension between family members or there being nothing to do if they did remain at home. The 'marketisation' of leisure facilities (sports and leisure centres for example) has put these beyond the economic reach of many young people (Bradford and Gough 1993). Public space – 'the street' – is often the alternative, with young people becoming the potential target of unsympathetic adults and aggressive police practices.

Whatever else youth work might offer, easily accessible, supportive and safe places for young people to meet their friends and youth workers play an important role. Often, such spaces are established in youth clubs and centres, or other project locations – information and counselling services or activity centres for example. Detached youth workers operating on the streets of housing estates, towns or village centres create 'virtually' enclosed spaces in which relationships between those involved – young people and youth workers – gradually mark out geographical and social boundaries in locations which young people recognise as partially their own. In these spaces, the organisation and management of a constellation of relationships between young people themselves and youth workers, constitutes the underlying 'social' dimension of 'social education'. The DfE research indicates that the main reason given by current participants for valuing the youth service is that 'I can meet my friends or make new friends' at youth service provision. Overall, 84 per cent of current participants gave this as a reason for their participation: 61 per cent said that youth service provision is 'somewhere to go', and 45 per cent of participants identified youth service provision as a 'safe place to go' (Department for Education 1995). Other research indicated that the majority of youth workers believed that the main reason for young people's use of provision was to meet their friends, although this was apparently less important to the young people (Love and Hendry 1994).

By initially offering accessible meeting places, youth workers can develop informal relationships with young people and respond to a wider range of needs and problems which *young people themselves* define as important to them. Provision of this kind is valued by young people because it can provide those who become involved with 'a sense of purpose, a sense of belonging, a sense somebody cares, a sense you're not alone, a sense that you're central to things, a sense of achievement' (Williamson *et al.* 1997, p.185). As Williamson and others point out, young people who participate in youth work provision are not necessarily looking for formal or 'expert' modes of intervention in their lives. Rather, they engage in relationships with youth workers who demonstrate respect for them 'as they are'. Throughout the youth work literature, the nature of relationships between young people and adults assumes critical importance. Appropriate relationships are seen by young people and youth workers alike as being characterised by trust and confidence. Indeed, in Love and Hendry's research (1994), the trustworthiness of youth workers, their friendliness and interest in them were identified as valuable qualities more by young people than by youth workers. The DfE research showed that about 30 per cent of current youth work participants between the ages of 13 and 19 cited 'supportive' youth workers as one of the reasons they used youth work provision (Department for Education 1995). Although resources are inevitably important, high quality youth work so often appears to hinge on youth workers' abilities to 'seize the moment', to start from where young people are' and from there to render the ordinary fabric of young people's lives a little more extraordinary. An acceptance of young people as *active agents* in the process of youth work also seems to be crucial. As one local authority Principal Youth Officer put it 'First of all it depends on the relationships with the youth worker... The other thing is that they need to know what they are getting out of it... [and] they need to have some element of control' (Maychell *et al.* 1996, p.53). It is these relationships and their constitutive characteristics which provide the basis for further extension of practice, potentially leading to young people's personal and social development, and in youth work terms, their 'empowerment' (Love and Hendry 1994; Treacy 1994; Maychell *et al.* 1996; Williamson *et al.* 1997).

Offering activities: developing young people's bodies and minds

A broad repertoire of 'leisure' and informal 'educational' activities provide content to youth work. DfE research shows that 'interesting activities' are cited by large numbers of young people using youth service provision: 61 per cent of male and 59 per cent of female participants aged between 13 and 19 refer to this (Department for Education 1995). Scottish research confirms a similar level of importance given by young people to 'games and sport' as a reason for attending youth groups (Love and Hendry 1994). Love and Hendry point out that there is some consensus between young people and youth workers on their perceptions of the significance of activities in making youth work provision attractive. Organised physical activities have always provided a structure through which youth work could initially attract young people and which subsequently enable youth workers to encourage young people to make considered choices about 'health and fitness'. An interest in young people's health is reflected in youth work's current work in dealing with matters like alcohol and drug use, sexuality and diet. Such 'issues' provide the basis for youth work intervention through informal health promotion which aim to encourage the moderation of 'risk' behaviours (Her Majesty's Inspectorate 1990).

Typically, a range of sports or arts activities, health promotion, or community involvement form the ongoing work of a youth club or centre (West Sussex County Council 1997), along with more complex activity programmes which offer recognised awards or qualifications based on the acquisition of particular skills and knowledge. The Duke of Edinburgh's Award scheme is one such example which has been flexibly used to offer under-achieving young people opportunities to develop skills, confidence and self-esteem (Maychell *et al.* 1996). In the DfE research, about half of male and female current participants identified the acquisition of skills, awards and records of achievement as a reason for their participation. However, 'fun' and 'enjoyment' seem to justify many young people's involvement in the youth service (Love and Hendry 1994; Department for Education 1995; Bradford and Martin 1996). For young people in urban and rural areas, boredom can be a corrosive and sometimes crushing force. Research in the West Midlands showed the extent to which it was acknowledged by young people as a contributory factor to their involvement in minor criminal activity, as well as a thoroughly demoralising force in itself (Bradford and Gough 1993). Reflecting this, recent research in Wales confirms that the need for 'something to do' is a central feature of the lives of many young people, and that activity programmes offered by youth workers combat boredom and may lead to the development of creative initiatives with the young people concerned. For young people who have left full-time education and who are not working this may be very important.

Although activities offered by youth workers were differentially valued by young people in the Welsh context, Williamson points out that they provide part of the basic framework within which effective youth work can occur. Informally structured activities in whose organisation young people had been involved were overwhelmingly identified by them as most likely to engage their attention. Formal 'issue-based' sessions on drugs or health for example were much less attractive to them (Williamson *et al.* 1997). In contrast, Love and Hendry observe that although youth workers' professional ideology emphasises young people's involvement in the organisation of programmes and activities as a desired 'learning outcome', it was apparently not particularly important to young people themselves (Love and Hendry 1994). DfE research supports this and indicates that only 35 per cent of current youth service participants aged 13–19 value the youth service because it provides them with an opportunity to 'have a say in what goes on'. As suggested earlier, participation and inclusion are central values in youth work and although there is some ambiguity in the research evidence, Williamson clearly shows the importance that some young people attach to the informal 'process' of youth work. Those who had experienced this were able to distinguish between 'how things were made available and what was actually available – a critical distinction reflecting levels of quality of young work practice' (Williamson *et al.* 1997, p.37). Although young people (like adults) inevitably value participation in different ways, it seems that when an inclusive and participative approach is actually experienced, it is identified by them as a significant factor in their involvement. Perhaps the DfE research and that of Love and Hendry indicate something of the limited extent to which this approach has been generally adopted in youth work.

Information, counselling and advice: new vocabularies of empowerment

One of youth work's principal concerns has always been to enhance young people's own capacity to make *rational* and *informed* decisions about their lives.

Since the early 1960s, 'official' youth work discourse has identified the provision of information, counselling and advice as an aspect of youth work which contributes to this aim (Ministry of Education 1960; Department of Education and Science 1982; National Youth Agency 1992). Perhaps surprisingly, neither the young people who participated in Love and Hendry's research nor those in the DfE research identified this as an immediate reason for participating in youth service provision.

At the current time there are about 300 services or projects in England and Wales undertaking this work, and most local authority youth services offer provision of this kind in one form or another. Sometimes young people need 'someone to talk to', perhaps to share a problem or get advice. For some young people, youth workers may be their only source of such support (Maychell *et al.* 1996). In contrast to 'formal' counselling and information services, most youth workers undertake elements of this work as part of the routine curriculum of youth work. If offered in a 'non-judgemental' and 'confidential' way such support may enable young people to resolve their own difficulties, and thus become more autonomous. Difficulties connected with the transition to adulthood (work and worklessness, and homelessness for example) have taken on a particular salience for some young people, and wider concerns about sex, sexuality, alcohol and drug use in the context of health and 'healthy lifestyles' are reflected in young people's demands for information and support, as well as in youth workers' perceptions of their own professional role (Surrey County Council 1997; Williamson *et al.* 1997). Most 'local' accounts and evaluations of youth work indicate that this area of work is an important and valued part of youth work provision and young people identify this work as responding to real issues which they face in their lives (for example, see Hampshire County Council 1996; Surrey County Council 1997; West Sussex County Council 1997). As suggested earlier, the provision of safe and accessible space and interesting activities may be only the beginning of a developing process of youth work which may subsequently incorporate the provision of information, counselling and advice. Reflecting the significance of transition, Williamson suggests that older participants in youth work are most likely to use informal guidance and information provision. As one 16-year-old young woman in his sample put it:

> if I had a problem I could go to the workers and I could trust them to keep what I say confidential and I could trust them to help… I suppose I could go to profes-

sional (counsellors) but I find it better to talk to someone I know quite well than I could with a stranger. (Williamson *et al.* 1997, p.40)

This quote exemplifies important elements of the youth work approach, and indicates the particular nature of youth workers' transactions with young people. They are *informal* (contrasted in this case with 'professional' counsellors), based on mutual *trust*, and help or support is given in the context of a close *relationship* which is likely to have developed as part of a continuing process of youth work intervention and support.

Focusing youth work: responses to young people 'at risk'

Because of youth work's informal approach, its capacity to reach 'difficult' and marginalised young people and its aim of encouraging young people to become *self*-regulating, rational and responsible, youth work has inevitably been drawn into a corpus of work concerned with crime prevention. Although exacerbating the tension between the principle of a 'universal' youth service and youth work 'targeted' on specific groups of young people, work with 'at risk' young people nevertheless accords with current public and political priorities.

Great symbolic significance is currently attached to 'risk' populations, particularly the constituent groups of the so-called 'underclass': lone parents; truants; drug abusers; the young homeless and perhaps particularly young offenders. Home Office research has suggested that youth workers may be the only adults 'able to reach and establish a basis of trust and mutual respect… with some "at risk" young people' (Graham and Bowling 1995, p.96). As one account puts it, these young people 'often occupy a twilight world and adopt unconventional lifestyles. This, combined with an acquired mistrust of those in authority, makes it difficult to reach them, p.2' (Office for Standards in Education 1993). OFSTED has identified youth service projects with homeless young people, young offenders, 'at risk' young women and young people absent from school. OFSTED's evaluation of this work concentrates mainly on managerial criteria which contributed to the effectiveness of these projects (clear needs analysis, realistic planning, clear staff roles and accountability, appropriate resource levels, strict monitoring and use of performance indicators). However, it is clear that the projects adopted a 'process oriented' approach which entailed the careful development of relationships with specific groups of young people in which their confidence and trust in the youth workers was built up gradually. The work was characterised by young people's *active participation* in decisions about the direction in which the work should go, rather than this being determined by professional fiat. Working alongside young people, youth workers were able to touch on sensitive areas of their lives: mediating in the context of broken relationships, encouraging young people to make responsible choices about drug and substance use, supporting young women in danger of being drawn into prostitution and providing informal counselling and advice to homeless young people. Although OFSTED points out that indicators of effectiveness are insufficiently developed in this work, judgements of achievement should take account of the 'slow, developmental process required to bring about changes' (Office for Standards in Education 1993, p.11). Its report points to three broad factors which seem to underlie effective youth work with 'at risk' young people. First, secure and informally organised accommodation appropriately supported by detached and outreach work can provide opportunities for advice, counselling and the provision of information on benefits, health or educational opportunities for example. Second, well established 'networking' with other professionals and agencies was a feature of the projects reviewed by OFSTED. Networking opened up possibilities of youth workers engaging in advocacy on young people's behalf, or linking young people to other specialist services which they might not otherwise have known about or used. Various multiagency or partnership approaches to project work seemed to facilitate the development of effective networks. Third, youth workers, skilled in building relationships with young people in groups or as individuals can 'meet young people on their terms, at times and in places that the young people themselves determine' (Office for Standards in Education 1993, p.11) and in so doing engage them as active participants contributing to their own personal and social development.

Youth work's formal deployment in initiatives with actual or potential young offenders has increased in recent years. This has been encouraged by some practitioners and by an academic constituency for whom youth work's informal approach offers an ideologically acceptable form of 'social crime prevention' which challenges the orthodoxy of the 'right-wing Realist social policy' pursued during the Thatcher years (Pitts 1992). A number of arguments have been used to justify youth work's involvement in this area of work (Bradford 1997), one of which is that youth work is effective and efficient in work with young offenders.

Paraskeva (1992) suggests that 'at risk' young people (like others) need to develop their communication skills, participate in exciting and stimulating activities, and gain access to education and training which develops their self-esteem and reflexive capacities. However, it is difficult to locate specific evidence which demonstrates that youth work is especially effective in diverting young people from crime. As Graham and Bowling show, the factors which encourage young people's involvement in crime, and which sustain that involvement are complex and wide-ranging. The modest resources available to the youth service are unlikely to have much *overall* impact on the numbers of young people involved, although youth workers may be influential with some individuals and small groups (Graham and Bowling 1995). Perhaps, unsurprisingly therefore, the evaluation of the 'Youth Action Schemes' (YAS) established to reduce youth crime by working with 13 to 17 year olds 'at risk of drifting into crime' (Department for Education 1993) was unable to come up with clear evidence of success in terms of young people's changed behaviour or attitudes. The authors of the national evaluation of the 60 YAS projects which operated in 28 local authorities were able to say much about successful managerial aspects of these projects. However, because of apparent weaknesses in local evaluation they were unable to 'answer the critical question of whether the Youth Action Scheme projects significantly changed their members' behaviour or attitudes. We have the evidence from the project's line managers that they believed that they had been successful... but the objective, independent evidence for this is not terribly good' (France and Wiles 1996, p.46). Despite this, France and Wiles suggest that youth workers have the capacity and the skills to 'identify and work with' young people who are likely to offend.

Although attitudes and behaviour are notoriously difficult to alter, youth work can offer valuable informal educational opportunities to young people actually or potentially involved in offending. Community-based projects designed to target youth crime in Hackney and Newcastle have provided some evidence that youth work has potential in diverting young people from crime, as well as engaging them in activities designed to enhance their social skills and political literacy. On one high-crime Hackney estate a 'state-of-the-art' project was established in 1996 with the aim of preventing youth crime and reducing residents' fear of crime. Detached youth workers on the project demonstrated how it was possible to contact and establish relationships with young people considered difficult to reach and involve them in initiatives designed to give them a say in improving their neighbourhood. Through sensitive work on the part of the youth workers, young people were encouraged to participate in a number of political activities and structures in which they were able to express their views about life on their estate and have some influence in the development of local facilities (Irving 1996). Although Irving does not claim a reduction in youth crime as a direct result of this work, he outlines valuable educational work with these young people which may have the incidental effect of reducing crime. In Newcastle, a similar project offering activities and programmes of social education during the school holidays calculated its cost-benefits using figures prepared by the accountants Coopers Lybrand, who estimated a cost of £30 per annum for each potential participant in youth work, against a short-term saving of £2300 on each youth crime prevented (Coopers Lybrand 1994). Police data for the project's area showed that the number of incidents reported to the police during the project's operations was lower than that of a comparable area. Young people themselves reported that their involvement in crime diminished while they were involed on the project. The level of acknowledged offences was less than that of a comparable group of young people who were not involved on such a project. Despite well-known difficulties associated with the validity of inferences drawn from self-report studies and police statistics the project claims impressive cost-benefit savings. As Barna (1995) points out, these were in addition to the project's contribution to reducing the fear of crime in the area (demonstrated through surveys of local people), and any other benefits that young people and others in the community derived from such a project.

Conclusion

This chapter has identified the diversity of provisions and interventions which comprise youth work. It has been acknowledged in the chapter that there is an absence of systematic external research on youth work's effectiveness, although a range of more 'impressionistic' evidence of effectiveness has been discussed. However, the data which have been collected on youth work say little about its impact on the acquisition and development of skills, knowledge or dispositions which official youth work discourse suggests constitute young people's 'empowerment'. For example, research on whether youth work increases young people's 'autonomy' or enables them to engage in 'active citizenship' seems not to have been undertaken. There may be three main reasons for the absence of such studies. First, the search for 'hard' outcome measures of effectiveness may conflict with youth work's traditional 'person-centred' and informal approach. Second, youth work's informal and sometimes intermittent contact with young people, some of whom may be extremely disaffected, means that follow-up can be problematic and research seeking to identify outcomes over a protracted period may not be achievable. Third, youth work's somewhat vague statements of purpose are not entirely susceptible to outcome analysis. Indeed as specified, youth work's objectives are long-term, essentially 'moral' in nature and open to argument and debate. This leads to difficulties of a methodological kind. What for example would count as an 'autonomous' individual, or an 'active' or 'responsible' citizen? Given the ambiguity of such terms, it may not be so surprising that limited hard data exists on long-term youth work outcomes.

In the context of wide public and political concerns about specific groups of young people, youth work has recently become increasingly deployed in the management of so-called 'at risk' young people, and in particular young people considered to be 'at risk' of engaging in criminality. This involvement has heightened a long-standing debate about whether youth work should retain its (official) purpose as a 'universal' service or whether it should fully acknowledge its de facto targeting of specific groups of young people. This debate has assumed particular salience at a time when 'official' figures suggest that the overall number of young people participating in youth work is relatively low (although consistent) and seem to undermine the idea that the youth service can claim a universal relevance or mandate. Work targeted on identifiable groups of young people (young offenders or homeless young people for example) or on issues of social or political concern (health or sexuality for example) may seem to give youth work a more relevant and socially-valued role and may be thought to offer the possibility of specifying clear objectives amenable to various 'outcome measures' and 'performance indicators'. However, the recent national evaluation of the Youth Action Schemes which targeted 'at risk' young people across England and Wales was unable to come up with firm evidence of youth work's effectiveness in this field.

Despite the limitations, research reviewed in this chapter suggests that there are five underlying factors which support effective youth work, whether 'targeted' or not. First, the provision of secure and accessible places for young people to meet and get help or support *as they determine appropriate* appears to form the basis of effective contact between youth workers and young people. Second, it seems important to create a balanced combination of relevant and interesting 'leisure' and 'educational' opportunities for young people as a vehicle for initially attracting them to youth work provision. A number of commentators suggest (see for example Maychell *et al.* 1996; Williamson *et al.* 1997) that the nature of the relationships established between youth workers and young people is important in determining young people's experience of youth work and whether *they* believe it to be effective. Third, young people themselves identify the provision of relevant information, informal counselling and advice as valued elements of youth work. Fourth, it seems important that youth work is undertaken in the context of partnership with related agencies and professionals where appropriate. This enables youth workers to advocate on young people's behalf, and to support young people in making links with other professionals and agencies who may offer them particular help. Finally, underlying youth work is a 'process-oriented' and 'person-centred' approach which emphasises informality, the willingness of youth workers to engage with young people on negotiable terms and a recognition of young people's status as active partners rather than passive consumers.

There is clear scope for more research into youth work's capacity to work effectively with young people. Whilst 'local' and small-scale evidence of the achievement of youth work's socially inclusive aspirations undoubtedly exists, evidence of a broader and more reliable kind is ambiguous. Perhaps the government's commitment to 'lifelong learning' will lead to a proper analysis of youth work's contribution to this objective.

References

Barna, D. (1995) 'Breakout: School holiday activities and their impact on youth crime.' *Youth and Policy 50,* 59–64.

Bradford, S. (1997) 'The management of growing up: Youth work in community settings.' In J. Roche and S. Tucker (eds) *Youth in Society.* London: Sage Publications.

Bradford, S. and Gough, S. (1993) *Encounters With Young People: A Report of Research Completed in the Metropolitan Borough of Dudley.* Egham: Department of Education, Brunel University.

Bradford, S. and Martin, W. (1996) *'Shaping the Future', A Review of the Youth and Community Service in the London Borough of Redbridge.* Egham: School of Education, Brunel University.

Burchell, G., Gordon, C. and Miller, P. (eds) (1991) *The Foucault Effect. Studies in Governmentality.* London: Harvester Wheatsheaf.

Butters, S. and Newell, S. (1978) *Realities of Training, A Review of the Training of Adults Who Volunteer to Work with Young People in the Youth and Community Service.* Leicester: National Youth Bureau.

Clarke, J., Cochrane, A. and McLaughlin, E. (eds) (1994) *Managing Social Policy.* London: Sage Publications.

Coleman, J. and Warren-Adamson, C. (eds) (1992) *Youth Policy in the 1990s, the Way Forward.* London: Routledge.

Coles, B. (1995) *Youth and Social Policy. Youth Citizenship and Young Careers.* London: UCL Press.

Coopers Lybrand (1994) *Preventive Strategy for Young People in Trouble.* London: ITV Telethon and Prince's Trust.

Davies, B. and Gibson, A. (1967) *The Social Education of the Adolescent.* London: University of London Press.

Department for Education (1993) *GEST, Youth Action Scheme, Arrangements for Evaluation and Reporting.* London: Youth Service Unit.

Department for Education (1995) *OPCS Survey of Youth Service Participation.* London: HMSO.

Department of Education and Science (1982) *Experience and Participation, Report of the Review Group on the Youth Service in England and Wales.* Cmnd. 8686. London: HMSO.

Foucault, M. (1991) 'Governmentality.' In G. Burchell, C. Gordon and P. Miller (eds) *The Foucault Effect. Studies in Governmentality.* London: Harvester Wheatsheaf.

France, A. and Wiles, P. (1996) *The Youth Action Scheme, A Report of the National Evaluation.* London: Department for Education and Employment.

Graham, J. and Bowling, B. (1995) *Young People and Crime.* Home Office Research Study 145. London: Home Office.

Hampshire County Council (1996) *Snapshots of Practice, Annual Report of the County Youth Service.* Winchester:

Hampshire County Council. Her Majesty's Inspectorate (1990) *Responsive Youth Work. The Youth Service and Urgent Social Needs.* London: Department of Education and Science.

Irving, D. (1996) 'The voices from the hill.' *Social Action Today 3,* 8–10. ——

Jeffs, T. and Smith, M. (eds) (1990) *Using Informal Education: An Alternative to Casework, Teaching and Control?* Milton Keynes: Open University Press.

Jones, G. and Wallace, C. (1992) *Youth, Family and Citizenship.* Buckingham: Open University Press.

Karsh, H. (1984) 'Social education defined?' *Inner London Education Authority newsletter editorial.* London: ILEA.

Love, J.G. and Hendry, L.B. (1994) 'Youth workers and youth participants: two perspectives of youth work?' *Youth and Policy 46,* 43–55.

Maychell, K., Pathak, S. and Cato, V. (1996) *Providing for Young People. Local Authority Youth Services in the 1990s.* Slough: National Foundation for Educational Research.

Ministry of Education (1960) *The Youth Service in England and Wales.* Report of the Committee Appointed by the Minister of Education in November, 1958 (Cmnd. 929). London: HMSO.

Morley, L. (1995) 'Empowerment and the New Right, culture of change.' *Youth and Policy 51,* 1–10.

National Youth Agency (1992) *Background Papers to the Third Ministerial Conference for the Youth Service.* Leicester: National Youth Agency.

Office for Standards in Education (1993) *Youth Work Responses to Young People At Risk*. London: OFSTED.

Office for Standards in Education (1997) *Inspecting Youth Work: A Revised Inspection Schedule*. London: OFSTED.

Paraskeva, J. (1992) 'Keeping out of trouble.' *Times Educational Supplement,* 21 October.

Pitts, J. (1992) 'Juvenile-justice policy in England and Wales.' In J. Coleman and C. Warren-Adamson (eds) *Youth Policy in the 1990s, The Way Forward*. London: Routledge.

Roche, J. and Tucker, S. (eds) (1997) *Youth in Society*. London: Sage Publications.

Smith, M. (1988) *Developing Youth Work*. Milton Keynes: Open University Press.

Surrey County Council (1997) *Developing the Vision – Towards a Surrey Youth Strategy*. Addlestone: Surrey Youth Strategy.

Treacy, D. (1994) *A Review of Youth Work Practice in Community-Based Projects*. Dublin: Government of Ireland.

West Sussex County Council (1997) *Windows on Practice: Staffing, Curriculum Provision, Targeting and the Concerns of Young People*. Chichester: West Sussex Youth Service.

Williamson, H., Afzal, S., Eason, C. and Williams, N. (1997) *The Needs of Young People aged 15–19 and the Youth Work Response*. Cardiff: Wales Youth Agency and University of Wales Research Partnership.

CHAPTER 10

Child and Adolescent Psychiatry Services

Joanne Barton

It is important when describing current psychiatric service provision for children and adolescents, to consider their historical development. This has been eloquently reviewed by Parry-Jones (1989) and will be briefly summarised here.

The medical speciality of paediatrics emerged relatively recently in the mid nineteenth century and the first children's hospital opened in 1852 (Great Ormond Street, London). Interest in childhood mental illness is even more recent. The scientific opinion in the early nineteenth century was that insanity could not occur before puberty because the brains of children were not sufficiently developed to go wrong! By the middle of the nineteenth century mental illness in children was referred to in the literature and children were admitted to mental hospitals, although no special provision was made for them.

The developments in psychology and psychoanalytic theory in the early twentieth century had a significant influence on studies of the child. The development of services for children was influenced by the Child Guidance Movement which developed in the United States in the 1920s creating a model for multidisciplinary work. At the same time paediatricians were becoming more interested in the nervous diseases of childhood and links between paediatrics and psychiatry began to emerge. The first child psychiatry out-patient clinics appeared in the 1920s and 1930s. Significant advances in the care of children and young people with psychiatric illness occurred following World War II with the development of out-patient services and in-patient departments in hospitals. Also the need for separate services for adolescents was recognised. The ideal model for service delivery remains a contentious issue with a lack of standardisation of service provision throughout the UK today.

The range of psychiatric disorders seen in children and young people includes all of the major illnesses seen in adults, such as schizophrenia, manic depressive illness and obsessive compulsive disorders. In addition, a group of disorders is encountered which is characterised by having onset specifically in childhood or adolescence. Such disorders include emotional and behavioural disorders.

These disorders are responsible for significant morbidity in affected individuals. Children usually live within a family with responsible adults required to care for them and siblings or other children who share their living environment. The presence of a child affected by mental illness within a family group will have consequences for their normal day-to-day functioning.

Some child and adolescent psychiatric disorders are transient and affected individuals go on to lead fulfilling lives. In other cases, the condition persists into adulthood and is responsible for considerable disability. The economic implications of this are as yet unclear but require consideration (Knapp 1997).

Prognoses of childhood psychiatric disorders can only be examined by long-term longitudinal studies which are complicated and expensive but, nevertheless, essential (Verhulst and Koot 1991). In general, emotional disorders have a better prognosis than disorders such as schizophrenia and obsessive compulsive disorder.

The prevalence of psychiatric disorders of moderate to severe degree in the child and adolescent population is estimated to be between 14 and 20 per cent (Brandenburg, Freidman and Silver 1990). Offord *et al.* (1987) found that the prevalence of disorder was related to age and sex, with disorder being more common in boys up to the age of 11 years but more common in girls during adolescence. A variety of factors are known to affect adversely the rate of mental illness in children and young people including race, ethnicity, chronic physical illness, learning disability, lower social class, urban residence and parental psychopathology (Offord and Fleming 1991).

Many children and young people with psychiatric illness are not under the care of psychiatric services; those who are, tend to be male, have a more severe disorder and come from families with high levels of psychosocial stress (Garralda and Bailey 1988).

Child and adolescent mental health services are under resourced and show wide variation across the UK. Services operate from a range of settings including hospital out-patient clinics, community clinics in general practitioners' surgeries and child development clinics. In-patient units are scarce and are generally small units operating at regional level. Services are commonly based on the work of a multidisciplinary team, variably composed of child psychiatrists, psychologists, psychotherapists, social workers, specialist nurses and play therapists. A range of treatments are available and the relative contribution of psychological and physical components varies considerably. In view of the relationship between psychiatric problems and educational and social difficulties, liaison with professionals in education and social work is a common feature of child and adolescent psychiatry practice.

Methodological issues

In keeping with medical practice generally, research evidence is increasingly used to guide clinical practice in the provision of child and adolescent mental health services. Outcome research, which measures the effect of an intervention, is essential to service planning. Instruments which assess the mental health of children and adolescents are, and have been, used in case identification and in research trials. No one tool provides a comprehensive evaluation, so combinations of measures are required (Hunter, Higginson and Garralda 1996).

The randomised controlled trial is commonly seen as the gold standard of outcome research. Such trials may not, however, provide a comprehensive assessment of outcome or be a true reflection of what actually happens in everyday clinical practice. It is important, therefore, that some consideration be given to future study designs that are a closer representation of actual clinical work (Barnes McGuire, Stein and Rosenberg 1997).

Quantitative measures, such as change in symptom levels, are frequently used to evaluate outcome. A more important question however is a qualitative one: do treated children and young people lead more fulfilled and productive lives? Adding qualitative data from youngsters, such as their accounts of success in achieving 'normal' day-to-day activities, could make a significant contribution to determining what are useful treatments. Consumer satisfaction must also be considered in the evaluation of interventions. To date, however, there is a lack of standardisation of instruments and methods of collecting information (Young, Nicholson and Davis 1995).

Treatment methods

Conclusions about the effectiveness of interventions employed in child and adolescent psychiatry are summarised here, with reference to other reading material which provides comprehensive data. Interventions have been divided into physical and psychosocial. In clinical practice, the treatment of children should be based on individualised treatment packages often calling upon more than one form of intervention. Research into the effects of combinations of treatments is limited although clinical trials of multimodal interventions are beginning to be reported (Sprenger and Josephson 1998).

Much of the research evidence is American in origin, but in most instances the findings are applicable to the UK. Family therapy is commonly used in child and adolescent psychiatry, but its role in services for children and young people will not be discussed here as this was addressed in Chapter 7. Similarly, cognitive behaviour therapy is frequently called upon in the treatment of child and adolescent psychiatric disorders and, whilst this is discussed briefly here, it has been addressed more comprehensively elsewhere in this book (see Chapter 5).

Psychosocial treatments

Prevention

Preventive interventions can be divided into those which (a) aim to prevent disorder developing in the first place (primary prevention), (b) target groups felt to be at high risk of developing problems (secondary prevention) or (c) aim to treat established problems (tertiary prevention). The relative merits of the different forms of prevention are reviewed by Offord *et al.* (1998).

When considering primary prevention programmes it might be thought that by improving the socio-economic circumstances of children, their mental health would improve. In fact this is not the case, although there does appear to be a relationship between aspects of a child's physical environment and mental health. For example, children living in homeless accommodation are at greater risk of emotional and behavioural problems as well as developmental delay. (Fox *et al.* 1990). A study of 2000 young people in Norway demonstrated that unemployment had a significant impact on mental health (Hammer 1993). It is likely, therefore, that investment in strategies to achieve full employment will have a beneficial effect on the mental health of young people and, indirectly, an effect on the mental health of the children of parents who are unemployed.

Considerable information about prevention programmes in the pre-school age group was derived from the Headstart Program established in the United States in the 1960s. Programmes targeted emotional, behavioural and educational problems of children and it was found that intensive and structured programmes were successful in reducing rates of referral to special classes and enhancing social and emotional development (Woodhead 1988).

Children of primary and secondary school age are readily available for preventive interventions because of the requirement that they attend school. O'Donnell *et al.* (1995) describe a programme to reduce delinquency, school failure and drug abuse among children living in low income urban families. There is less data about prevention programmes targeting adolescents. Suicide is a cause for particular concern in this age group and prevention programmes have addressed this (Shaffer *et al.* 1988).

Preventive activities can be targeted at groups felt to be at particular risk such as young, socially disadvantaged pregnant women and mothers (Olds *et al.* 1986) or children affected by separation and divorce (Rae-Grant and Robson 1988). Children of parents with mental illness are known to be at increased risk of psychiatric problems, but there is little systematic research examining the effect of preventive activities in this group.

Psychotherapy

The term psychotherapy is used to describe a variety of interventions, the intentions of which are to improve the psychosocial functioning of children. Such interventions include psychoanalytic, psychodynamic, client centred, behavioural, cognitive behavioural and group therapy. These therapies are applied to a wide range of disorders and problems.

Research into the effectiveness of psychotherapy for children and young people with mental health problems is relatively recent. Over the last decade, however, meta-analyses describing a range of treatment methods applied to a variety of problems suggest that psychotherapy may have significant benefits. For example, Weisz *et al.* (1995) examined 150 outcome studies and found that overall there was a positive effect from therapy. In general, behavioural forms of therapy were more effective than non-behavioural approaches and adolescent girls had on average better outcomes than other age and gender groups. Although meta-analyses suggest that psychotherapy works, there are important questions remaining such as which form of treatment works, for which individuals, with which disorders, at which time? There follows a brief description of some of the 'psychotherapies'.

INDIVIDUAL PSYCHOTHERAPY

The techniques available for individual psychotherapy are numerous and the goals and duration of treatment are varied. The range extends from highly intensive psychoanalysis occurring three to five times per week over a period of several years, to short-term, focused work aimed at solving an acute problem. There are significant methodological problems associated with outcome research in such psychotherapeutic interventions including the lack of standardisation of inclusion criteria and treatment methods and therapist variables.

COGNITIVE BEHAVIOUR THERAPIES

Cognitive behaviour therapy (CBT) describes a group of techniques designed to produce changes in thinking, feeling and behaviour. Strategies used include relaxation training, modelling of desired behaviour, educational approaches and teaching of positive self-statements. CBT is used in the management of disorders including, Attention Deficit Hyperactivity Disorder (ADHD), anxiety, depression (Kaplan, Thompson and Searson 1995) and obsessive compulsive disorder (March 1995).

Important questions remain regarding the efficacy of these treatments such as whether generalisation occurs across situations and over time. Also, further research is required to address the effects of CBT in combination with other treatments such as medication.

BEHAVIOUR THERAPY

Behavioural interventions, as distinct from CBT, are employed naturally by parents every day to influence children's behaviour. Material and emotional rewards and punishment are all forms of behavioural intervention. Behavioural therapies are used to address a number of disorders in child and adolescent psychiatry. Research evidence supports the effectiveness of such interventions in children with oppositional behaviour (Forehand and MacMahon 1981) and sleep disorders (Richman *et al.* 1985).

GROUP PSYCHOTHERAPY

Group psychotherapy involves the treatment of a group of children by a therapist, often accompanied by a co-therapist. The theoretical base derives from various disciplines, but often involves either psychodynamic principles or those of CBT. There are several advantages to group psychotherapy. For example, children can learn from each others' strengths and weaknesses, while the sense of isolation felt by many children with psychiatric problems may be relieved. In addition there are benefits for the clinician and service provider. It is cost effective to see groups of children rather than individuals. Group psychotherapy is undertaken by a range of professionals, but a period of training under the supervision of experienced professionals should be mandatory. Children with various problems can make use of group therapy, for example peer interaction difficulties and obesity (Reid and Kolvin 1993).

SOCIAL SKILLS TRAINING

Being able to mix well with peers is an important skill. Children who find this difficult are at risk of later psychopathology, particularly peer rejection, aggressive behaviour, delinquency and adult criminality. Interventions to improve social skills draw upon a variety of strategies and may be conducted in individual or group therapy sessions. Strategies include techniques to foster pro-social behaviours: modelling, in which children observe the appropriate behaviour of adults or peers and coaching, where children are taught the general principles of social interaction. The effectiveness of social skills training has been evaluated in a number of studies and the evidence suggests that a variety of interventions are effective. Pellegrini (1994) provides an overview of training in social skills.

PARENT TRAINING

Parent training describes a group of interventions aimed at helping parents relate better to their children. The approaches used include courses, self-help and support groups, training manuals and handbooks. An advantage of parent training is that it addresses the question of generalisability of effect discussed earlier. Parents are trained to carry out behavioural interventions which they apply at home, or in any setting, and to prevent future problems.

Parent training interventions have been used to address various problems including conduct disorders (Webster-Stratton 1991) and sleep disorders (Richman *et al.* 1985). Interventions are often targeted at nursery and primary school ages. The focus of many of these programmes is on parent education and training, with children and young people being involved to varying degrees. In some cases, children take part in the training sessions; in others, parents attend a training session at which they are given 'tasks' or homework to carry out with the child or young person at home, with a requirement that they report back at the next session.

Studies examining the effectiveness of parent training are fraught with methodological problems. Most are descriptions of specific projects, so generalisable conclusions are not possible.

Physical treatments
Drugs

The use of psychotropic drugs in the management of children and young people with psychiatric illness is controversial. Nevertheless, pharmacotherapy is an important aspect of treatment which should be available in all child and adolescent mental health services. The use of drugs is complex and requires a thorough knowledge on the part of the practitioner of the range of effects of drugs on behaviours and psychological processes. Side effects must be considered and the benefits of the drug weighed against risks. The effectiveness of treatment must be constantly evaluated. A variety of drugs are used in the treatment of child and adolescent psychiatric disorders and there is increasing evidence for their usefulness and limitations (Kaplan and Hussain 1995; Popper and Zimnitzky 1996).

STIMULANTS

Psychostimulants (methylphenidate and dexamphetamine) are the most extensively researched drugs in child and adolescent psychiatry. They are used in the treatment of hyperactivity disorders (ADHD and Hyperkinetic Disorder), which are commonly seen in child and adolescent psychiatry clinics. Their core features are motor overactivity, impulsivity and impaired attention span. Considerable evidence supports the usefulness of psychostimulants in reducing activity level, impulsivity and in improving concentration (Taylor 1986; Greenhill

1992). Verbal and physical aggression are reduced as are some anti-social behaviours (Hinshaw, Heller and McHale 1992). Stimulants may also improve parent–child interaction and peer relationships. Side effects of the stimulants are usually mild and easily reversed. There is no evidence that drug abuse develops, although it is sensible to exercise caution when there is a history of associated conduct problems or chaotic family life. Although psychostimulants produce dramatic improvement in the short term, there is a lack of evidence of benefit from long term outcome studies (Schachar and Tannock 1993).

ANTIPSYCHOTICS

Antipsychotic drugs, also referred to as neuroleptics or major tranquillisers, include phenothiazines, butyrophenones and thioxanthenes. They have proven value in the treatment of psychotic conditions in adults. In children and young people, they are used to treat conditions such as schizophrenia, pervasive developmental disorders, aggression and tic disorders.

There are few studies looking at the use of neuroleptics in children and adolescents with schizophrenia, but they appear to be less effective than in adults (Campbell *et al.* 1993). Clozapine, a newer antipsychotic with fewer side effects, produced significant improvement in one open trial of 36 treatment resistant schizophrenic adolescents (Remschmidt, Schulz and Matthias Martin 1994).

Haloperidol is used to reduce stereotyped behaviours, social withdrawal and emotional lability in children with pervasive developmental disorders, such as autism and other communication disorders (Anderson *et al.* 1989). Side effects are a problem but this may be due to the high doses required by these children.

Neuroleptics are used to control aggressive behaviour, although their mechanism of action may be sedation rather than any specific antiaggression effect. Aggression is complex and it is preferable to use psychological or behavioural strategies, with neuroleptics being reserved for children who do not respond.

There are few controlled studies of the use of neuroleptics in tic disorders and Gilles de la Tourette's syndrome (the combination of motor and vocal tics). Haloperidol and Pimozide are the most frequently studied drugs (Shapiro *et al.* 1989).

ANTIDEPRESSANTS

This group of drugs includes tricyclic antidepressants (TCAs) (Imipramine, Desipramine and Clomipramine), mono-amine oxidase inhibitors (MOAIs) (Phenelzine) and newer antidepressants, selective serotonin re-uptake inhibitors (SSRIs) (Fluvoxamine and Fluoxetine).

The demonstrated effectiveness of these drugs in the treatment of depression in adults would suggest that they would also be helpful in the management of depression in children and young people. However, evidence for their effectiveness is limited but strongest for the SSRIs such as Fluoxetine (Prozac) (Kutcher 1997). The SSRIs are also preferable in view of their less problematic side effect profile.

Imipramine is used in the treatment of hyperactivity disorders. It does have an antihyperkinetic effect and is particularly useful in the treatment of children who also have anxiety symptoms. It is less potent than stimulants and can produce cardiac side effects, so that it is not the drug of first choice for these disorders (Spencer *et al.* 1996). Imipramine is effective in stopping bed wetting although the problem often returns on discontinuing medication. Its use has, however, been superseded by Desmopressin, which has fewer side effects.

Obsessive compulsive disorder (OCD) comprises the combination of obsessional thoughts (images or impulses, recognised as senseless by the individual but intruding involuntarily into their consciousness) and compulsions (acts which the individual feels driven to carry out, often to follow certain rules or ward off obsessional thoughts or impulses). Clomipramine is effective in the treatment of OCD (DeVeaugh-Geiss *et al.* 1992). Fluvoxamine (Goodman *et al.* 1989) and Fluoxetine (Riddle *et al.* 1992) have also been used, but studies to date have involved small samples.

The use of antidepressants in the treatment of phobias (specific fears associated with avoidance behaviour, resulting in functional or social impairment) and panic disorder, requires further investigation as most of the evidence is derived from case studies not controlled trials. As effective behavioural interventions exist for such disorders, medication should be considered as second line treatment.

ANTICONVULSANTS

Anticonvulsants are used in the management of epilepsy. They may indirectly improve behaviour by virtue of reducing the disturbance caused by fits, but they are not generally useful in the treatment of psychiatric disorders. An exception to this is Carbamazepine which is used in the treatment of rapid cycling manic depressive illness (in this disorder the individual moves between depression and mania rapidly) and in the management of unpredictable aggressive outbursts (Evans, Clay and Gualtieri 1987).

ANXIOLYTICS

Benzodiazepines (Valium, Lorazepam), antihistamines (Phenergan, Vallergan), Beta blockers (Propranolol) and Buspirone, have antianxiety properties and may be used in the management of anxiety disorders in children and young people. Most anxieties are normal and adaptive and childhood fears are usually transitory, but those which are excessive, or developmentally inappropriate and disrupt a child's normal day-to-day life, are maladaptive. To date, there is a lack of rigorously controlled evidence for the use of anxiolytics in children and young people (Coffey 1990).

OTHER DRUGS

Lithium is effective in the management of manic-depressive illness (bipolar disorder) in adult patients. The literature describing its use in young people with this disorder is limited but, in general, it seems useful (Alessi *et al.* 1994). It may help to contain unpredictable, explosive aggressive outbursts which cannot be controlled by psychological interventions.

Clonidine is an antihypertensive agent used in the treatment of Tourettes, ADHD, aggressive outburst and manic episodes (Hunt, Carper and O'Connell 1990).

ELECTRO-CONVULSIVE THERAPY (ECT)

ECT is rarely used in children and young people and there are no guidelines for its use. It is reserved for severe disorders which have not shown response to adequate trials of other interventions, e.g. severe catatonic depression. A review of the literature describing the use of ECT in adolescents suggests that it has similar effectiveness and side effects to those seen in adults (Rey and Walter 1997). Further rigorously controlled research is required.

Other physical treatment

Diet

The role of food allergies in the causation of childhood behavioural problems remains controversial. The use of dietary manipulation in the management of child psychiatric disorders generally has not been investigated with sufficient scientific rigour to allow conclusions to be drawn about its effectiveness.

Homoeopathic preparations

There is increased interest in the use of homoeopathic preparations but, to date, there is insufficient research evidence describing the effectiveness of such preparations in child and adolescent psychiatry.

Liaison psychiatry

Psychological dysfunction arising from medical and surgical problems and psychological disorder manifesting as physical illness, require the intervention of a specialist trained in paediatric liaison psychiatry.

Studies have examined the psychological reactions of children suffering from physical illness but there has been little evaluation of the effectiveness of paediatric liaison services. There are methodological problems in such evaluations, but the effectiveness of these costly and demanding services must be examined if paediatric liaison psychiatry is to survive in the current economic climate. Paediatricians appear to want access to psychiatrists for consultation purposes and value a rapid response (Burket and Hodgin 1993).

In-patient and day-patient units

Child and adolescent psychiatry in-patient units tend to be small. Admission is the treatment of choice for children whose presentation is so severe that it precludes out-patient management. Other reasons for admission include complex presentations requiring specialised intervention, a life threatening condition, such as suicidal depression, or where dysfunctional family interaction is interfering significantly with a child's development.

The environments of in-patient units vary according to a number of factors, but the usual aim is to provide a therapeutic milieu which, whilst containing, will facilitate assessment and treatment. A range of treatments are employed within units including psychotherapy, cognitive and behavioural interventions and pharmacotherapy.

There are relatively few studies examining the outcome of in-patient intervention (Winsberg *et al.* 1980). There are problems in studying the effects of such units because they refer to different populations in different settings using different measures.

Day-hospital services are valuable for children who do not require hospitalisation, but do require more intensive input than can be provided on an out-patient basis. Specialist interventions for particular disorders are also usefully provided on a day-patient basis, for example, interventions for autistic children. Few conclusions can be drawn from evidence available thus far. Generally, it would appear that children benefit from day-patient services, particularly younger children, although improvement may be limited (Richman, Graham and Stevenson 1983).

Adolescent services

Adolescence is often assumed to be a period of good physical health, but psychiatric morbidity is a significant problem with up to 20 per cent of young people experiencing mental health problems of some kind. Adolescence brings with it considerable stress, and interruption of normal maturational processes can occur as a result of both physical and psychiatric illness. The management of psychiatrically disturbed adolescents in services for children or adults is inappropriate. The exposure of adolescents to severely psychiatrically ill adults may be disturbing. Equally, adolescent behaviour may be regarded as a problem in either child or adult psychiatric units (Parry-Jones 1996).

Psychiatric disorders presenting in adolescence include those continuing from childhood, for example emotional and behavioural disorders, and also the major psychiatric illnesses of adulthood, schizophrenia and manic depressive psychoses. The presentation of such disorders is affected by maturational processes and the assessment, diagnosis and treatment of psychiatric illness in this age group requires the specialist expertise of the adolescent psychiatrist. The evaluation of adolescent services remains limited, although there have been a few studies examining the outcome of admission to adolescent units (Wrate, Rothery and McCabe 1994; Rothery *et al.* 1995).

Services for children with learning disabilities

Children and young people with learning disabilities are at above average risk of psychiatric disorders. They require specialist expertise in terms of assessment and management. Service provision is grossly inadequate, with most learning disability services being directed to people of 16 years and older. Children and young people with learning disabilities are looked after primarily by their families or foster carers in the community. They ideally require support, with access to resources addressing the special needs of the young person.

Challenging behaviour is a major problem and is responsible for significant distress in families. Drug treatment (particularly neuroleptics) is common but few controlled trials have been carried out to test their usefulness. Behavioural intervention has become more sophisticated, with the development of new methods of functional analysis of behaviour and an emphasis on promoting positive behaviour.

Implications for practice, service delivery and policy

With the current trend in psychiatric service provision being directed towards cost effective and inexpensive interventions, it is essential that rigorous evaluation of treatment programmes be undertaken including economic appraisal.

There is conclusive evidence for the effectiveness of certain drugs in the management of specific disorders (ADHD and OCD) but further work is required to determine the effectiveness of other medications. There is also evidence for the effectiveness of cognitive behavioural therapies and behaviour modification in certain disorders. Also, parent training has been shown to be of benefit for a variety of problems. Considerable work is required to determine the effectiveness of the various forms of psychotherapy. In particular, important questions remain about what is the most effective treatment, for which child or young person, with which disorder, at what time. Whilst in-patient units are expensive, there will always be a number of children and young people suffering from severe psychiatric illness who require such facilities.

Further rigorous evaluation is required in most areas of treatment in child and adolescent psychiatry. What denotes effectiveness is an important question requiring consideration. Large scale, randomised, experimental design studies are required in order to demonstrate the long term effectiveness of interventions. Such studies are complex and expensive and, therefore, uncommon at present, but they would inform the development of effective services and facilitate standardisation of service.

The particular needs of adolescents require attention. Mental disorders in this age group are serious and are responsible for significant mortality and morbidity. Adolescent medicine is beginning to address the requirements of young people, but psychiatric services have made less significant advances in this area. The importance of prevention of mental health disorders in young people must be investigated, taking into consideration the potential long-term benefits of apparently expensive interventions.

References

Alessi, N., Naylor, M.W., Ghazziudin, M. and Kar Zubieta, J. (1994) 'Up-date on lithium carbonate therapy in children and adolescents.' *Journal of the American Academy of Child and Adolescent Psychiatry 33*, 3, 291–304.

Anderson, L.T., Campbell, M., Adams, P., Small, A., Perry, R. and Shell, J. (1989) 'The effects of haloperidol on discrimination learning and behavioural symptoms in autistic children.' *Journal of Autism and Developmental Disorders 19*, 2, 227–239.

Barnes McGuire, J., Stein, A. and Rosenberg, W. (1997) 'Evidence-based medicine and child mental health services. A broad approach to evaluation is needed.' *Children and Society 11*, 89–96.

Brandenburg, N.A., Freidman, R.M. and Silver, S.E. (1990) 'The epidemiology of childhood psychiatric disorders: Prevalence findings from recent studies.' *Journal of the American Academy of Child and Adolescent Psychiatry 29*, 76–83.

Burket, R.C. and Hodgin, J.D. (1993) 'Pediatricians' perceptions of child psychiatry consultations.' *Psychosomatics 34*, 5, 402–408.

Campbell, M. *et al.* (1993) 'Antipsychotics (neuroleptics)'. In J.S. Werry and M.G. Aman (eds) *Practitioner's Guide to Psychoactive Drugs for Children and Adolescents.* New York, NY: Plenum Medical.

Coffey, B.J. (1990) 'Anxiolytics for children and adolescents: Traditional and New drugs.' *Journal of Child and Adolescent Psychopharmacology 1*, 57–83.

DeVeaugh-Geiss, J., Moroz, G., Beiderman, J. *et al.* (1992) 'Clomipramine hydrochloride in childhood and adolescent obsessive compulsive disorder: A multicentre trial.' *Journal of the American Academy of Child and Adolescent Psychiatry 31*, 45–49.

Evans, R.W., Clay, T.H. and Gualtieri, C.T. (1987) 'Carbamazepine in pediatric psychiatry.' *Journal of the American Academy of Child and Adolescent Psychiatry 26*, 1, 2–8.

Forehand and MacMahon (1981) *Helping the Noncompliant Child: A Clinician's Guide to Parent Training.* New York, NY: Guilford Press.

Fox, S.J., Barnett, J., Davies, M. and Bird, H.R. (1990) 'Psychopathology and developmental delay in homeless children.' *Journal of the American Academy of Child and Adolescent Psychiatry 29*, 5, 732–735.

Garralda, M.E. and Bailey, D. (1988) 'Child and family factors associated with referral to child psychiatrists.' *British Journal of Psychiatry 153*, 81–89.

Goodman, W.K., Price, L.H., Rasmussen, S.A. *et al.* (1989) 'Efficacy of fluvoxamine in obsessive compulsive disorder. A double blind comparison with placebo.' *Archives of General Psychiatry 47*, 36–44.

Greenhill, L.L. (1992) 'Pharmacological treatment of attention-deficit hyperactivity disorder.' *Psychiatric Clinics of North America 15*, 1, 1–27.

Hammer, T. (1993) 'Unemployment and mental health among young people: A longitudinal study.' *Journal of Adolescence 16*, 4, 407–420.

Harris-Hendricks, J. and Black, M. (eds) (1996) *Child and Adolescent Psychiatry. A New Century.* Royal College of Psychiatrists Occasional Paper OP 33. London: Royal College of Psychiatrists.

Hinshaw, S.P., Heller, T. and McHale, J.P. (1992) 'Covert antisocial behaviour in boys with attention deficit hyperactivity disorder: External validation and effects of methylphenidate.' *Journal of Consulting and Clinical Psychology 60*, 2, 274–281.

Hunt, R.D., Carper, L.S. and O'Connell, B. (1990) 'Clonidine in child and adolescent psychiatry.' *Journal of Child and Adolescent Psychopharmacology 1*, 1, 87–102.

Hunter, J., Higginson, I. and Garralda, E. (1996) 'Systematic literature review: Outcome measures for child and adolescent mental health services.' *Journal of Public Health Medicine 18*, 197–206.

Kaplan, C.A. and Hussain, S. (1995) 'Use of drugs in child and adolescent psychiatry.' *British Journal of Psychiatry 166*, 291–298.

Kaplan, C.A., Thompson, A.E. and Searson, S.M. (1995) 'Cognitive behaviour therapy in children and adolescents.' *Archives of Diseases in Childhood 73*, 472–475.

Knapp, M. (1997) 'Economic evaluations and interventions for children and adolescents with mental health problems.' *Journal of Child Psychology and Psychiatry 38*, 1, 3–25.

Kutcher S. (1997) 'Practitioner review: The pharmacotherapy of adolescent depression.' *Journal of Child Psychology and Psychiatry 38*, 7, 755–767.

Lewis, M. (ed) (1991) *Child and Adolescent Psychiatry. A Comprehensive Textbook.* Baltimore, MD: Williams and Wilkin.

March, J.S. (1995) 'Cognitive-behavioural psychotherapy for children and adolescents with OCD: A review and recommendations for treatment.' *Journal of the American Academy of Child and Adolescent Psychiatry 34*, 1, 7–18.

O'Donnell, J., Hawkins, J.D., Catalano, R.F. *et al.* (1995) 'Preventing school failure, drug use and delinquency among low-income children: Long term intervention in elementary schools.' *American Journal of Orthopsychiatry 65*, 1, 87–100.

Offord, D.R., Boyle, M.H., Szatmari, P., Rae-Grant, N.I. *et al.* (1987) 'Ontario Child Health Study. II. Six-month prevalence of disorder and rates of service utilization. *Archives of General Psychiatry 44*, 832–836.

Offord, D.R., Chmura Kraemer, H., Kazdin, A.E., *et al.* (1998) 'Lowering the burden of suffering from child psychiatric disorder: Trade-offs among clinical, targeted and universal interventions.' *Journal of the American Academy of Child and Adolescent Psychiatry 37*, 7, 686–694.

Offord, D.R and Fleming, J.E. (1991) 'Epidemiology.' In M. Lewis (ed) *Child and Adolescent Psychiatry. A Comprehensive Textbook.* Baltimore, MD: Williams and Wilkins.

Olds, D., Henderson, C., Tatelbaum, R. and Chamberlin, R. (1986) 'Improving the delivery of pre-natal care and outcomes of pregnancy: A randomized trial of home visitation.' *Pediatrics* 77, 1, 16–28.

Parry-Jones, W.L. (1989) 'Annotation: The history of child and adolescent psychiatry: Its present day relevance.' *Journal of Child Psychology and Psychiatry 30*, 3–11.

Parry-Jones, W.L. (1996) 'Adolescent psychiatric services: Development and expansion.' In J. Harris-Hendricks and M. Black (eds) *Child and Adolescent Psychiatry. A New Century.* Royal College of Psychiatrists Occasional Paper OP 33. London: Royal College of Psychiatrists.

Pellegrini D.S. (1994) 'Training in interpersonal cognitive problem-solving.' In M. Rutter, E. Taylor and L. Hersov (eds) *Child and Adolescent Psychiatry: Modern Approaches.* Oxford: Blackwell Scientific Publications.

Popper, C.W. and Zimnitzky, B. (1996) 'Child and adolescent psychopharmacology update; January 1995–December 1995.' *Journal of Child and Adolescent Psychopharmacology 6*, 2, 85–118.

Rae-Grant, Q. and Robson, B.E. (1988) 'Moderating the morbidity of divorce.' *Canadian Journal of Psychiatry 33*, 443–452.

Reid, S. and Kolvin, I. (1993) 'Group psychotherapy for children and adolescents.' *Archives of Diseases in Childhood 69*, 244–250.

Remschmidt, H., Schulz, E. and Matthias Martin, P.D. (1994) 'An open trial of Clozapine in thirty-six adolescents with schizophrenia.' *Journal of Child and Adolescent Psychopharmacology 4*, 31–41.

Rey, J.M. and Walter, G. (1997) 'Half a century of ECT use in young people.' *American Journal of Psychiatry 154*, 5, 595–602.

Richman, N., Douglas, J., Hunt, H., Landsdown, R. and Levere, R. (1985) 'Behavioural methods in the treatment of sleep disorders – a pilot study.' *Journal of Child Psychology and Psychiatry 26*, 581–590.

Richman, N., Graham, P., Stevenson, J. (1983) 'Long-term effects of treatment in a pre-school day centre.' *British Journal of Psychiatry 142*, 71–77.

Riddle, M.A., Scahill, L., King, R.A. *et al.* (1992) 'Double-blind, crossover trial of fluoxetine and placebo in children and adolescents with obsessive-compulsive disorder.' *Journal of the American Academy of Child and Adolescent Psychiatry 31*, 6, 1062–1069.

Rothery, D.J., Wrate, R.M. and McCabe, R.J.R. *et al.* (1995) 'Treatment goal planning: Outcome findings of a British prospective multi-centre study of adolescent in-patient units.' *European Child and Adolescent Psychiatry 4*, 3, 209–221.

Rutter, M., Taylor, E. and Hersov, L. (eds) (1994) *Child and Adolescent Psychiatric: Modern Approach.* Oxford: Blackwell Scientific Publications.

Schachar, R. and Tannock, R. (1993) 'Childhood hyperactivity and psychostimulants: a review of extended treatment studies.' *Journal of Child and Adolescent Psychopharmacology 3*, 2, 81–97.

Shaffer, D., Garland, A,. Gould, M., Fisher, P. and Trautman, P. (1988) 'Preventing teenage suicide: A critical review.' *Journal of the American Academy of Child and Adolescent Psychiatry 27*, 6, 675–687.

Shapiro, E., Shapiro A.K., Fulop, G. *et al.* (1989) 'Controlled study of haloperidol, pimozide and placebo for the treatment of Gilles de la Tourette's syndrome.' *Archives of General Psychiatry 46*, 8, 722–730.

Spencer, T. Beiderman, J. Wilens, T. *et al.* (1996) 'Pharmacotherapy of attention deficit hyperactivity disorder across the life cycle.' *Journal of the American Academy of Child and Adolescent Psychiatry 35,* 4, 409–432.

Sprenger, D.L. and Josephson, A.M. (1998) 'Integration of pharmacotherapy and family therapy in the treatment of children and adolescents.' *Journal of the American Academy of Child and Adolescent Psychiatry 37,* 8, 887–889.

Taylor, E. (1986) 'Childhood hyperactivity.' *British Journal of Psychiatry 149,* 562–573.

Verhulst, F.C. and Koot, H.M. (1991) 'Longitudinal research in child and adolescent psychiatry'. *Journal of the American Academy of Child and Adolescent Psychiatry 30,* 3, 361–368.

Webster-Stratton, C. (1991) 'Annotation: strategies for helping families with conduct disordered children.' *Journal of Child Psychology and Psychiatry 32,* 7, 1047–1062.

Weisz, J.R., Weiss, B., Han, S.S. Granger, D. and Morton, T. (1995) 'Effects of psychotherapy with children and adolescents revisited: A meta-analysis of treatment outcome studies.' *Psychological Bulletin 117,* 3, 450–468.

Werry, J.S. and Aman, M.G. (eds) (1993) *Practitioner's Guide to Psychoactive Drugs for Children and Adolescents.* New York, NY: Plenum Medical.

Winsberg, B.G., Bailer, I., Kupietz, S., Botti, E. and Balka, E.B. (1980) 'Home versus hospital care of children with behaviour disorders.' *Archives of General Psychiatry 37,* 413–418.

—— Woodhead, M. (1988) 'When psychology informs public policy: The case of early childhood intervention.' *American Psychologist 43,* 6, 443–454.

Wrate, R.M., Rothery, D.J. and McCabe, R.J.R (1994) 'A prospective multi-centre study of admissions to adolescent in-patient units.' *Journal of Adolescence 17,* 3,221–237.

Young, S.C., Nicholson, J. and Davis, M. (1995) 'An overview of issues in research on consumer satisfaction with child and adolescent mental health services.' *Journal of Child and Family Studies 4,* 219–238.

Treatment Issues in Child Sexual Abuse

Kathleen Murray

The nature and scale of child sexual abuse

During the last 15 years it has increasingly been recognised that the sexual victimisation of children is an international problem affecting children of all social and economic backgrounds (Finkelhor 1994). As the horrific disclosures of children alleging sexual abuse have multiplied, policy makers and practitioners have been increasingly concerned to provide appropriate protection and treatment for children at risk.

Child sexual abuse has a number of distinctive characteristics that make understanding and responding to the problem an especially difficult task. First, the term 'child sexual abuse' covers a wide range of behaviour. The acts of abuse can vary in nature, frequency, duration and intensity. Second, the abuser may be a family member, friend, acquaintance or stranger. Third, the act itself typically takes place in private and rarely leaves physical signs, making detection difficult. Thus unless secrecy is somehow broken it is difficult to protect the victims of sexual abuse or stop the offenders. Fourth, the fact that the children are of all ages and stages of development increases the complexity of responding to the problem (Larson *et al.* 1994).

Because the sexual abuse of children is typically shrouded in secrecy there are no statistics on the number of cases occurring each year. The national child protection statistics that are published annually by the Department of Health and The Scottish Office provide data on the number of children on local authority child protection registers who are considered at risk of abuse. Gough (1993) noted that in the early 1980s there was no category of sexual abuse on local child abuse registers in Britain. By 1994, 27 per cent of registrations and 28 per cent of children on the register in England and Wales had an identified sexual abuse component; between 1994 and 1997 these proportions fell to 22 per cent and 24 per cent respectively (Department of Health 1997, p.7, Table A). In Scotland, the most recent available statistics show that sexual abuse was the main category in 23 per cent of registrations in 1996 (Scottish Office 1997, para. 22.3).

Currently, the favoured method of determining the scale of child sexual abuse is through population surveys of adults' retrospective recall of childhood sexual experiences. Between 3 and 30 per cent of males and between 6 and 62 per cent of females report having such experiences before the age of 18 years (Elliott and Briere 1995). The high variation in reported rates of sexual abuse between studies may be due to differences between samples, but is more likely to be a function of differences in methodology, in interviewing and in definitions of sexual abuse (Gough 1993).

Data derived from general population surveys (Finkelhor *et al.* 1990) indicate that abuse by parents or step parents constitutes between 6 and 16 per cent of all sexual abuse cases and abuse by any relative comprises approximately 25 per cent of cases. Between 5 and 15 per cent are stranger abuse cases and the remainder are individuals known to the child or family. In clinical samples, however, parents comprise about 33 per cent of the offenders (Gomes-Schwartz, Horowitz and Cardarelli 1990). Thus in any clinical sample intrafamilial sexual abuse tends to be over represented.

Impact of child sexual abuse

During the past decade a large body of literature has emerged describing the short- and long-term effects of child sexual abuse (Wyatt and Powell 1988; Finkelhor 1990; Gomes-Schwartz *et al.* 1990; Kendall-Tackett, Williams and Finkelhor 1993). Whilst no universal or uniform effect has been identified, the aftermath for many sexually abused children can be severe, including emotional dysfunction, behaviour problems, relationship difficulties, cognitive distortions, and post traumatic stress (Berliner and Elliott 1996). The experience can not only cause children immediate difficulties but constitutes a significant risk factor for the development of psychological problems in adult life (Finkelhor 1990).

Despite the seriousness of these effects, they are not experienced by all victims, with as many as 40 per cent being symptom free (Kendall-Tackett *et al.* 1993;

Mullen *et al.* 1996). More distress is found in cases involving penetrative sex, violence, a closer relationship to the offender, multiple offenders, longer duration and more frequent contact (Conte and Schuerman 1987). Other important factors are age and gender of victims, their cognitive appraisal of their victimisation, and their family and wider social environment, including the presence or absence of a close supportive relationship (Briere and Elliott 1993). Maternal support also predicts the reaction of child protective services with non-believed and unsupported children more likely to be received into care (Hunter *et al.* 1990).

A number of longitudinal studies has shown that the symptoms of the majority of sexually abused children improve over time, whether or not they receive therapy (Runyan *et al.* 1988; Gomes-Schwartz *et al.* 1990). However, between 10 and 24 per cent of child victims either do not improve or deteriorate (Kendall-Tackett *et al.* 1993). In addition, Gomes-Schwartz *et al.* (1990) found that abused children who were initially least symptomatic had more problems 18 months afterwards than did their initially more highly symptomatic peers. This finding could be explained by suppression and avoidance strategies that are commonly used as a way of coping with abuse, or by delayed responses to earlier sexual abuse (sometimes called 'sleeper effects') that are triggered by later developmental challenges (Leitenberg, Greenwald and Cado 1992; Finkelhor and Berliner 1995). For example, sexually inappropriate behaviour may not be exhibited until adolescence when sexuality usually becomes a salient issue.

Treatment needs of sexually abused children

Children are usually referred for psychotherapy because of symptoms of emotional or behavioural disturbance. By contrast, sexually abused children are referred for treatment because of the discovery that they had a particular kind of experience. Consequently, child sexual abuse treatment involves children of all ages, with a variety of histories and presentations, with many different kinds of symptoms, and some without symptoms at all. These realities have implications for the organisation of treatment services and their evaluation (Beutler, Williams and Zetzer 1994; Finkelhor and Berliner 1995).

In the UK, recent concern has centred on the tendency to be preoccupied with investigation and preparing for court, while overlooking the treatment needs of sexually abused children. Lynch and Browne (1995) cite several studies where after the initial investigation was completed, it was rare to formulate a comprehensive assessment, and few children were referred for psychological or psychiatric treatment (Prior, Lynch and Glaser 1994). The lack of follow-up services had a marked negative impact on the well-being of both children and parents (Sharland *et al.* 1995). Berliner and Elliott (1996) argue that most children who have been sexually abused should receive therapeutic assistance. The aims are not only to provide immediate help for the child and reduce current symptoms but also to prevent the development of problems at a later date. As previously mentioned, children who are symptom-free shortly after the abuse is discovered may experience later psychological difficulties. There may also be some potential impacts of sexual abuse experiences that cannot be dealt with until the child reaches a later developmental stage. For example, a young person's sexuality may not be addressed in a meaningful way until adolescence. However, since very few studies have documented the course of children's symptom development, little is known about the process of recovery subsequent to abuse.

Guiding philosophies

The philosophies that guide treatment embody different strategies and different aims. Some theories, such as those guiding psychoanalytic therapies, emphasise the importance of uncovering repressed and forgotten material (Loftus and Yapko 1995). Others, such as the behavioural and cognitive behavioural therapies, focus directly on the events of the abuse and seek to change the victim's perceptions, social adjustment and adaptive behaviour (Deblinger and Heflin 1996; see also Chapter 5).

The post traumatic stress disorder (PTSD) model

The PTSD model emphasises that child sexual abuse is a traumatic and frightening experience that produces an anxiety disorder. The physiological response of fear becomes conditioned or associated with aspects of the abuse situation. A wide range of stimuli may then induce fear and prompt intrusive recollections or nightmares, disturbing thoughts and flashbacks, avoidance and withdrawal behaviour (McLeer *et al.* 1988). A primary coping strategy is cognitive, affective and behavioural avoidance to reduce anxiety. The result may be a temporary adjustment, but unresolved trauma. For example, a sexually abused child who is coping primarily through avoidance or is having concentration problems because of intrusive thoughts may be unable to perform to his or her ability in school and then associates with a deviant peer group.

Treatment techniques derived from this approach include anxiety reduction strategies as well as cognitive restructuring where the child is taught to recognise and alter abuse-distorted thoughts, beliefs and perceptions, such as making clear that sexual abuse is the offender's responsibility rather than the child's. Conditioned stimuli (i.e. stimuli present in the abuse environment, such as getting undressed, darkness, men), can continue to elicit fear and anxiety. Berliner and Saunders (1996) have demonstrated that the power of these stimuli can be reduced through several mechanisms, including habituation through repeated exposure, pairing negative stimuli with relaxation responses and thereby dislodging their association with fear and anxiety.

The traumagenic factors model

The effects of sexual assault include not only anxiety but cognitive and behavioural adjustment to the meaning of the experience (Finkelhor 1988). It has been observed: 'The experience of being a victim of sexual abuse is likely to affect people's self-perceptions as they try to ascertain the implications of being a victim for their perceptions of themselves, of their role in the world and their relationships with others' (Berliner 1991, p.150). One approach to understanding these kinds of effects is to use the four traumagenic factors model developed by Finkelhor and Browne (1985). They hypothesise that an experience of sexual abuse might affect four different areas of human experience. These are traumatic sexualisation, betrayal, powerlessness and stigmatisation. By being abused, children learn things in these four areas, either through direct reinforcement and modelling or cognitive learning in terms of making sense of the experience. How children explain what happened to them may affect whether or not they feel guilt, anger or other feelings and reactions. For example, abused adolescents commonly report that they are struggling with beliefs about their own internalised stigmatisation, powerlessness and shame. As one adolescent girl said when asked to describe how the abuse had affected her life: 'I have felt so bad about myself... What kind of person lets their father molest them?' (Chaffin *et al.* 1996, p.121).

This model is extremely helpful in identifying the broad range of possible treatment needs, but it does not suggest specific interventions (Friedrich 1995).

Developmental model

A number of writers have referred to the various ways in which sexual abuse or other traumatic experience can affect neurological, affective, cognitive and social development (Finkelhor 1995; Christo 1997). Psychologists typically conceptualise development as being a process that builds from one stage to the next, with certain tasks and activities being salient at particular ages (Erikson 1950). If a child fails to engage in or successfully master these tasks then the normal developmental process may be arrested (Berliner 1997).

Children may be affected by sexual abuse differently because their developmental level may provide them with a different understanding or interpretation of sexual acts. For example, a major developmental task during adolescence is forming a self-concept in which the several roles a person has are merged into a coherent psychosocial identity (Erikson 1968). Child sexual abuse can seriously undermine healthy identity development, giving the chronically abused child an overwhelming sense of shame, and confusion about psychosexual identity (Bagley and Thurston 1996).

Attachment theory

Attachment theory, as articulated by Bowlby (1969), is commonly advanced as a framework for understanding the familiar antecedents and long-term consequences of child sexual abuse (Alexander 1992).

The key features of attachment theory have been broadly confirmed by empirical research (Rutter 1995). They are:

1. An attachment is a biologically-based bond between a child and one or more people (attachment figures)

2. Attachment plays an important role in promoting security and encouraging independence

3. Attachment relationships can be classified into four categories – secure attachment, which is the healthiest, and three types of insecure attachment; resistant, avoidance and disorganised

4. The effects of early attachment experiences are carried forward into later relationships by means of 'internal working models', that is, internalised

representations of relationships as tending to be, for example, accepting, rejecting or inconsistent.

QUALITIES OF ATTACHMENT

Securely attached children have a sense of inner confidence and competence, have the capacity to be emotionally close, to seek and receive care, and to give care. They have an internal working model of caregivers as consistent, supportive in times of stress, attuned to their needs and reciprocal. Insecurely attached children come to see themselves as unworthy of others' attention: they see other people as untrustworthy, unresponsive and perhaps abusive. 'Resistant' attachment is associated with attention seeking, impulsiveness, frustration and helplessness; 'avoidance' attachment with emotional insulation, hostility and anti-social behaviour; and 'disorganised' attachment with controlling behaviour.

FAMILIAR ANTECEDENTS OF SEXUAL ABUSE

Attachment theory can be used to explain the individual and family dysfunction that frequently sets the stage for sexual abuse (Alexander 1992). Lack of maternal warmth, parental conflict, the presence of a step-father and disruptions in the mother–child relationship are some of the family features that can place a child at risk of attachment problems that predate abuse. Insecure attachment may preclude impulse control in the abuser, or interfere with the protectiveness of the non-abusing parent, or increase the vulnerability of the child to abuse.

CONSEQUENCES OF CHILD SEXUAL ABUSE

Research has demonstrated that there are a number of environmental factors that can act in a protective manner either to cut short the sexual abuse or to ameliorate the impact once it has occurred. For example, perceived parental warmth has been shown to mediate the relationship between childhood intra-familiar abuse and depression and low self-esteem in adult women (Alexander 1992). Recent research on adult attachment and long-term effects in incest survivors suggests that while attachment and abuse severity are not significantly related, they each appear to make significant contributions to the prediction of post-abuse symptoms, distress and personality disorders (Alexander et al. 1998).

IMPLICATIONS FOR TREATMENT

The attachment model helps the therapist to appreciate:

- the origin and diversity of relationships between children and parents
- the influence of internal working models on the formation of the treatment relationships and all other social relationships
- the need to improve attachment relationships if the therapist is to alter basic assumptions children have about themselves (Friedrich 1996; Berliner 1997).

Therapy itself can be interpreted as an attachment relationship whose purpose is to alter negative models of the self and others by providing the child with a secure base from which to explore his or her inner world and actual relationships (Alexander *et al.* 1998).

Transactional model

Christo (1997) explains that development proceeds through a series of transactions between the individual and the environment. From this perspective sexual abuse is viewed in terms of the entire impact of the abuse on the child's family and community environment.

Spaccarelli (1994) used the transactional approach to develop a general theoretical framework which predicts that a survivor's risk of poor mental health outcome increases as a function of the total stress generated by three categories of stressful events:

1. *Abuse events*, such as, sexual exposure, coercion, denigration, and trust violation

2. *Abuse-related events*, such as, family dysfunction, marital separation, and loss of social contacts

3. *Disclosure-related events*, such as, non-supportive responses to disclosure, child removal from the home, family relocation, therapeutic and investigative interventions.

In the transactional model the stressful effects of sexual abuse and abuse related events are mediated by the formation of 'negative cognitive appraisals', such as self-blame, and the use of 'problematic coping strategies', such as being physically and psychologically unavailable, that are the immediate causes of increased symptomatology (Spaccarelli 1994, p.343).

Approaches to treatment

There is an extensive clinical literature describing treatment approaches for sexually abused children. These are based on different theoretical perspectives and make use of a number of treatment formats, including group, individual and family therapy. When Keller, Cicchinelli and Gardner (1989) surveyed more than 400 treatment programmes across the United States they found individual therapy most commonly used with sexually abused children although group and family therapy were also frequently employed, either alone or in combination with individual therapy. About one-third of the programmes surveyed included the offender in family treatment (Beutler *et al.* 1994).

Within each of the treatment formats there are variations in philosophy that result in different goals and treatment methods. The aims may include one or more of the following:

- relieving symptoms, which may be accomplished by encouraging the child to think differently about the event, facilitating the expression of negative feelings, affirming the child's experience and providing emotional support
- destigmatising, which may be achieved by group affirmation from other child victims and the therapist's supportive stance
- increasing self-esteem through cognitive and interpersonal exercises, role plays, and games
- preventing future abuse by changing either the victim's environment or his or her behaviours and awareness in that environment (Beutler *et al.* 1994).

In recent times the emphasis has been on family-based interventions (Giarretto 1982), abuse-focused therapy (Friedrich 1990; Deblinger and Heflin 1996) and cognitive-behavioural techniques (Deblinger, McLeer and Henry 1990). Psychoanalytic therapy has also been widely used (Kazdin 1991) as have amalgams of psychodynamic, cognitive behavioural and family systems intervention (Friedrich 1990).

Family-based interventions

Because family functioning and family disruption are commonly associated with both increased risk of abuse and psychological distress to children, family-based interventions are often considered appropriate (Berliner and Elliott 1996; Crittenden 1996). The importance of the family is shown by Kinzl *et al.* (1996)

who report that sexual dysfunction in males is better predicted by family background than by any history of abuse.

The humanistic approach of Giarretto (1982) has reported positive results. Ten years ago the Giarretto model was said to be the most commonly used treatment model in the United States and Canada, though often modified in practice to suit local needs (Keller *et al.* 1989). The main features of the programme are:

- the child victim is best served if returned to his or her own family

- to accomplish this aim the family system must be changed from an abusive to a nurturing one

- to expedite the return of the child to a healthy family environment, systematic collaboration is required among police, legal-judicial personnel, social workers, therapists and the family members themselves (through professionally-guided self-help groups, Parents United and Daughters & Sons United).

It has been reported that where the police and criminal justice system failed to collaborate, the programme operated less successfully (Giarretto and Enfield-Giarretto 1990).

In the UK, the Giarretto model was developed by staff at the Great Ormond Street Hospital for Sick Children in London. The follow up study of this programme indicated that the child welfare systems often fail to support or co-operate in therapy, many families drop out of therapy, and girls of families resistant to therapy are often re-victimised (Bentovim, van Elberg and Boston 1988).

Winton (1990) reported favourably on a parent support group. Cohen and Mannarino (1996a) demonstrated that appropriate psychotherapeutic interventions for distressed parents may be of critical importance in resolving a young child's emotional and behavioural difficulties. Meinig and Bonner (1990) described a method that aims to reunite offenders with the family, although there has been no formal investigation of this type of therapeutic intervention.

Despite the widespread use of the family systems approach there is scant empirical evidence of its effectiveness. There are also dangers contained in family based intervention. First, they may inadvertently place responsibility at the level of the family (including the child as a member) rather than the perpetrator who committed the abuse. Second, an overemphasis on the family may lead to an underemphasis on the protection of the child from further abuse, with the child pressured by the family to withhold the full details of the abuse suffered (Gough and Murray 1996).

Abuse-focused therapy

'Abuse-focused' is the term used to describe treatment that is directed towards the child and organised around the abuse experience. This approach is not based on a single psychological theory but borrows from a wide variety of clinical techniques. Its guiding principle is that abuse is a form of victimisation by the powerful against the powerless and that effects of abuse are a readily understandable adaptation to an abnormal experience (James 1989).

The common elements of abuse-focused treatment usually include:

1. Encouraging the child to express abuse-related feelings (e.g. anger, ambivalence, fear)

2. Clarifying erroneous beliefs that might lead to negative attributions about self or others (for example self-blame)

3. Teaching abuse prevention skills

4. Diminishing the sense of stigma and isolation through reassurance or exposure to other victims (e.g. through group therapy) (Finkelhor and Berliner 1995, pp.1418–1419).

Parents may receive a form of parallel treatment or participate in joint sessions with the child. However the focus is on helping the child to come to terms with the abuse rather than expecting the parents to change.

According to Berliner (1997), the desirable outcomes of successful abuse-focused therapy are:

- the children understand that what happened was abuse, that it was wrong and that it may have caused them some temporary problems

- they no longer suffer from abuse related emotional and behavioural problems and they have the skills and knowledge to deal with future problems

- supportive relationships with caretakers are established

- the children's development is proceeding normally.

Cognitive behavioural therapy

Cognitive behavioural therapy has been described as 'treatment that is theoretically driven, empirically grounded and relatively straightforward to deliver' (Berliner 1996, p.viii). It aims to provide techniques for dealing with distress, to correct irrational thinking and to clarify the basis of beliefs that victims have regarding the meaning of abuse and their role in the victimisation. The methods include thought stopping, guided self-dialogue and cognitive re-structuring (Lipovsky 1992; Berliner 1997).

Deblinger and Heflin (1996) argue that cognitive behavioural interventions may be particularly appropriate for sexual abuse victims and their families for the following reasons:

1. Cognitive behavioural therapy targets many symptoms which are manifested by abused children and their families.

2. The therapeutic plan is made explicit so that children can determine for themselves whether or not the therapy will suit their needs, thus giving them some control over their situation.

3. The clients and therapist work collaboratively thus promoting a greater sense of control and self-respect.

4. Children and parents are provided with skills that are useful in therapy and also in the event of post-abuse difficulties in later life.

5. Cognitive behavioural therapy appears to be effective with children and families from diverse cultures.

6. The effectiveness of cognitive behavioural therapy has been empirically tested.

Treatment issues

A number of issues arise in the research and clinical literature that have implications for practitioners in the sexual abuse field and for future research strategy.

Treatment effectiveness

When Gough (1993) reviewed the research literature on child abuse interventions he reported very little data on the treatment of victims and survivors of child sexual abuse. He found some research support for the benefits of group therapy and of certain individual therapies, but little to indicate that one approach was superior to another or that a particular method was more appropriate to one individual rather than another. There were few research reports on interventions with male victims and most of the published work focused on intra-familial as opposed to extra-familial abuse.

In their scholarly review of treatment outcome research, Finkelhor and Berliner (1995) located only 29 published and unpublished studies of treatment outcome for sexually abused children. In the majority of studies children were tested at two points in time during which they received some kind of professional intervention (pre-post design). The main findings of their review were:

- aggressiveness and sexualised behaviours resulting from abuse are resistant to treatment
- although uncontrolled pre-post designs report improvements over time in terms of means for the whole sample, some children do not improve
- some interventions described as specific for sexual abuse treatment show few positive effects in pre-post studies or little difference in effect from other interventions. (Finkelhor and Berliner 1995)

The British study (Monck *et al.* 1996) reviewed by Finkelhor and Berliner compared family network treatment with and without group work. Positive outcomes resulted for both programmes but there were no significant differences between them. The absence of an untreated comparison group made it impossible to determine how much improvement was due to the passage of time and how much to treatment.

There is some encouraging evidence of the effectiveness of cognitive behavioural group interventions with sexually abused pre-schoolers and their non-offending mothers (Stauffer and Deblinger 1996). These group interventions were effective in improving the parenting practices of non-offending mothers and in producing a marked reduction in maternal reports of the children's sexualised behaviour.

There is also some emerging research support for the effectiveness of structured cognitive behavioural therapy (Berliner 1997). These are relatively brief, structured, cognitive behavioural treatments that include both child victims and their carers. This approach is designed to target specific difficulties that many sexually abused children and their parents experience. Specific parent issues include ambivalence in belief of the child's abuse, ambivalent feelings towards the perpetrator, attributions regarding the abuse, feeling that the child is damaged, providing appropriate emotional support to the child, management of inappropriate child behaviours (Cohen and Mannarino 1993).

Preliminary studies by Cohen and Mannarino (1996b) provide empirical support for therapy addressing the problems of both emotional and cognitive processing so that the child can recall traumatic experiences without significant distress and can develop an accurate and meaningful explanation of what happened. This approach also fits the findings of Himelein and McElrath (1996) that higher levels of post abuse adjustment were found in victims who disclosed and discussed the abuse, yet refused to dwell on the experience, and minimised and managed positively to reframe it. This suggests that how the child interprets the causes of the abuse and the responsibility for it are important in responding to abuse.

Monck and New (1996) tracked the progress of 239 sexually abused children through specialised treatment delivered in local voluntary agency centres in England, Wales and Northern Ireland. Children appeared to be allocated to therapeutic services without any systematic formulation of their difficulties or what led up to them. It appeared that intervention was prompted purely by a diagnosis of sexual abuse, rather than a thorough assessment of the symptoms and complex family problems which may surround a particular case. Based on these findings, the researchers put forward recommendations for therapists to develop more effective ways of monitoring their own treatment and intervention programmes.

CONTEXTUAL FACTORS IN TREATMENT EFFECTIVENESS

A key question in developing treatment for child sexual abuse victims is why different victims demonstrate such wide variations in the levels and types of effects experienced. Many children who enter a sexual abuse treatment programme will have experienced other traumas in their lives, such as family disruption, poverty or criminality, while they themselves may suffer from difficulties unrelated to the abuse. Therefore, sexual abuse may be only one of the traumas to which the child is exposed.

Berliner (1997) cautions that in this wider context of troubled children's lives it is easy to exaggerate the significance of sexual abuse. She believes that the other factors contributing to the child's difficulties should also be subjected to therapeutic intervention. There is always the possibility that success in addressing the negative effects of sexual abuse will enhance feelings of self-worth and strengthen the will of parents and children to comply with treatment for other problems.

RESEARCH ISSUES

A number of important lessons for research methodology can be drawn from the early studies of treatment outcome (Babiker and Herbert 1996; Briere 1996; Monck *et al.* 1996). Whilst random assignment to treatment and comparison groups is rarely possible, studies should employ reliable and valid measures that are relevant to the goals of treatment, should avoid systematic bias and should have some level of generalisability to the real world of clinical practice (Briere 1996).

Finkelhor and Berliner (1995) draw attention to increasing concern with making research results more clinically relevant. Instead of presenting findings simply as a comparison of group means and significance tests, Jacobson and Truax (1991) suggest a statistical method that will throw light on variability of individual responses to treatment, will help clinicians to understand why improvement occurs or does not occur and will give useful feedback to clinicians and researchers on the specific characteristics of individuals who respond less well to treatment.

Monck and New (1996) suggest moving away from time limited 'external' research projects in favour of an integral approach to monitoring and evaluation where research is a component part of service delivery and the responsibility of the providers of the service. They also speculate about the value of multicentre co-ordination where, for example, the large voluntary agencies collaborating on data collection gather the same core information on all pre-defined groups of cases.

Lynch and Browne (1995) caution that the need for more evaluative research should not be used as an excuse for restricting access to treatment services. They believe that the negative consequences of sexual abuse amply justify comprehensive assessment of the treatment needs of the child and family. 'For some children realistic aims of intervention may include preventing the escalation of existing difficulties or the development of additional ones' (Lynch and Browne 1995, p.236).

Parental participation in treatment of sexually abused children

There is accumulating research evidence that the involvement of non-abusive mothers in the treatment of their sexually abused children leads to improved parenting practices and to decreased behavioural difficulties and less depression in the children (Deblinger, Lippmann and Steer 1996). Deblinger and colleagues argue that treatment that includes a behaviour management strategy gives the parent the skills and a sense of competence to deal with behavioural problems in their children. However, it does little for the internal psychological distress of the children if the children are not themselves receiving treatment.

Berliner (1997) suggests that further research should be carried out with the aim of discovering whether it is the behaviour management component or whether it is the abuse focus with the child that is associated with the change, or both.

Duration of treatment

In view of the limited resources available, the duration of treatment is an especially important issue. Most studies have examined relatively brief interventions of between 6 and 20 sessions but without varying the duration as an experimental factor. Lanktree and Briere (1995) have found that sexual abuse symptoms continue to improve as therapy extends for as long as 12 months. They also found that different symptoms respond to intervention at different points in time. Identification of persistent symptoms and continuing cognitive distortions suggests where and what interventions need to be employed.

It seems likely that short-term treatments which can demonstrate effectiveness will be favoured in the future and that practitioners who prefer more extended provision will need to demonstrate its value from the results of empirical research.

Treatment drop out

Many children who enter a treatment programme fail to complete the course or attend only intermittently, yet none of the treatment evaluation studies reported to date have examined the problem. Finkelhor and Berliner (1995) suggest offering a brief prophylactic intervention for all children that contains the messages crucial for all victims and families to hear. The treatment would be continued only for those subjects who were assessed to have continuing significant levels of distress and the commitment to proceed.

There remains a great deal to be learned about which children drop out of treatment and why. Research in this area would help to identify ways in which current intervention approaches are failing to meet the needs of certain groups of children and families. It will be important to know whether social, ethnic or psychological characteristics are most relevant. Practitioners might then be encouraged to test specific strategies for attracting and holding resistant users of their services. Drop-outs from treatment are also an important group to consider when judging whether or not a treatment approach made a difference (Finkelhor and Berliner 1995).

The child victim as a witness

Part of the therapist's task may be to assist the child through his or her contacts with the medical and law enforcement systems as well as through traumatic court testimony. Whether a child's participation in counselling undermines the reliability of a child's subsequent statements is a recurring issue in the American literature (Myers 1996). Two respected scholars in the area of children's memory and suggestibility advise that since therapeutic techniques may pose too great a risk to the child's testimonial accuracy, their presumed benefits are undermined by the likelihood of the case failing to stand up in court (Ceci and Bruck 1995).

One way of helping children to cope with the court process is to prepare them for the experience. This does not mean coaching the witnesses but guiding and informing them on the nature of the process and being available for support both prior to and during the trial. Currently the provision of pre-court preparation varies widely across the UK ranging from specialist services to complete lack of provision (Murray 1997).

Children's and carers' perspectives

In recent years the perceptions of children and carers regarding the child protection process have been the subject of study (Prior *et al.* 1994; Berliner and Conte 1995; McGee and Westcott 1996). While there are similarities between children's and carers' views of their interaction with professionals, children's experiences tend to be more favourable than their carers'.

According to McGee and Westcott (1996), children comment positively on professionals' intervention and in most cases report feeling better after contact. Children value being believed, and want professionals to be easily accessible, non-judgemental and to keep their promises. Children want to be treated with respect and kept informed about what is happening in their case.

In a number of studies of social work–family interaction, the children and carers have valued friendliness, warmth, courtesy, honesty, directness in approach, sensitivity and sympathy (Butler and Williamson 1994; Prior *et al.* 1994). Humour, trust and privacy are also important factors in the positive feelings of children and parents (Westcott 1995).

Gender differences, ethnicity and disability

GENDER DIFFERENCES

There is a growing awareness that in considering approaches to treatment gender differences need to be considered (Friedrich 1995). Empirical research indicates that greater levels of sexual behaviour are seen in sexually abused boys, when contrasted with sexually abused girls, particularly during the ages 7 to 12 years. Sexually abused boys are also more often implicated in sexual aggression (Friedrich *et al.* 1992). Three sexual abuse effects are said to be more or less unique to male victims:

- confusion or anxiety over sexual identity
- inappropriate attempts to reassert masculinity
- recapitulation of the victimising experience. (Watkins and Bentovim 1992, p.216)

Each of these relates to some aspect of sexual behaviour. Consequently, sexual behaviour is likely to be a more frequent treatment target for boys than for girls.

ETHNICITY

Research on the particular problems facing families from different races and cultures is scarce. Bernard (1995) reported on a study with 30 black mothers whose children were sexually abused. Some of the factors making black mothers reluctant to report their suspicions of sexual abuse to child protection agencies include feeling torn about going outside their families and communities, fearing the agencies would take a blaming or dismissive attitude towards them because they were black, and fearing that the authorities would take a heavy handed approach. The mothers reported that some of these feelings were confirmed by their experiences of investigations. For example, their approaches to agencies were met with resistance and hostility, leaving them feeling isolated and betrayed.

If professional treatment services are to be successful in meeting the needs of different cultural groups they will have to become more culturally competent and relevant.

DISABILITY

Although children with disabilities are particularly vulnerable to sexual abuse, very little is known about their coping strategies and appropriate therapeutic intervention. Without more research in this area Kennedy and Kelly (1992) fear that the background to policy and practice will continue to be one of discrimination, myths and prejudice. They ask, 'How many of the forms of treatment and therapy developed for children and adults presume speech, hearing, mobility, dexterity and literacy?' (Kennedy and Kelly 1992, p.149).

McGee and Westcott (1996) draw attention to the findings of a small study that aimed to investigate the perceptions of children with disabilities and their carers on child abuse investigations. Parents tended to deny the validity of their children's allegations and parents had more influence over the process. The children were 'objectified and depersonalised' by the adults, a situation compounded by inadequate and inappropriate methods of communication (p.176). Parents were judged to be compliant and relatively powerless in comparison to the social workers. Yet social workers reported feeling powerless and inadequate as a result of their limited training and experience in disability issues.

In a study of sexual abuse victims with a disability, Mansell, Sobsey and Calder (1992) found that over half of their sample of 170 victims had difficulty obtaining treatment services because of their disability, and those with severe disability were most affected. Few received treatment appropriate to their individual needs. Negative attitudes towards persons with disabilities, particularly myths about asexuality, are cited as reasons for the poor response of the professionals. Other problems in services relate to resources, physical access and lack of training among staff.

Conclusion

Sexual victimisation in childhood is an experience that can never be forgotten. But there is no reason to believe that the experience will determine the course of children's lives or leave residual problems. There will be some children who suffer, particularly those where the abuse was severe or the abuser was a close relative. Some children will also have psychological or developmental difficulties that are unrelated to the sexual abuse but need therapy.

Until now many of the therapeutic responses to child victims of sexual abuse and their families have been based on the need to do something rather than on the basis of empirical evidence. The way forward is to empirically assess the efficacy of different treatment approaches. The usefulness of this multiplies if it is linked to a theoretical framework that hypothesises certain effects and outcomes. By continuing to base interventions upon strong research knowledge and empirically sound procedures, the efficiency of treatment programmes and the well-being of the children they serve will be greatly enhanced.

References

Alexander, P.C. (1992) 'Application of attachment theory to the study of sexual abuse.' *Journal of Consulting and Clinical Psychology 60,* 1, 185–195.

Alexander, P.C., Anderson, C.L., Brand, B., Schaeffer, C.M., Grelling, B.Z. and Kretz, L. (1998) 'Adult attachment and longterm effects in survivors of incest.' *Child Abuse and Neglect 22,* 1, 45–62.

Babiker, G. and Herbert, M. (1996) 'The role of psychological instruments in the assessment of child sexual abuse.' *Child Abuse Review 5,* 4, 239–252.

Bagley, C. and Thurston, W.E. (1996) *Understanding and Preventing Child Sexual Abuse. Vol. 1.* Aldershot: Arena.

Bentovim, A., van Elberg, A. and Boston, P. (1988) 'The results of treatment.' In A. Bentovim, A. Elton, J. Hildebrand, M. Tranter and E. Vizard (eds) *Child Sexual Abuse within the Family: Assessment and Treatment.* London: Wright.

Bentovim, A., Elton, A., Hildebrand, J., Tranter, M. and Vizard, E. (eds) (1988) *Child Sexual Abuse within the Family: Assessment and Treatment.* London: Wight.

Berliner, L. (1991) 'Treating the effects of child sexual abuse.' In K. Murray and D.A. Gough (eds) *Intervening in Child Sexual Abuse.* Edinburgh: Scottish Academic Press.

Berliner, L. (1996) 'Foreword.' In E. Deblinger and A.H. Heflin *Treating Sexually Abused Children and their Nonoffending Parents.* Thousand Oaks, CA: Sage.

Berliner, L. (1997) 'Trauma-specific therapy for sexually abused children.' In D.A. Wolfe, R.J. McMahon and R.D. Peters (eds) *Child Abuse: New Directions in Prevention and Treatment Across the Lifespan.* Thousand Oaks, CA: Sage.

Berliner, L. and Conte, J. (1995) 'The effects of disclosure and intervention on sexually abused children.' *Child Abuse and Neglect 19,* 3, 371–384.

Berliner, L. and Elliot, D.M. (1996) 'Sexual abuse of children.' In J. Briere, L. Berliner, J.A. Bulkey, C. Jenny and T. Reid (eds) *The APSAC Handbook on Child Maltreatment*. Thousand Oaks, CA: Sage.

Berliner, L. and Saunders, B.E. (1996) 'Treating fear and anxiety in sexually abused children: Results of a 2-year follow-up study.' *Child Maltreatment 1*, 4, 294–309.

Bernard, C. (1995) 'A study of black mothers' emotional and behavioural responses to the sexual abuse of their children.' *Paper presented to the 4th International Family Violence Research Conference*, 21–24 July, University of New Hampshire, Durham.

Beutler, L.E., Williams, R.E. and Zetzer, H.A. (1994) 'Efficacy of treatment for victims of child sexual abuse.' *Future of Children 4*, 2, 156–175.

Bowlby, J. (1969) *Attachment and Loss: Vol. 1 Attachment*. New York: Basic Books.

Briere, J.N. (1996) 'Treatment outcome research with abused children: Methodological considerations in three studies.' *Child Maltreatment 1*, 4, 348–352.

Briere, J. and Elliott, D.M. (1993) 'Sexual abuse, family environment, and psychological symptoms: On the validity of statistical control.' *Journal of Consulting and Clinical Psychology 61*, 2, 284–288.

Briere, J., Berliner, L. Bulkey, J.A., Jenny, C. and Reid, T. (eds) (1996) *The APSAC Handbook on Child Maltreatment*. Thousand Oaks, CA: Sage.

Butler, I. and Williamson, H. (1994) *Children Speak: Children, Trauma and Social Work*. Harlow: Longman.

Ceci, S.J. and Bruck, M. (1995) *Jeopardy in the Courtroom: A Scientific Analysis of Children's Testimony*. Washington: American Psychological Association.

Chaffin, M., Bonner, B., Worley, K.B. and Lawson, L. (1996) 'Treating abused adolescents.' In J. Briere, L. Berliner, J.A. Bulkey, C. Jenny and T. Reid (eds) *The APSAC Handbook on Child Maltreatment*. Thousand Oaks, CA: Sage.

Christo, G. (1997) 'Child sexual abuse: Psychological consequences.' *The Psychologist 10*, 5, 205–209.

Cloke, C. and Davies, M. (eds) (1995) *Participation and Empowerment in Child Protection*. London: Pitman Publishing.

Cohen, J.A. and Mannarino, A.P. (1993) 'A treatment model for sexually abused preschoolers.' *Journal of Interpersonal Violence 8*, 1, 115–131.

Cohen, J.A. and Mannarino, A.P. (1996a) 'Factors that mediate treatment outcome of sexually abused preschool children.' *Journal of the American Academy of Child and Adolescent Psychiatry 34*, 10, 1402–1410.

Cohen, J.A. and Mannarino, A.P. (1996b) 'A treatment outcome study for sexually abused preschool children: Initial findings.' *Journal of the American Academy of Child and Adolescent Psychiatry 35*, 1, 42–50.

Conte, J.R. and Schuerman, J.R. (1987) 'Factors associated with an increased impact of child sexual abuse.' *Child Abuse and Neglect 11*, 2, 201–211.

Crittenden, P.M. (1996) 'Research on maltreating families.' In J. Briere, L. Berliner, J.A. Bulkey, C. Jenny and T. Reid (eds) *The APSAC Handbook on Child Maltreatment*. Thousand Oaks, CA: Sage.

Deblinger, E. and Heflin, A.H. (1996) *Treating Sexually Abused Children and their Nonoffending Parents.* London: Sage Publications.

Deblinger, E., Lippmann, J. and Steer, R. (1996) 'Sexually abused children suffering posttraumatic stress symptoms: initial treatment outcome findings.' *Child Maltreatment 1,* 4, 310–321.

Deblinger, E., McLeer, M.D. and Henry, D. (1990) 'Cognitive behavioural treatment for sexually abused children suffering post-traumatic stress: Preliminary findings.' *Journal of the American Academy of Child and Adolescent Psychiatry 29,* 5, 747–752.

Department of Health (1997) *Children and Young People on Child Protection Registers Year Ending 31 March 1997 England.* London: Government Statistical Service.

Elliott, D.M. and Briere, J. (1995) 'Posttraumatic stress associated with delayed recall of sexual abuse: A general population study.' *Journal of Traumatic Stress Studies 8,* 4, 629–648.

Erikson, E.H. (1950) *Childhood and Society.* New York: Norton Books.

Erikson, E.H. (1968) *Identity: Youth and Crisis.* New York: Norton Books.

Finkelhor, D. (1988) 'The trauma of child sexual abuse: Two models.' In G. Wyatt and G. Powell (eds) *Lasting Effects of Child Sexual Abuse.* Newbury Park, CA: Sage.

Finkelhor, D. (1990) 'Early and long term effects of child sexual abuse: An update.' *Professional Psychology 21,* 325–330.

Finkelhor, D. (1994) 'Current information on the scope and nature of child sexual abuse.' *The Future of Children 4,* 2, 31–53.

Finkelhor, D. (1995) 'The victimisation of children: A developmental perspective.' *American Journal of Orthopsychiatry 65,* 2, 176–193.

Finkelhor, D. and Berliner, L. (1995) 'Research on the treatment of sexually abused children: A review and recommendations.' *Journal of the American Academy of Child and Adolescent Psychiatry 34,* 11, 1408–1423.

Finkelhor, D. and Browne, A. (1985) 'The traumatic impact of child sexual abuse: A conceptualisation.' *American Journal of Orthopsychiatry 55,* 4, 530–541.

Finkelhor, D., Hotaling, G., Lewis, I.A. and Smith, C. (1990) 'Sexual abuse in a national survey of adult men and women: Prevalence, characteristics and risk factors.' *Child Abuse and Neglect 14,* 1, 19–28.

Foy, D.W. (ed) (1992) *Treating PTSD: Cognitive-Behavioural Strategies.* New York, NY: Guilford.

Friedrich, W.N. (ed.) (1990) *Psychotherapy of Sexually Abused Children and Their Families.* New York: Norton.

Friedrich, W.N. (1995) *Psychotherapy with Sexually Abused Boys.* Thousand Oaks, CA: Sage.

Friedrich, W.N. (1996) 'An integrated model of psychotherapy for abused children.' In J. Briere, L. Berliner, J.A. Bulkey, C. Jenny and T. Reid (eds) *The APSAC Handbook on Child Maltreatment.* Thousand Oaks, CA: Sage.

Friedrich, W.N., Luecke, W.J., Beilke, R.L. and Place, V. (1992) 'Psychotherapy outcome of sexually abused boys: An agency study.' *Journal of Interpersonal Violence 7,* 3, 396–409.

Giarretto, H. (1982) *Integrated Treatment of Child Sexual Abuse: A Treatment and Training Manual.* Palo Alto, CA: Science and Behaviour Books.

Giarretto, H. and Enfield-Giarretto, H. (1990) 'Integrated treatment: The self-help factor.' In A. Horton, B. Johnson, L. Roundy and D. Williams (eds) *The Incest Perpetrator: The Family Member No One Wants to Treat.* Newbury Park, CA: Sage.

Gomes-Schwartz, B., Horowitz, J.M. and Cardarelli, A.P. (1990) *Child Sexual Abuse: The Initial Effects.* London: Sage.

Gough, D.A. (1993) *Child Abuse Interventions: A Review of the Research Literature.* London: HMSO.

Gough, D.A. and Murray, K. (1996) 'The research literature on the prevention of child abuse.' In Commission of Inquiry into the Prevention of Child Abuse *Childhood Matters, Volume 2.* London: The Stationery Office.

Himelein, M.J. and McElrath, J.A.V. (1996) 'Resilient child sexual abuse survivors: Cognitive coping and illusion.' *Child Abuse and Neglect 20,* 8, 747–758.

Horton, A., Johnson, B., Roundy, L. and Williams, D. (eds) *The Incest Perpetrator: The Family Member No One Wants to Treat.* Newbury Park, CA: Sage.

Hunter, W.M., Coulter, M.L., Runyan, D.K. and Everson, M.D. (1990) 'Determinants of placement for sexually abused children.' *Child Abuse and Neglect 14,* 3, 407–418.

Jacobson, N.S. and Truax, P. (1991) 'Clinical significance: A statistical approach to defining meaningful change in psychotherapy research.' *Journal of Consulting Clinical Psychology 59,* 12–19.

James, B. (1989) *Treating Traumatised Children.* Lexington, MA: Lexington Books.

Kazdin, A.E. (1991) 'Effectiveness of psychotherapy with children and adolescents.' *Journal of Consulting Clinical Psychology 59,* 6, 785–798.

Keller, R.A., Cicchinelli, L.F. and Gardner, D.M. (1989) 'Characteristics of child sexual abuse treatment programs.' *Child Abuse and Neglect 13,* 3, 361–368.

Kendall-Tackett, K.A., Williams, L.M. and Finkelhor, D. (1993) 'Impact of sexual abuse on children: A review and synthesis of recent empirical studies.' *Psychological Bulletin 113,* 1, 164–180.

Kennedy, M. and Kelly, L. (1992) 'Inclusion not exclusion.' *Child Abuse Review 1,* 3, 147–149.

Kinzl, J.F., Mangweth, B., Traweger, C. and Biebl, W. (1996) 'Sexual dysfunction in males: Significance of adverse childhood experiences.' *Child Abuse and Neglect 20,* 8, 759–766.

Lanktree, C.B. and Briere, J. (1995) 'Outcome of therapy for sexually abused children: A repeated measures study.' *Child Abuse and Neglect 19,* 9, 1145–1156.

Larson, C.S., Terman, D.L., Gomby, D.S., Quinn, L.S. and Behrman, R.E. (1994) 'Sexual abuse of children: Recommendations and analysis.' *The Future of Children 4,* 2, 4–30.

Leitenberg, H., Greenwald, E. and Cado, S. (1992) 'A retrospective study of long term methods of coping with having been sexually abused during childhood.' *Child Abuse and Neglect 16,* 3, 399–407.

Lipovsky, J.A. (1992) 'Assessment and treatment of post-traumatic stress disorder in child survivors of sexual assault.' In D.W. Foy (ed) *Treating PTSD: Cognitive-Behavioural Strategies.* New York: Guilford.

Loftus, E.F. and Yapko, M.D. (1995) 'Psychotherapy and the recovery of repressed memories.' In T. Ney (ed.) *True and False Allegations of Child Sexual Abuse.* New York: Bruner Mazel.

Lynch, M.A. and Browne, K.D. (1995) 'Working together to provide services.' *Child Abuse Review 4,* 4, 235–238.

Mansell, S., Sobsey, D. and Calder, P. (1992) 'Sexual abuse treatment for persons with developmental disabilities.' *Professional Psychology: Research and Practice 23,* 5, 404–409.

McGee, C. and Westcott, H.L. (1996) 'System abuse: Towards a greater understanding from the perspectives of children and parents.' *Child and Family Social Work 1, 2,* 169–180.

McLeer, S., Deblinger, E., Atkins, M., Foa, E. and Ralphe, D. (1988) 'Post-traumatic stress disorder in sexually abused children.' *Journal of the American Academy of Child and Adolescent Psychiatry 27,* 5, 650–654.

Meinig, M. and Bonner, B.L. (1990) 'Intrafamilial sexual abuse: A structured approach to family intervention.' *Violence Update, 1,* 11, 1–5.

Monck, E., Bentovim, A., Goodall, G., Hyde, C., Lewin, R., Sharland, E. with Elton, A. (1996) *Child Sexual Abuse: A Descriptive and Treatment Study.* London: HMSO.

Monck, E. and New, M. (1996) *Report of a Study of Sexually Abused Children and Adolescents and of Young Perpetrators of Sexual Abuse who were Treated in Voluntary Agency Community Facilities.* London: HMSO.

Mullen, P.E., Martin, J.L., Anderson, J.C., Romans, S.E. and Herbison, G.P. (1996) 'The long-term impact of the physical, emotional and sexual abuse of children: A community study.' *Child Abuse and Neglect 20,* 1, 7–21.

Murray, K. (1997) *Preparing Child Witnesses for Court.* Edinburgh: The Scottish Office Central Research Unit.

Myers, J. (1996) 'A decade of international reform to accommodate child witnesses.' *Criminal Justice and Behaviour 23,* 2, 402–422.

Murray, K. and Gough, D.A. (eds) (1991) *Intervening in Child Sexual Abuse.* Edinburgh: Scottish Academic Press.

Ney, T. (ed) (1995) *True and False Allegations of Child Sexual Abuse.* New York, NY: Bruner Mazel.

Prior, V., Lynch, M.A. and Glaser, D. (1994) *Messages from Children.* London: NCH Action for Children.

Runyan, D.K., Everson, M.D., Edelsohn, D.J., Hunter, W.M. and Coulter, M.L. (1988) 'Impact of legal intervention on sexually abused children.' *Journal of Paediatrics 113,* 4, 647–653.

Rutter, M. (1995) 'Clinical implications of attachment concepts: retrospect and prospect.' *Child Psychology and Psychiatry 4,* 36, 549–571.

Scottish Office (1997) *Child Protection Management Information 1995-96.* Edinburgh: Government Statistical Service.

Sharland, E., Jones, D., Aldgate, J., Seal, H. and Croucher, M. (1995) *Professional Intervention in Child Sexual Abuse.* London: HMSO.

Spaccarelli, S. (1994) 'Stress, appraisal, and coping in child sexual abuse: A theoretical and empirical review.' *Psychological Bulletin 116,* 2, 340–362.

Stauffer, L. and Deblinger, E. (1996) 'Cognitive behavioural groups for nonoffending mothers and their young sexually abused children: A preliminary treatment outcome study.' *Child Maltreatment 1,* 1, 65–76.

Watkins, B. and Bentovim, A. (1992) 'The sexual abuse of male children and adolescents: A review of current research.' *Journal of Child Psychology and Psychiatry 33,* 1, 197–248.

Westcott, H.L. (1995) 'Perceptions of child protection casework: Views from children, parents and practitioners.' In C. Cloke and M. Davies (eds) *Participation and Empowerment in Child Protection.* London: Pitman Publishing.

Winton, M.A. (1990) 'An evaluation of a support group for parents who have a sexually abused child.' *Child Abuse and Neglect 14,* 3, 397–406.

Wolfe, D.A., McMahon, R.J. and Peters, R.D. (eds) (1997) *Child Abuse: New Directions in Prevention and Treatment Across the Lifespan.* Thousand Oaks, CA: Sage.

Wyatt, G.E. and Powell, G.F. (eds) (1988) *Lasting Effects of Child Sexual Abuse.* Beverly Hills: Sage.

CHAPTER 12

Work with Fostered Children and their Families

David Berridge

Introduction

After many years of neglect, there has recently been something of an upsurge of interest in the UK in foster care. Compared with the residential sector, there have been thankfully very few publicised episodes of malpractice or abuse of children living in foster homes. This probably led to a general feeling of complacency whereby the difficulties confronting foster carers and the sophisticated skills they require have been taken too much for granted. This attitude brings with it considerable risks and the sector has not received the attention it both needs and deserves.

However at long last there are signs that matters may be changing. For things to alter, action needs to come from the top and the Department of Health Social Services Inspectorate (1995b) inspected local authority fostering services for the first time in over a decade. The Association of Directors of Social Services (ADSS) (1997) responded by expressing long overdue interest. Furthermore the National Foster Care Association (NFCA) left no doubts about the seriousness of the situation in the title of its hard hitting report *Foster Care in Crisis* (1997). The impact of this was increased when professionals and public at large were shocked by the disclosure that a convicted sex offender had been allowed to foster children with the awareness of local authorities concerned (*Community Care* 1997, p.1).

As part of this increasing interest in foster care, this chapter attempts to take stock of the situation by bringing together what we know from the research evidence about effective ways of working with children living in foster homes and their families. But here we run into immediate problems in that, despite progress in a number of areas, the relative professional neglect of the service has been matched by a lack of research attention. Indeed a recent review of foster care research concluded that over the past 20 years barely 13 studies in the UK have had foster care as their main focus (Berridge 1997). In contrast the residential sector has attracted much greater attention, despite catering for far fewer children. Yet, once again, the situation seems to be changing. Apart from the review just mentioned, Barnardo's has published a useful report on what works in family placement (Sellick and Thoburn 1996). Waterhouse (1997) has focused on the organisation of fostering services. New research is underway at universities as far afield as Bristol, East Anglia, Edinburgh, Glasgow, Leicester and York as well as NFCA. The era of complacency is hopefully ended.

Background

Before concentrating on the research messages, it is first necessary to sketch some more details about the current context of foster care as we approach the new millennium. At any one time some 35,000 children and young people are living in foster homes in the UK. Many more move in and out each year. Foster care caters for some two-thirds of all children looked after by local authorities and is thus an essential part of family support and community services for children. Those concerned are among the most deprived and rejected children in our society with some of the worst prospects. They enter care for reasons including temporary relief from family difficulties or having experienced physical, sexual and emotional abuse or neglect. Many display emotional and behavioural difficulties as a consequence. The proportion of children in public care living in foster homes has doubled over the past 20 years. However, surprisingly to many, the *number* has remained virtually constant: there are thus no more foster carers today than there were 10 or 20 years ago and the increase in the proportion has been achieved by a decline in the total number of children looked after. Foster care has not expanded.

Despite limitations in the data and issues of definition, which are discussed later, researchers and professionals alike have felt that foster care mostly works well. The bulk of the work has entailed short-term, temporary care for children, often quite young, who usually return home rapidly and effectively (Berridge and Cleaver 1987; Rowe, Hundleby and Garnett 1989). Greater concern has been expressed about fostering older children, particularly adolescents posing behavioural difficulties, where discontinuity in placements has been a problem.

Indeed foster care has changed considerably over the years, partly as a result of the closure of many residential homes, so that older and more challenging children have been placed. It is ironic that this trend has occurred during a period in which, as indicated earlier, the service has been very much disregarded, particularly at a national level. A further significant achievement has been the successful placement of severely disabled children in long-term family placements, who would previously have remained permanently in residential care or hospital.

Attention is increasingly focused on the status of foster care and foster carers. Most local authority foster carers are not employees but in fact volunteers, receiving payments intended to cover the living expenses of bringing up children but not any element of reward. This traditional approach has led to ambiguities in foster carers' parenting roles with expectations to act more like birth parents than temporary carers. Deriving satisfaction from day-to-day care of children, many experience discomfort about taking on a wider role to help the birth family resume care, as social workers increasingly expect. Long-term foster care in the past tended to be more a form of quasi-adoption rather than a skilled child welfare service (Rowe *et al.* 1984). It has also on occasions led to problems of accountability in the form of social workers' reluctance to intervene when concerns over caring practices have existed, as well as an unwelcoming 'exclusive' rather than 'inclusive' approach towards birth parents and other family members (Holman 1975). We do not yet know the extent to which this has changed following the Children Act 1989, with its greater emphasis on partnership with families (Department of Health 1991). Foster carers have also been excluded from professional teams and their contribution undervalued. There have been more specialist or professionalised approaches in which carers have been paid fees and an important recent trend has been the growth in independent fostering agencies, which have adopted this style. Indeed it was probably this creeping privatisation, reduced supply and prospect of increased costs that triggered Directors of Social Services to act, as much as altruism or concerns over standards.

Foster care takes several forms though it is impossible to do them all justice in this short chapter. Observers now frequently distinguish between *task-focused, temporary care* – where the goal is usually to return home or some other specific objective – and *long-term, more permanent placements* (Triseliotis, Sellick and Short 1995; Sellick and Thoburn 1996). The wide range of types and functions is illustrated in the following extract:

These foster homes are of very different types and cater for children in a range of circumstances. Some will admit children at very short notice in the midst of emergencies or to provide a period of respite for them and their families. Others offer long-term or permanent homes to children who are unable to return to their own families... 'Bridging' placements also exist for children in intermediate circumstances, such as those in preparation for permanent homes... Foster care may also offer remand placements or be a venue for assessments. Children involved can be young, old, male, female and from different ethnic groups. Foster carers may be relatives or unrelated and contact may or may not continue with birth families. (Berridge 1997, pp.7–8)

In addition, unlike for example the USA, it is unusual for foster care to be underpinned by specific theoretical or therapeutic approaches – such as behaviourism – but for more general parenting to be offered (Hill *et al.* 1993). The existence of, and adherence to, care planning varies.

The nature of the research evidence

Having briefly set the scene, attention now focuses on what the research concludes are effective ways of working with children in foster care and their families. Four points need to be clarified at the outset. First, all evidence reviewed here is from the UK only. Whereas research for example from the USA can give useful indicators, there are important differences in service organisation and delivery which mean that its relevance cannot automatically be assumed. Second, in considering effective ways of working in foster care we shall concern ourselves directly with the impact on children and families rather than, for example, positive ways of recruiting and retaining foster carers. The latter, no doubt, can have certain indirect benefits but there is not the space to deal with it all here. Third, and for similar reasons, the chapter attempts to generalise across different types of foster care. There are important variations, as shown already, but this brief chapter would be unsatisfactory and repetitive if continual qualifications had to be made to statements. Readers seeking a more detailed discussion should consult the reports mentioned in the introduction to this chapter.

The fourth point to raise is more complex and requires rather more detailed explanation. As we have seen, the underlying rationale to this book is to collate research evidence about what are known to be effective methods of working with children and their families. Furthermore, independent evaluations are to be preferred to more subjective accounts. This poses a major problem for foster care in that there is so little research evidence in the first place. Consequently, if we were only to proceed where there is clear research evidence to guide us, foster care would have few operational guidelines and the service may not even exist! For example, short-term foster care has received very sparse attention from researchers and there is probably still only one significant study focusing specifically on the educational experiences of foster children (Heath, Colton and Aldgate 1994).

If we want to give further guidance to those involved in foster care, and unless this is to be a very brief chapter, we need to broaden our approach and be more pragmatic. Apart from research evidence with its academic rigour, there is also a body of professional knowledge about foster care – 'practice wisdom' – which we should not simply disregard. We should obviously be careful in that it was once considered 'good practice', for example, to send large numbers of separated children to the far reaches of Australia and Canada, and some residential communities have been based on regimes of military precision, morning runs and cold showers. Nonetheless, a number of practitioners and adult educators would argue that 'evidence-based social work' should consist not only of academic research findings but also that there should be a role for 'reflective practice' (Schön 1983; Gould 1989). The line to be taken here will be that some areas of established practice wisdom may be included so long as they have not been negated by research findings.

Before turning to the evidence itself, there are metaphorically a few additional cards that need first to be laid on the table concerning the nature of previous research. In foster care, as in most social research, it is very difficult to demonstrate that certain approaches lead unquestionably to improved 'outcomes' for children and their families. Natural scientists in the laboratory have advantages over social researchers in this respect and the latter are faced with more complicated, uncontrollable variables (see Cheetham *et al.* 1992; Sellick and Thoburn 1996). The effects of a foster placement will be a complex interplay between the characteristics, situation and actions of children, foster carers, parents, social workers, teachers and several others. Some ways around this might include very large scale or experimental, 'randomised controlled trials', more popular in the USA, where subjects are allocated randomly to different approaches and their effects measured and compared. However UK child welfare researchers have chosen not to go down this route for practical, theoretical and ethical reasons.

Instead we often take advantage of 'natural experiments' which occur spontaneously (Rutter 1995). Furthermore, there is little long-term follow-up research attempting to trace through into adulthood the effects of child welfare interventions, although this again runs into many of the problems just mentioned.

Another shortcoming in existing knowledge about foster care concerns limitations in exactly how placement 'outcomes' are defined and measured. Useful work has recently taken place on this issue (Parker *et al.* 1991), which has been incorporated in the Department of Health's (1995) progressive *Looking After Children* planning and assessment package. However, prior to this researchers tended to evaluate foster care outcomes in less sophisticated terms, including whether or not placements broke down prematurely and social workers', children's and parents' subjective perceptions of the contributions of placements (see Sellick and Thoburn 1996; Berridge 1997). While in themselves these are useful indicators, they only go so far.

Readers' patience is now rewarded and we turn to the evidence itself. In terms of organising the material it has been decided to keep to the threefold division developed in a previous publication by the author (Berridge and Cleaver 1987). Thus, first we deal with *child-related factors,* second comes *social networks and care careers* – these could obviously be approached as separate elements but one can also significantly affect the other – and finally, there are *placement-related factors.*

Evidence on effective foster care
Child-related factors

The literature reveals that it is more difficult to deliver effective foster care to some groups of children than to others. This does not necessarily mean that it is the children themselves who determine outcomes – a recent study of residential care discovered that the quality of care offered was unrelated to the backgrounds of residents and the problems they presented (Berridge and Brodie 1997). Nevertheless, it should alert social workers and carers to the fact that problems are likely to ensue in particular circumstances and contingency plans should be in place.

Studies have generally found that foster placements of older children are more prone to breakdown than those with their younger peers; similarly placement aims are more difficult to achieve (Rowe *et al.* 1989). Linked to this is the finding that children posing behavioural problems have been less successfully fostered than others. Key issues in fostering adolescents from young people's and parents' points of view have been carers' attitudes towards family contact and the level of autonomy the young person will have (Triseliotis, Borland, Hill and Lambert 1995). Downes (1992) expressed this as the need for foster carers to adjust to children's learned attachment patterns. Interestingly, disabled children who are fostered seem to do better or at least as well as children without physical and learning impairments (Thoburn, Murdoch and O'Brien 1986). Once other factors are taken into account there is no clear evidence that fostering outcomes are related to a child's gender.

A rather obvious point perhaps is that foster placements have been found to be more likely to fail when children's needs are not met. Triseliotis, Sellick and Short (1995) concluded that it is important for young people to feel cared for and respected, and elsewhere Triseliotis (1989) stressed the need for children to have a proper understanding of their circumstances.

A complicated and controversial issue concerns foster care for children from ethnic minority groups, in particular the merits of 'same-race' or ethnic matching in placements. The term 'black' is avoided here as, whatever its political advantages, it masks important differences between ethnic groups both in the care system (Rowe *et al.* 1989) and society at large (Policy Studies Institute 1997). There is also the complex situation of mixed parentage children, a significant minority group in the looked after population. Most authorities now seem to have increased the number of foster carers from minority ethnic groups (Barn, Sinclair and Ferdinand 1997) and the National Foster Care Association (1997) linked this to the presence of multi-ethnic family placement teams.

The reality then is that authorities, if they so wish, should be able to recruit foster carers to match children's ethnic backgrounds. But does this matter? Here we enter disputed territory and the research findings are not as clear cut as many would imagine. Indeed the research is inconclusive as to whether children fare better if placed with carers from the same ethnic background and this topic needs to be investigated in greater depth. A detailed study of mixed parentage children in the wider community, though acknowledging sampling and methodological problems, concluded that they often maintained dual racial identities; moreover the development of a 'positive racial identity', and ability to deal with racism, did not depend on the ethnic background of parents children were growing up with (Tizard and Phoenix 1993).

In the light of perhaps conflicting information, each situation should always be carefully assessed on an individual basis rather than following any rigid procedures. However, given the developments in recruitment, in the absence of evidence to the contrary and in line with Children Act 1989 guidance, the conclusion here remains that 'children should be placed with families with as similar an ethnic, religious and linguistic background as possible' (Smith and Berridge 1993, p.33).

Social networks and care careers

Some of the strongest research evidence on foster care in the UK concerns the role of birth families. We obviously need to be cautious where child protection concerns exist and individual care plans should be carefully drawn up and enforced for all children. A consistent research finding is that foster placements with relatives have generally been more successful than those with unrelated carers. In view of this it is surprising that foster placements with relatives have not been used more frequently, although sometimes this may have occurred under alternative legal and financial procedures. The Children Act 1989 sought to standardise these arrangements in England and Wales (Department of Health 1991). 'Kinship care' is reported to be much more extensively used in the USA as well as some other countries and no doubt it will develop here (Colton and Williams 1997).

Most researchers have concluded that continued structured contact with birth parents generally benefits children living away from home. Studies in the 1980s discovered that parents were often excluded or marginalised from the care process once children moved into foster or residential care (Department of Health and Social Security 1985). This contributed to the Children Act 1989 in England and Wales and its emphasis on partnership with parents. Exclusion of parents was not intended by social workers but more a by-product of the way the care system operated. Barriers existed not so much as a result of formal restrictions, such as court orders or regularity of contact permitted, but more due to *implicit* constraints such as distance to placements, carers' attitudes, and anxieties and uncertainties in how to behave (Millham *et al.* 1986). Social workers and carers who wish to encourage parental contact will need to consider carefully how it can be facilitated – it will not automatically occur unassisted.

The researchers quoted above showed that placements in which parental contact continued tended to be more stable and children benefited psychologically, socially and educationally. Elsewhere the same research team revealed that return home is more likely to occur where positive relationships are maintained between social workers, carers, parents and children (Bullock, Little and Millham 1993).

As with parental contact, it would generally now be considered good practice to maintain relationships between brothers and sisters and to place them in the same foster family wherever possible. However, conflicting results have emerged. There are also practical problems associated with large sibling groups and when permanent families become available for some but not all. Indeed when siblings are separated it is usually because of placement problems and lack of choice rather than to meet children's different needs. As with the research relating to ethnicity, it has been concluded that sibling groups should be kept together wherever possible unless there is firm evidence to the contrary (Triseliotis 1989).

Moving beyond the family, school is a key social institution for children, not only to enhance learning and career prospects but also in developing peer relationships and interpersonal skills. For some it can provide an element of continuity in their lives that has otherwise been lacking. Once again, very little research attention has focused on the educational experiences of children in foster care, although the evidence that exists is far from encouraging (Berridge 1997). For example the most detailed study of this subject concluded that the educational contribution of the placements studied was at best neutral (Heath *et al.* 1994). Even in stable, rewarding long-term foster placements, school progress was limited. One investigation found that placements were less likely to break down when pupils did not also change schools on arrival (Berridge and Cleaver 1987). Messages from the research include the point that educational considerations should play a more important part than hitherto in social services policy and individual care planning. In addition, carers and social workers need to think carefully about ways in which learning, attendance and achievement can be reinforced and how effective school liaison can be maintained.

Related to the care process itself, studies have found that pre-placement preparation is extremely important for the child, parents and carers alike. Yet this is often compromised due to the haste with which placements occur and the absence of choice between foster homes (National Foster Care Association 1997). Especially for long-term or permanent placements, different parties need time to come to terms with the new arrangement, adapt their lives and for expectations to be made explicit. It has been found that planning tends to concentrate too much on short-term rather than long-term objectives (Department of Health Social Services Inspectorate 1994). There is also some evidence that foster care can be more successful if preceded by planned *short-term* use of residential care (Berridge 1997). It can allow for proper matching to occur rather than an inappropriate setting being seized. However, children who have languished in residential care and subsequently become 'institutionalised' can find it very difficult to adapt to family life.

Placement-related factors

Much of the research evidence about effective work with fostered children and their families relates to the placement itself. Social workers when interviewed have been mostly positive about the skills of foster carers, although looking after adolescents as we saw has been more problematic. One study (Berridge and Cleaver 1987) found that older and more experienced foster carers achieved better results but supportive evidence is lacking. Social workers have felt that successful carers possess the following qualities:

- they should enjoy being with children
- carers need to be family-centred, although family life can take different forms – including for example single parent households
- flexibility but firmness are important and carers should be prepared to tolerate difference and accept the child
- emotional and behavioural problems should be expected and foster carers will need emotional resilience
- they should be willing to communicate openly and honestly
- be able to seek and receive support from outside the family. (Sellick and Thoburn 1996; Berridge 1997)

Our discussion of foster care should not be one-sided and research has explored also foster carers' views about what they want from social workers and link workers (in family placement teams) (Sellick and Thoburn 1996). For example they should be well informed, accessible, reliable and develop a relationship of trust with carers. Workers need to liaise effectively on their behalf. Direct support of placements is valued, including having arrangements in place when link workers are unavailable such as at weekends. The opportunity to benefit from relevant training, meet other carers and participate in support groups is also welcomed. Building into the placement short breaks or 'respite care' arrangements should be considered. Foster carers appreciate social workers who gain access to help from specialist professionals when required, such as educational psychologists or child psychiatrists. In addition adequate management systems need to be in place, for example to pay carers fairly and promptly, deal with compensation claims, offer appropriate support for carers involved in disputes and ensure that legal advice is provided. Regrettably, research shows that these are usually the exception rather than the rule (Sellick 1992).

In corroboration of the above, studies have concluded that support to carers, practical and personal, plays an important part in delivering effective foster care – both in terms of sustaining placements and helping to retain families. This applies to young and old children alike and we should not assume that the former are unproblematic. Feeling involved and consulted in planning and decision making are also important, as is efficient and frank communication from social workers and link workers (Aldgate and Hawley 1986; Berridge and Cleaver 1987). Similarly, studies have indicated the general benefits of training, although more detailed research is required to differentiate between particular forms of training and their exact impact.

One very specific and interesting point to have emerged consistently from research studies concerns the greater likelihood of failure where foster carers have a daughter or son of their own similar in age to the child being placed (Parker 1966; Berridge 1997). Jealousies and rivalries can ensue from perceived competition for attention and affection. Agencies should try to avoid such situations or, if not, build in additional safeguards including alerting carers to the likely difficulties. Indeed, agencies and carers should not underestimate the effects of fostering on the carers' own families, and the stresses on and needs of their own children should be acknowledged (Ames 1993). Some children may initially disclose evidence of abuse to other children, who may be shocked or overwhelmed by such information but may also give comfort and support (Pugh 1996).

Finally, there has been little investigation to date of the influence of particular forms of organisation of fostering services on outcomes for children, although additional work on this complex topic is currently underway at NFCA.

Conclusion

We round off the chapter by first summarising the main preceding messages from the research. Initially it was seen that the existing knowledge base about foster care is limited. This has not been a major area of academic interest and, consequently, there is not a great deal of 'hard' information about effective methods of working with children and families. Thus the chapter cast its net slightly more widely. Nonetheless the evidence revealed that most foster care has been felt to work positively, although there have been particular problems concerning placements of older children and those with behavioural problems. Foster care with relatives has tended to be very successful, though underdeveloped.

Indeed, there is now strong evidence about the benefits for most children of continued, structured contact between absent children and birth parents, as well as other family members. We also have better understanding of the mechanisms by which parents have been unintentionally excluded from the care process. Pre-placement planning has been found to play an important part in successful foster care. The qualities required by carers and social workers have been highlighted. Furthermore, there is consensus that practical and personal support are important for foster carers, as well as training. Involving and consulting carers and open communication are also key. In all this the impact of fostering on carers' own families should not be overlooked. A controversial topic has been family placements involving children from ethnic minority groups. The evidence is less clear cut than many would assume but the conclusion here is in line with existing practice wisdom, namely that when making placements continuities should be sought with ethnic, religious and linguistic background.

The major conclusion from examining foster care research is concern about the relative neglect of the service. We should not overlook the improvements that have occurred in specific authorities or more generally, such as involving experienced foster carers in training. Notwithstanding this, however, foster care has received inadequate attention from the Government, managers, professional bodies and researchers alike. The Children Act 1989 and guidance on family placements (Department of Health 1991) provide a useful framework but are insufficient.

Foster care has become progressively more difficult over the years and the continuing closure of residential homes will add to this trend. Foster families are now accepting older children, more are known to have been ill-treated and they pose greater problems at home, school and in the community. In the light of this, continuing professional negligence is unacceptable.

It has often been asserted that a major shift needs to take place in the *status* of foster care (Sellick 1992; Triseliotis, Borland and Hill 1998). Some carers find an almost magical solution if they join the better voluntary or independent fostering agencies, which pay more, provide training and support and value what families offer. Local authorities often seem willing to fund adequately independent placements but not to invest in their own services. Unless this changes, carers will probably continue to vote with their feet and local authorities will find that their bills rise inexorably. However the independent sector by no means automatically guarantees superior care for individual children and there are concerns for example about distance, separation, the quality of care for ethnic minority groups and schooling, let alone arrangements for inspection and scrutinising carers' backgrounds (Department of Health Social Services Inspectorate 1995a).

Enhanced status for foster care and foster carers needs to be achieved both individually and structurally. In specific cases, social workers can demonstrate that they value the contributions of carers, involve them in planning and making decisions, tell them what is going on and listen to what they have to say. Many carers are very experienced. This would be more likely to occur if, structurally, foster care were to become more professionalised. We can contrast *traditional* with *professionalised* approaches to foster care. In the former, carers are volunteers, paid at minimum rates, unwelcoming to birth family and social work involvement, and act essentially intuitively. A more professionalised approach, in contrast, is one in which carers are skilled and proficient, receive fees, accept external involvement, and are trained.

As with many things in life, unfortunately, changes and improvements have cost implications. At present the majority of local authorities pay carers below the recommended NFCA rate and therefore do not even meet what are calculated to be the essential living costs of looking after children. Foster carers, therefore, are subsidising the state. At present, twice as much is spent in total on residential care in Britain compared with foster care despite catering for a third the number of children. Reimbursing carers more adequately would make it possible to insist that they attend training, which is voluntary at present. Such developments seem inevitable.

Specific practice reforms would appear piecemeal unless the above were also addressed. Nevertheless, there is clearly a crisis in supply of foster carers in many parts of the UK that urgently needs to be tackled (National Foster Care Association 1997). It is no solution, however, if family placement workers concentrate on recruitment to such a degree that they neglect existing carers, who leave due to dissatisfaction on feeling unsupported. In addition, administrative systems for foster care need to be improved and there are concerns specifically over procedures when allegations are made against carers. Furthermore, good care planning is at the heart of effective practice, yet an official report discovered that thorough assessments and care plans were absent for two-thirds of children in the authorities inspected (Department of Health Social Services Inspectorate 1996).

Finally, it is encouraging that, enticed by offers of funding, researchers are more active in the field of foster care. Some of the key issues are now being studied, including recruitment and retention of carers, support, birth parent contact and working with abused children. Numerous gaps still exist, such as the education of fostered children, aftercare and the functioning of the independent sector. There are also very few intensive qualitative studies of how arrangements work in detail. In all, therefore, there is a quite considerable agenda that needs to be tackled to enhance the understanding and operation of foster care for children and their families.

Acknowledgement

The author is grateful to Isabelle Brodie, Malcolm Hill, Clive Sellick and Pat Verity for comments on an earlier version of this chapter.

References

Aldgate, J. and Hawley, D. (1986) 'Preventing disruption in long-term foster care.' *Adoption and Fostering 10*, 3, 23–30.

Ames, J. (1993) *'We Have Learned a Lot from Them': Foster Care for Young People With Learning Disabilities.* Barkingside: Barnardo's/National Children's Bureau.

Association of Directors of Social Services (1997) *The Foster Care Market: A National Perspective.* Ipswich: Suffolk Social Services.

Barn, R., Sinclair, R. and Ferdinand, D. (1997) *Acting on Principle: An Examination of Race and Ethnicity in Social Services Provision for Children and Families.* London: Batsford.

Berridge, D. (1997) *Foster Care: A Research Review.* London: The Stationery Office.

Berridge, D. and Brodie, I. (1997) *Children's Homes Revisited.* London: Jessica Kingsley Publishers.

Berridge, D. and Cleaver, H. (1987) *Foster Home Breakdown.* Oxford: Blackwell.

Bullock, R., Little, M. and Millham, S. (1993) *Going Home: The Return of Children Separated from their Families.* Aldershot: Dartmouth.

Cheetham, J., Fuller, R., McIvor, G. and Petch, A. (1992) *Evaluating Social Work Effectiveness.* Buckingham: Open University Press.

Colton, M. and Williams, M. (1997) 'The nature of foster care: International trends.' *Adoption and Fostering 21,* 1, 44–49.

Community Care Newspoint (1997) 'Boateng closes door to stop abusers fostering.' *Community Care 1174,* 29 May.

Department of Health (1991) *The Children Act 1989. Guidance and Regulations: Volume 3 – Family Placements.* London: HMSO.

Department of Health (1995) *Looking After Children.* London: HMSO.

Department of Health and Social Security (1985) *Social Work Decisions in Child Care: Recent Research Findings and their Implications.* London: HMSO.

Department of Health Social Services Inspectorate (1994) *Planning Long-Term Placements Study.* London: Department of Health Social Services Inspectorate.

Department of Health Social Services Inspectorate (1995a) *Independent Fostering Agencies Study.* London: HMSO.

Department of Health Social Services Inspectorate (1995b) *Inspection of Local Authority Fostering 1994-5.* London: Department of Health.

Department of Health Social Services Inspectorate (1996) *Inspection of Local Authority Fostering 1995–1996 National Summary Report.* London: Department of Health Social Services Inspectorate.

Downes, C. (1992) *Separation Revisited: Adolescents in Foster Family Care.* Aldershot: Ashgate.

Gould, N. (1989) 'Reflective learning for social work practice.' *Social Work Education 8,* 2, 9–19.

Heath, A., Colton, M. and Aldgate, J. (1994) 'Failure to escape: A longitudinal study of foster children's educational attainment.' *British Journal of Social Work 24,* 3, 241–260.

Hill, M., Nutter, R., Giltinan, D., Hudson, J. and Galaway, B. (1993) 'A comparative survey of specialist fostering in the UK and North America.' *Adoption and Fostering 17,* 2, 17–23.

Holman, R. (1975) 'The place of fostering in social work.' *British Journal of Social Work 5,* 1, 3–29.

Millham, S., Bullock, R., Hosie, K. and Haak, M. (1986) *Lost in Care.* Aldershot: Gower.

National Foster Care Association (1997) *Foster Care in Crisis.* London: NFCA.

Parker, R. (1966) *Decision in Child Care.* London: Allen & Unwin.

Parker, R., Ward, H., Jackson, S., Aldgate, J. and Wedge, P. (1991) *Looking After Children: Assessing Outcomes in Child Care.* London: HMSO.

Policy Studies Institute (1997) *Ethnic Minorities in Britain.* London: PSI.

Pugh, G. (1996) 'Seen but not heard? Assessing the needs of children who foster.' *Adoption and Fostering 20,* 1, 35–41.

Rowe, J., Caine, M., Hundleby, M. and Keane, A. (1984) *Long-Term Foster Care.* London: Batsford.

Rowe, J., Hundleby, M. and Garnett, L. (1989) *Child Care Now: A Survey of Placement Patterns.* London: British Agencies for Adoption and Fostering.

Rutter, M. (1995) 'Causal concepts and their testing.' In M. Rutter and D. Smith (eds) *Psychosocial Disorders in Young People: Time Trends and Their Causes.* Chichester: Wiley.

Rutter, M. and Smith, D. (eds) (1995) *Psychosocial Disorders in Young People: Time Trends and Their Causes.* Chichester: Wiley.

Schön, D. (1983) *The Reflective Practitioner: How Professionals Think.* London: Arena.

Sellick, C. (1992) *Supporting Short-Term Foster Carers.* Aldershot: Avebury.

Sellick, C. and Thoburn, J. (1996) *What Works in Family Placement?* Barkingside: Barnardo's.

Smith, P. and Berridge, D. (1993) *Ethnicity and Childcare Placements.* London: National Children's Bureau.

Thoburn, J., Murdoch, A. and O'Brien, A. (1986) *Permanence in Child Care.* Oxford: Blackwell.

Tizard, B. and Phoenix, A. (1993) *Black, White or Mixed Race? Race and Racism in the Lives of Young People of Mixed Parentage.* London: Routledge & Kegan Paul.

Triseliotis, J. (1989) 'Foster care outcomes: A review of key research findings.' *Adoption and Fostering 13,* 3, 5–17.

Triseliotis, J., Borland, M. and Hill, M. (1998) *Fostering Good Relations: A Study of Foster Care and Foster Carers in Scotland.* Report to the Scottish Office. Edinburgh: Scottish Office.

Triseliotis, J., Borland, M., Hill, M. and Lambert, L. (1995) *Teenagers and the Social Work Services.* London: HMSO.

Triseliotis, J., Sellick, C. and Short, R. (1995) *Foster Care: Theory and Practice.* London: Batsford.

Waterhouse, S. (1997) *The Organisation of Fostering Services.* London: NFCA.

CHAPTER 13

Work with Children in Residential Care

Roger Bullock

The role and context of residential care

The first point to make about residential child care is that it cannot be understood in isolation. Without knowing its context, much of the provision and activities within it appear bizarre. The alarms on bedroom doors in a children's home or the long silences of group meetings in a therapeutic community only make sense in light of the aims, structure and processes of each establishment.

Residential care forms an important part of the services specified in Part III of the Children Act 1989 but its uses for children in care or accommodation have changed considerably in recent years. The most notable feature is a marked decline in usage. The numbers of young people under the age of 18 living in residential establishments at any one time for welfare, criminal or special education reasons fell in England and Wales by 59 per cent in the 20 years between 1971 and 1991, the dates used for two accurate surveys by Moss (1975) and Gooch (1996). The figure is now 32,000 (Department of Health, 1998). The drop in annual throughput of children, however, may be less as fewer young people than formerly enter residential care before the age of 11, so the potential for long stays is reduced. A Dartington Social Research Unit (1996) study of all admissions to residential care in one county found that twice as many children were admitted to residential care over a year as were resident at any one time. Some young people were admitted more than once and one emergency unit averaged nine annual admissions per bed.

A sizeable proportion of adolescents who are looked after away from home are still likely to have a residential experience. Because of practice changes over the last decade the present figure is less than the 80 per cent found 15 years ago for those admitted to care over the age of ten (Millham *et al.* 1986); it is probably nearer 60 per cent (Bullock, Gooch and Little 1998b). Moreover, as Cliffe and Berridge (1992) report in *Closing Children's Homes,* those local authorities that have stopped providing children's residential care themselves, such as Solihull and Warwickshire, have found that for a proportion of adolescents (some 10–15%) there is no viable alternative to residential placement. An analysis of referrals to several social services departments based on the planning tool *Matching Needs and Services* (Dartington Social Research Unit 1995) identified a small number of children whose needs were best met by residential care, although not always of the type available. But, despite this continuing demand, further decline seems likely as discriminating purchasers seek value for money and cheaper alternatives.

Social workers' attitudes to the types of accommodation needed and the implementation of other policies, such as bail support for offenders, must affect the residential services provided. The growing tendency to choose residence late in young people's care careers would suggest those admitted will be older than in the past and will present complex and challenging needs. Individually, the young people are probably no more difficult than their predecessors but today the most challenging youngsters come together in small groups, with few straightforward cases to ease the burden for hard pressed staff. Dartington's study of approved schoolboys in the late 1960s (Millham, Bullock and Cherrett 1975) found that 30 per cent had serious psychological problems while the remainder could be categorised as socialised delinquents. They were certainly anti-social and emotionally deprived but posed residential staff relatively few problems. Few of these young men would be in residential establishments today.

Caution must be taken when generalising about residential services. Any search for single-issue explanations of developments must account for the revival in usage in the 1970s as well as the decline of the 1980s. Neither should the fact that children in residential care undoubtedly have complex needs be confused with myths that they are all delinquent or are all victims of sexual abuse. Nonetheless, at least a dozen separate trends within the residential sector as a whole can be identified. These are:

- the replacement of single-sex establishments by ones that are co-educational but which, in practice, are dominated by boys
- the increasing age of residents at entry; more young people with health problems, behaviour disorders and disabilities

- greater racial and ethnic mix
- larger catchment areas, raising problems for educational continuity and contact with home
- more provision by private agencies
- less specialisation by sector with a resulting mix of needs in each establishment
- assessment by need criteria rather than social role categories, such as disabled or special educational needs
- a more generalist service
- shorter stays
- rising cost
- more concerns about rights and protection
- further reductions in the size of units and in the numbers accommodated by the system but, paradoxically, a larger proportion of the total places in secure accommodation or other specialist centres such as therapeutic communities.

Naturally, the factors that explain changes in the use of private boarding schools, schools for children with special educational needs and penal institutions may be different from those that affect child care establishments but in all of these sectors viable alternatives have been created. Even in those primarily concerned with the delinquent and disruptive adolescent, the emergence of a coherent system of intermediate treatment has been of major importance, although there is still considerable reliance on residence as a last resort.

The Children Act 1989 echoes previous attempts, such as the Wagner Report (National Institute for Social Work, 1988) to shed the last resort image of residential care and ensure that it is integral to children's services. It should be used as a 'positive choice' whenever needed and should be sufficiently attractive to young people for them to request it. The strengths of the best residential approaches have been laid out in several papers (see Bullock 1992; Kahan 1994) and it is encouraging that recent studies of teenagers in community homes have found that many young people speak favourably about their experiences (Sinclair and Gibbs 1998). All children in need have a right to these services if it can be shown to be in their best interests. Sadly, some residential care falls short of providing this but, as recent studies show, some works well.

Research into residential care

Studies of residential care in the immediate post-war years were undertaken chiefly with the aim of informing some wider social or psychological theory. Bowlby (1944), for example, studied juvenile offenders while developing his views on attachment and separation. In the 1960s, for a variety of reasons, research interest shifted from the development of an academic discipline to the institutions themselves, gaining impetus, paradoxically, from theoretical dissertations rather than empirical evidence. In 1961, the American author Goffman published *Asylums*, which elaborated the influential concept of the total institution. A year later came Polsky's *Cottage Six* which illuminated the inner world of residence. At the same time, in Britain, Barton (1959) was highlighting the apathy and dependency exhibited by institutionalised patients in mental hospitals. Organisational theory was also beginning to suggest links between the various components of institutions, indicating connections between residents' behaviour and aspects of regimes.

Thus, an interest in research into residential care for children took root and several groups in Britain developed models by which institutions might be explored. At the King's College Research Centre in Cambridge, Lambert, Millham and Bullock (1975) published *A Manual to the Sociology of the School* which offered a conceptual framework and a methodology for understanding boarding schools. At the Thomas Coram Research Unit and the Maudsley Hospital, Bartak and Rutter (1975) and King, Raynes and Tizards (1971) devised methodologies for comparing and evaluating different residential approaches. The Home Office Research Unit, too, made pioneering studies of the effects of different regimes, good examples of which are Dunlop's (1974) work on approved schools, Heal and Cawson's (1975) analysis of institutional climates and Sinclair's (1971) comparative study of probation hostels. In addition, two experimental modifications of regimes were evaluated: Cornish and Clarke (1975) conducted a controlled trial in which approved schoolboys deemed suitable for therapeutic care were randomly allocated to contrasting regimes while Bottoms and McClintock (1973) at the Cambridge Institute of Criminology meticulously traced changes in the regime at Dover Borstal.

An examination of these studies shows that certain aspects of the subject received greater attention than others (Bullock, Little and Millham 1993). Facilities for children with physical and mental disabilities and for the seriously delinquent were given copious coverage. On the other hand, ordinary children's homes in England and Wales, which in 1971 sheltered over 30,000 young people, were virtually ignored. Most residential studies of the period thus concentrated on long stays; residential facilities offering brief placements were little considered. It is also evident that the focus was on organisational goals, regimes and structures and on staff and residents' adaptations; less notice was taken of the historical antecedents of services or of the routes or avenues young people took before entering residential care. What we now call consumer studies were virtually unknown.

The major contribution of subsequent research was to improve understanding of the functions of residential care for the wider childcare system, but the relevance of the findings was restricted by a limited understanding of children's background characteristics and needs, a situation that has only been remedied since the implementation of the Children Act 1989. Recent studies have scrutinised a range of establishments from secure treatment units (Bullock, Little and Millham 1998a), therapeutic communities (Little and Kelly 1995), children's homes (Berridge and Brodie 1996; Sinclair and Gibbs 1996; Whitaker, Archer and Hicks 1998) and boarding schools for children with emotional and behavioural difficulties (Grimshaw and Berridge 1995).

This recent information has the advantage of viewing residential care in the current legal and practice framework which should, in theory, mean less use of residential placements for young offenders but more respite and short-term accommodation. It also benefits from the collective wisdom of earlier studies combining an interest in the role of residential care in a comprehensive childcare service with knowledge about what homes can actually achieve. Many of the earlier research findings have been confirmed but understanding of the relationship between causal factors and processes has been increased. Within the general context of knowledge about the strengths and weaknesses of residential approaches, the qualities displayed by effective establishments are clearer.

Summary of research findings

Initially, the evidence about residential care overall will be reviewed, followed by a consideration of more specific aspects and interventions.

Young people placed in residential care are increasingly older adolescents, many of whom present special difficulties. They display varied characteristics and a range of presenting needs and problems. Many say they prefer residential care to fostering because it is less restrictive and minimises conflict with family loyalties, so preserving trust and confidence. However, there is an ever present risk of poor outcomes and the experience may be of limited value. The Children Act 1989 stresses the need to respect children's wishes but their expressed preferences may spring from insecurity and isolation more than a knowledge of what is available or an understanding of what research shows to be in their long-term interests.

The sequence of decisions and placements prior to admission is well established. Decisions made by professionals largely determine the avenues along which young people move. Sometimes these decisions aggravate a child's problems, for example by placing a 'runaway' in a setting with a high absconding rate or one that is a long way from home. Concern about the risks inherent in the childcare process has generated research interest in the consequences of well-intentioned placement decisions for children.

Follow-up studies of looked after children show that residence is used more frequently than commonly thought. Three-fifths of children separated from their families for more than two years have at least a taste of residential care. Also, residential care can be used at different points in a child's care career, such as when first looked after or subsequent to a foster home breakdown. Frequently it is not the only intervention: nearly one-third of long-stay cases experience both foster and residential care. In the context of a child's wider care career, the residential experience may also be of marginal significance; major effects on behaviour are seldom to be expected.

Residential institutions emerge as complex organisations impossible to classify on the basis of simple criteria. For example, a liberal regime may accompany a strong, intolerant child culture. Similarly, depending on the susceptibilities of the individual, expressive sanctions, such as moral opprobrium or adult disapproval, may be as painful as the loss of liberty. Rarely can institutions be assessed according to clear continua, such as might connect the liberal at one extreme to the repressive at the other, or a 'group' as opposed to an 'individual' orientation.

When the strengths and weaknesses of residential care are evaluated (Bullock 1992), it is found that good residential care can provide children with a stable home and a stimulating educational environment. It can widen their cultural horizons and create a framework for emotionally secure relationships with adults. It can also provide a basis for intensive therapeutic work. Generally, the less punitive and overtly caring the regime, the better the outcome for children, from the point of view of their education, personal growth, development and social conduct.

The weaknesses of residential settings lie in their inability to give continuing unconditional love, the constraints they place on a child's emotional development, their inability to ensure staff continuity and the peripheral role they often allocate to children's families. These deficiencies were probably less serious in an era when residential care could lead to employment in domestic service and the armed services but today no such links exist and there are few compensations for these difficulties.

Admission to residential care also creates secondary problems associated with stigma, separation and strained relationships within the institution. These can so preoccupy the child and carers that the primary problems which necessitated removal from home are forgotten. The problems separated children experience as they try to preserve the continuity of their personal and family relationships may overwhelm any benefit that might reasonably be expected to accrue. Institutional neglect, whereby children's education, family relations and health care are adversely affected, is an ever present risk (Ward 1995). With the exception of persistent offenders, young people leaving residential care face problems markedly different from those that necessitated entry. Impetuous and difficult behaviour usually declines, but now unemployment, isolation and homelessness loom.

It should be borne in mind that the strengths and weaknesses of residential care may not always be apparent from studies of young people while they are resident. Follow-up research suggests that some children who are difficult and unsettled while there do quite well in the longer term – some girls for example – while others, such as withdrawn institutionalised boys, generally fare badly, drifting into homelessness and recidivism (Bullock, Millham and Little 1998a).

The immediate impact of residence on young people while they are there is particularly evident in differences across establishments in the incidence of running away and of violent behaviour, contrasts that endure when young people's background characteristics are taken into account. The cultures that prevail among staff and children are especially significant in this respect. In successful institutions, they reinforce childcare aims of promoting children's welfare; in poor quality establishments, hostile cultures seriously undermine effectiveness by encouraging cynicism about the homes, aims and minimal involvement in their work. This contribution is very significant in the context of the tariff system whereby running away and violent behaviour usually result in transfer to more controlling environments. Thus, any improvement in behaviour, self image and criminal identity is a contribution to welfare.

The impact of a residential experience on the behaviour of young people is less discernible after they have left, although this finding rests largely on studies of persistent property offenders for whom the prognosis is generally poor whatever form the intervention takes. Neither do good outcomes automatically follow stays in good homes. Some young people find the contrast between the caring home and the uncaring community too much to handle. Nevertheless, while there is much less difference in young people's difficult behaviour after leaving, whatever the establishment, the pattern of good and bad homes is usually maintained. This suggests that the influence on young people's potentially damaging behaviour while they are resident is mirrored by a smaller but still significant effect on behaviour after departure (Sinclair and Gibbs 1998).

A problem inherent in discussions about research findings has been the tendency to confuse the shortcomings of residential care with those of state care generally. In other contexts, such as in elite boarding schools, research has produced far less criticism. We need to differentiate the categories of care placements more carefully in evaluations, so that the different nature and quality of inputs can be compared. We also need to study the combinations and sequences of interventions likely to be employed under the 1989 Children Act, in order to assess care approaches more accurately. An analysis of the different dimensions of important factors, such as the different meanings children and administrators attribute to the size of groups, also needs to be undertaken. Finally, a sharper distinction needs to be drawn between studies of children in residential care, which suggests a process perspective, and residential care as a social service, which implies more of a systems approach.

Features of a good residential establishment

Various research studies have explored the conditions that facilitate the strengths of residential approaches. A Dartington Social Research Unit (Brown, Bullock, Hobson and Little 1998) study of nine children's homes found that a 'good' home is one where, in the context of aims that seek to promote children's welfare, the various components of the structure are concordant. The greater the concordance between the expectations of society, the law and professional guidance, the way the home is structured and resourced and what staff believe they can achieve, the better the establishment. A concordant structure leads to positive cultures among staff and children. These, in turn, lead to better outcomes both for the home and the young people who live there.

In another study of 48 children's homes, Sinclair and Gibbs (1998) found that a good home is likely to be one that is small, where the head of home feels that its role is clear, mutually compatible and not disturbed by frequent re-organisation and that he or she is given adequate autonomy to get on with the job. It also helps if staff are agreed about how the home should be run and are not at odds with each other. Such a home is likely to help children by having low sickness rates among staff, infrequent running away by children and good care plans for each resident as well as being a nice place to live, in terms of such things as the absence of bullying, feeling cared for and being in a friendly place.

Looking more generally at residential settings, Bullock (1992) concluded from a review of the research that the following conditions were necessary for a successful establishment:

1. The young people feel enriched by their residential experience and should perceive staff as caring.

2. The young people see themselves as acquiring clear instrumental skills during their stay.

3. The institution pursues a set of goals which are matched to the primary rather than the secondary needs of the children; that is to the needs which necessitated absence from home rather than those brought about by living away. These aims should be reiterated in a wide variety of ways and permeate the whole control process.

4. Some consensus exists among staff, children and parents about what these goals should be and how they should be achieved. To maintain this consensus, leadership should be clear and consistent. Staff should be reminded of the strengths of residential care as well as warned against its weaknesses.

5. Efforts are made to prevent staff and child cultures from cohering in a destructive way. It may be necessary to fragment the informal world of children by a variety of structural features, such as by creating small group

situations, by appointing senior children to positions of responsibility or by encouraging sensitive and informed staff–child relationships.

There are many special contributions to children's welfare facilitated by placing them in residential settings but two are particularly important. The first is predictability in that the whole of the young person's life is enacted in the same value framework. This enables a consistent approach to permeate education, relationships and social development. Second, the staff and resident groups can be used creatively, to develop good relations with a range of adults and to foster peer support and positive reinforcement.

The effects of specific interventions

With regard to the effects of specific interventions for particular behaviours, it is more difficult to be conclusive. Some problems, such as educational underachievement, can clearly be resolved with special effort but it is difficult when explaining outcomes to know how far residential care has been essential. In a comprehensive review of the evidence on juvenile offending, Sheldrake (1994, p.979) concludes, 'the relative merits of different approaches have yet to be determined.' Controlled trials and comparison studies (Bottoms and McClintock 1973; Cornish and Clarke 1975; Coates, Miller and Ohlin 1978) have found that young people's behaviour is altered while they are there but have failed to identify any clear long-term effects of residence.

There is a danger of interpreting the absence of clear findings on effects as indicating that 'nothing works'. Although it has to be acknowledged that some research results are disappointing, particularly for those working with persistent offenders and disturbed young people who have been long looked after, recent studies indicate some ways forward.

The first is to look more closely at the link between specific interventions and specific groups of adolescents. To do this, taxonomies, such as those constructed for young offenders by West (1982) and Little (1990), need to be further developed and related to a careful scrutiny of interventions. When this is done, more encouraging results emerge. For example, although persistent delinquency appears hard to stop, the outcomes for offenders who commit one-off grave crimes are encouraging. In addition, although past traumas are often difficult to heal, sophisticated family therapy has been found to have some beneficial effects on disordered adolescents (Bullock, Little and Millham 1998a). The effects were more marked for some 'career' groups than others and for subgroups within them, related to gender and ethnicity. Much replication is obviously needed before findings can be considered conclusive but initial results are promising. But one should not hope for too much. In these difficult areas, professionals can at best hope for relatively small improvements as a result of more targeted interventions, the benefits again most likely to be forthcoming while the young person is actually in residence.

But even when differences are found, there remains the problem of separating the residential intervention from other effects. As randomised control trials are unlikely to be feasible with troubled adolescents, other methods of teasing out treatment effects have to be devised. One solution is to use research knowledge to make blind predictions of outcome at the point of entry and to compare actual with predicted results later on. An exploration of the experiences of 56 young people leaving Youth Treatment Centres based on this technique (Bullock *et al.* 1998a) concluded that 75 per cent of leavers had done better than expected and that for 76 per cent of these the residential experience seemed to have helped. Nearly half (45%) of the leavers showed significantly changed behaviour in the areas which the intervention had addressed. However, the effects were again better for certain career groups, such as those young people whose disruptive behaviour had escalated in adolescence and one-off grave offenders. In another study (of a therapeutic community), the therapy was found to have more impact on children with behaviour problems than on those in need of long-term protection (Little and Kelly 1995). Thus, careful identification of needs groups and career pathways and the application of predictive techniques offer a way of identifying more clearly the effects of residential interventions.

A second development is to view residential care in the wider context of the young person's needs and the services that best meet them. Certainly, the wider package of services available for young people and their families needs to be incorporated into interventions with difficult adolescents as this will ensure that continuities are maintained and return problems forestalled. Contingency plans should also be made. The needs of young people and their families cannot be compartmentalised and an undue emphasis on one problem can lead to other aspects of the young person's needs being ignored. For instance, an adolescent may be helped with violent behaviour but remain depressed. The philosophy underpinning the 1989 Children Act facilitates both the focused approach that seems to work best and the wider strategies for helping children and families that research suggests are needed.

Conclusion

Residential interventions are, therefore, best viewed as neither inherently good nor bad. The important questions are whether they are appropriate and which one for whom? Current practice suggests that they are increasingly seen by decision makers as less desirable but for some young people there does not seem to be any alternative. To decide what is likely to be best, it is helpful to look beyond the residential intervention.

The starting point has to be the needs of the young person and what is deemed necessary to meet them. The first question to be asked, therefore, is what does the young person and his or her family need? Does he or she need residential care, and if so what for, of what type, for how long and with what else? For those selected, the next question is what regime and intervention are shown by research to be the most effective for meeting those needs? To answer this properly, we again need to develop a validated taxonomy of children who are looked after and to relate this to a taxonomy of careers derived from evidence on interventions and outcomes for each group. Residential settings are powerful environments where, if they are to be used effectively, the intervention must be appropriate to the needs of the young people and be morally acceptable in the demands it makes on them, otherwise the mistakes of Pindown will be repeated.

This sequence of questions focuses attention on the aims of residential care and highlights gaps between desired and actual outcomes. Interventions are thus related to each individual's needs and comprise two features explored by the research just reviewed, namely the creation of generally auspicious settings and effective interventions.

If these ideas inform answers to the questions posed earlier, the place of residential care in a comprehensive childcare service becomes clear. Approaches to difficult adolescents need to be multifaceted; prevention and diversion have their place as does residential treatment. A needs perspective has the advantage that when a new approach comes on stream, its relevance can be quickly gauged, so avoiding unhelpful 'for' and 'against' stances often taken by professionals. Considerable effort may be necessary to develop these suggestions, but the benefits of doing so should be apparent in improved outcomes for children and enhanced job satisfaction among professionals. This is the clear message from the comprehensive research commissioned by the Department of Health (1998).

Although residential care is likely to remain an important option for dealing with young people in need, it must change continually if it is not to fossilise. The system and the units within it are likely to become smaller than previously, but if it is to play a full role in the new range of services for children and families, it must be enabled to develop in other ways. It needs to be less isolated from wider childcare practice and not divided within itself. It will have to play a clear role in the wider welfare system and be closely integrated into other social services. Finally, it must be self-evaluating, maximising its effectiveness by encouraging critical scrutiny and avoiding pretentiousness.

References

Barton, R. (1959) *Institutional Neurosis.* London: Wright.

Berridge, D. and Brodie, I. (1996) *Children's Homes Revisited.* Luton: University of Luton.

Bottoms, A. and McClintock, F. (1973) *Criminals Coming of Age.* London: Heinemann.

Bowlby, J. (1944) 'Forty-four juvenile thieves: Their characters and home life.' *International Journal of Psycho-Analysis XXV,* 19–52 and 107–127.

Brown, E., Bullock, R., Hobson, C. and Little, M. (1998) *Making Residential Care Work: Structure and Culture in Children's Homes.* Aldershot: Ashgate.

Bullock, R. (1992) *Residential Care: What We Know and Don't Know.* London: National Children's Home.

Bullock, R., Gooch, D. and Little, M. (1998b) *Children Going Home: The Re-unification of Families.* Aldershot: Ashgate.

Bullock, R., Little, M. and Millham, S. (1993) *Residential Care for Children: A Review of the Research.* London: HMSO.

Bullock, R., Little, M. and Millham, S. (1998a) *Secure Treatment Outcomes: the Care Careers of Very Difficult Adolescents.* Aldershot: Ashgate.

Cliffe, D. and Berridge, D. (1992) *Closing Children's Homes.* London: National Children's Bureau.

Coates, R., Miller, A. and Ohlin, L. (1978) *Diversity in a Youth Correctional System.* Cambridge: Ballinger.

Cornish, D. and Clarke, R. (1975) *Residential Care and its Effects on Juvenile Delinquency.* London: HMSO.

Dartington Social Research Unit (1995) *Matching Needs and Services: The Audit and Planning of Provision for Children Looked After by Local Authorities.* Totnes: Dartington Social Research Unit.

Dartington Social Research Unit (1996) *Admissions to Residential Care in County C.* Totnes: Dartington Social Research Unit.

Department of Health (1998) *Caring for Children Away from Home: Messages from Research.* Chichester: Wiley.

Dunlop, A. (1974) *The Approved School Experience.* London: HMSO.

Goffman, E. (1961) *Asylums.* New York: Doubleday.

Gooch, D. (1996) 'Home and Away: The residential care, education and control of children in historical and political context.' *Child and Family Social Work 1,* 19–32.

Grimshaw, R. and Berridge, D. (1995) *Educating Disruptive Children.* London: National Children's Bureau.

Heal, K. and Cawson, P. (1975) 'Organisation and change in children's institutions.' In J. Tizard, I. Sinclair and R. Clarke (eds) *Varieties of Residential Experience.* London: Routledge & Kegan Paul.

Kahan, B. (1994) *Growing Up in Groups.* London: HMSO.

King, R., Raynes, N. and Tizard, J. (1971) *Patterns of Residential Care.* London: Routledge and Kegan Paul.

Lambert, R., Millham, S. and Bullock, R. (1975) *A Manual to the Sociology of the School.* London: Weidenfeld & Nicolson.

Little, M. (1990) *Young Men in Prison.* Aldershot: Dartmouth.

Little, M. and Kelly, S. (1995) *A Life Without Problems? The Achievements of a Therapeutic Community.* Aldershot: Arena.

Millham, S., Bullock, R. and Cherrett, P. (1975) *After Grace-Teeth: A Comparative Study of the Residential Experience of Approved School Boys.* London: Human Context Books.

Millham, S., Bullock, R., Hosie, K. and Haak, M. (1986) *Lost in Care: The Problems of Maintaining Links between Children in Care and their Families.* Aldershot: Gower.

Moss, P. (1975) 'Residential care of children: A general view.' In J. Tizard, I. Sinclair and R. Clarke (eds) *Varieties of Residential Experience.* London: Routledge & Kegan Paul.

National Institute for Social Work (1988) *Residential Care: A Positive Choice.* London: HMSO.

Polsky, H. (1962) *Cottage Six.* New York: Sage Foundation.

Rutter, M., Taylor, E. and Hersov, L. (eds) (1994) *Child and Adolescent Psychiatry: Modern Approaches.* Oxford: Blackwell.

Sheldrake, C. (1994) 'Treatment of delinquents.' In M. Rutter, E. Taylor and L. Hersov (eds) *Child and Adolescent Psychiatry: Modern Approaches.* Oxford: Blackwell.

Sinclair, I. (1971) *Hostels for Probationers.* London: HMSO.

Sinclair, I. and Gibbs, I. (1998) *Children's Homes: A Study in Diversity.* Chichester: Wiley and Son.

Tizard, J., Sinclair, I. and Clarke, R. (1975) *Varieties of Residential Experience.* London: Routledge & Kegan Paul.

Ward, H. (1995) *Looking After Children: Research into Practice.* London: HMSO.

West, D. (1982) *Delinquency: Its Roots, Careers and Prospects.* London: Heinemann.

Whitaker, D., Archer, L. and Hicks, L. (1998) *Working in Children's Homes: Challenges and Complexities.* Chichester: Wiley and Son.

CHAPTER 14

Towards Effective Ways of Working with Children and their Families

Malcolm Hill

Intervening with children and their families

A wide range of agencies and professionals seek to influence children and their families for the better. Preceding chapters have reviewed a number of these and examined evidence about which forms of intervention work well. In this final chapter, an attempt will be made to draw out some of the implications arising from these reviews of the different ways of working. The contributors have presented a range of methods, underpinning principles and forms of evaluation which reflect the variety of approaches available in practice. What they all share is a commitment to improving children's lives and ensuring that practice takes account of systematic evidence.

Each profession tends to have distinctive ways of framing the needs of those who use its services and of corresponding responses (Smith 1980). For instance, reference may be made to clients, users, patients, pupils, parents, families; to difficulties, problems, disorders or conditions; to interventions, ways of working, treatment, therapy and so on. Some activities like psychiatry and social work are primarily focused on children and families who have some kind of identified difficulty, even though both have broader responsibilities. Others, like youth and community work, have a wider remit to engage with 'ordinary' members of the public, though with a particular concern to improve the circumstances of those who are disadvantaged. A number of service areas, such as early years provision and youth services, embrace a mix of universalist, open access facilities and more specialist services with often restricted entry.

Approaches to problem definition vary. For some, the professional makes the assessment or diagnosis. Parents and children usually provide information for this purpose and may be involved in determining the goals and tasks, as in many behavioural approaches. In these circumstances the problem is seen to be largely located in the child, the parents or family interaction, although external influences are often acknowledged, as with new developments in family therapy. Lloyd and Munn (Chapter 8) take a more social constructivist approach, stating that the notion of 'behavioural problems' is itself problematic and often context-specific. The environment makes a significant contribution to problem definition. For example school policies, structures and practices as well as teachers' experience and attributions greatly affect children's behaviour, teachers' perceptions and responses, and hence children's subsequent behaviour. When tensions and disputes arise, the environment needs examining and perhaps changing as much as the child or group of children. For community work, too, the ultimate targets for practitioners are often modifications in social institutions and values, public agencies or policies, though an intermediate goal will be to increase local residents' confidence, self-determination, power and skills.

Approaches which target individual children and families are of course not incompatible with tackling broader causes and issues. Roberts and Macdonald (Chapter 2) describe a number of successful interventions at the family level, but note that these tend to diminish rather than do away with disadvantage, so that other policies are needed to prevent that arising in the first place. On the other hand, Barton (Chapter 10) warns against too simple assumptions that material and environmental changes will prevent problems arising.

What do we mean by success?

This book has sought to review evidence concerning what appear to be successful ways of working with children and their families. As was discussed in Chapter 1 and will be apparent from the range of evidence provided in the subsequent chapters, different views occur on how success is to be judged and by whom.

General agreement exists that it is important to assess the *outcomes* of intervention. In other words have the goals or desired changes been achieved or not? Although the research literature typically contrasts outcomes with processes (i.e. ends with means), it is clear that for some approaches like youth work and community work the process of intervention is vital and so constitutes an objective in itself. Both Henderson and Bradford (Chapters 4 and 9) stress the core principles that service users should participate as much as possible and be engaged in defining what issues ought to be tackled. This means that effectiveness in such cases needs to be judged according to objective or subjective measures of participation and according to the aims identified by service users. This can sometimes result in tensions between a commitment to children or parents defining goals and obligations to funders who may have quite different objectives, like crime prevention (Chapter 9).

Thus a vital stage in assessing success is to decide who should determine the goals and hence outcome criteria. The expectations of a service held by professionals, parents and children often diverge markedly (Triseliotis *et al.* 1995), so that what one party judges a success another may not. Different parties involved may want and gain different things. In family situations the interests of children, mother and father do not always coincide – most obviously in situations of domestic violence and separation. Mediation offers one way of seeking compromises and family therapy techniques also recognise that individuals may need to modify their own goals for the greater good (Chapters 6 and 7). Legislation and practice values require that children's welfare should have the primary claim, however.

Often interventions are judged according to changes in individual children. In psychology and psychiatry (Chapters 5 and 10) a distinction is commonly made between externalising problems (often taking the form of behaviour that causes difficulties in relationships with adults or peers) and internalised difficulties (such as depression, anxiety or low self-esteem). In the first case, intervention may be invoked to make life easier for others, although also with the intention (or rationalisation?) of assisting the child's social participation and inclusion. Internalising problems cause more direct distress to the child. Both types of difficulty can also impinge on school performance. *The Looking After Children* materials (Ward 1995) offer a comprehensive means of assessing children's progress across emotional, behavioural, social and cognitive development. Although developed for children in foster and residential care, they have been found to correspond with the concerns and aspirations of a community sample of parents (Ward 1995; 1998). Thus they have a wide applicability as a tool for making comprehensive assessments, though many useful and more specific measures have been developed and tested (Chapter 1).

Success can be judged at different points in time. The American pre-school programmes of the 1960s seemed to have immediate benefits, which were not necessarily sustained, but were then also discovered to produce long-range advantages (Chapters 2 and 10). Some young people who do well in residential care struggle after they have left, whilst some of those who were doing poorly during the placement have better longer term outcomes (Chapter 13).

The nature of evidence

Several contributors note that pressures from government and funding agencies for greater accountability have promoted much more attention to the need for careful evaluation. Yet by their association with over-simplified performance indicators, league tables and so on, these pressures also foster suspicion that generating statistics can be misleading and incompatible with the main aims of the profession (see for example Chapters 8 and 9 on schools and youth work). It is essential therefore that the nature of the evidence should be appropriate to the issue under consideration and used alongside theoretical understandings and professional values.

Chapter 1 discussed at some length what counts as evidence for success and that material will not be repeated here. Overall the book has indicated the value of having a range of sources of evidence available. Ideally the research base ought to be rigorous so that it produces conclusions which are reliable and generalisable. When systematic evidence is not available then it is necessary to use other data, preferably through triangulation, which means seeking convergent findings from a range of sources.

The research considered has varied greatly in nature and volume, often reflecting the state of play within any particular field of activity. Several chapters, particularly those considering interventions with a more cognitive-behavioural component have been able to draw on systematic, quantified quasi-experimental evaluations. Some of these have included randomly allocated control groups or, more often, comparison groups deemed to be matched with or similar to those receiving the service being evaluated (notably Chapters 2, 5, 7, 10 and 11). In other subject areas, the main data source has been surveys, providing feedback from users and professionals, and in some cases incorporating indicators of outcome, such as placement breakdown (Chapters 9, 12 and 13). Case studies, perhaps supplemented by user and professional observations or administrative data (like child abuse registrations), have furnished the principal evidence on other forms of intervention (Chapters 3, 4, 6 and 8). Research has often been important in establishing the basis for the principles of intervention, as with respect to social learning treatments, work with social networks and family mediation.

In some areas, carefully controlled trials have identified clear effects from particular forms of intervention in ways which help rule out competing explanations. This was most apparent in relation to psychological and psychiatric services, though it also applied to certain centres and projects, especially in the early years. Many though not all of the relevant studies are North American. These have yielded strong indications about what works. Nevertheless authors in this book have urged caution even about these most 'scientific' of studies. Some results are statistically significant but show only a small effect. Not uncommonly, results from different studies reach inconclusive or even opposite conclusions. High drop out rates from a service or from the research can leave large gaps in the data. Studies which indicate success often do not specify the precise components which may have contributed to the identified benefits.

As Berridge notes (Chapter 12) evidence for success is often based on proportions and probabilities affecting whole populations, yet many professionals have to decide what is right for a particular individual. Although something works for most children, it may not work for the child you are dealing with. It is possible to identify risk and protective factors, as in the case of placing together in foster care children who are close in age, but there are always exceptions to the rule. Although Treatment A may generally help a higher proportion of children than Treatment B, for some particular children Treatment B may be better (Graham 1996). Placing older children with behavioural problems for adoption heightens the risk of breakdown, but any particular child can be among those for whom the outlook will be good despite previous difficulties (Howe 1998). As Howe argues, it is necessary to make a decision based on weighing up all the probabilities and their applicability to the specific situation. When evidence indicates that chances of success for the proposed intervention are lower than usual, then it is particularly important to consider additional supportive services and have a contingency plan in case alternative action is required.

Key findings

The chapters in this book have provided a wide range of detailed guidance about what forms of intervention have been demonstrated to work well. A brief summary of each chapter was provided at the end of Chapter 1. Here an attempt will be made to connect and integrate a few core points.

Two themes about levels of intervention recur in many of the chapters. One stresses a precise narrow focus; the other invites taking a broad perspective. In the first place there is ample well-founded evidence that approaches using behavioural and cognitive principles are very successful in alleviating a wide range of problems (Chapter 5). These methods focus on the 'micro-level', usually targeting the child or the parent–child relationship to tackle specific issues in an explicit way. The benefits are not confined to externalising behaviours, but can also assist children overcome serious emotional traumas and distress (Chapters 10 and 11). Also they have proved effective in a range of settings, including community agencies, family therapy centres, psychiatric units and residential establishments (Chapters 5, 7 and 10). In the early years, too, programmes which have demonstrated long-lasting beneficial effects have had tight aims, often with a component based on social learning theory (Chapter 2). Sheldon (1987) argues that such research has not only demonstrated 'what works', but encouraged practitioners to be more specific in generating agendas for change with service users and in monitoring progress towards stated goals.

Although specificity of goals and close attention to the predisposing and reinforcing contexts of behaviour are usually common elements, the chapters also showed differential effects depending on the particular issues being dealt with. Graham (1996) summarised the links between the following types of child mental health problem and treatments shown to be effective in controlled trials:

anorexia nervosa	family therapy
mixed emotional and conduct disorders	school-based group work
enuresis and school refusal	behavioural programmes
obsessional disorder	medication
difficult to control diabetes	psychodynamic therapy

The second main lesson of this book is that it is helpful to adopt a wide or systemic perspective to take account of the multiple influences in children's lives beyond that of their immediate parents or carers. Children can be helped or hindered by members of their personal social networks, both individually and through collective action (Chapter 3). Professionals can work with neighbourhood networks, particularly though not exclusively involving peers, to help give children a voice and influence in their communities, as well as to tackle specific problems (Chapters 4 and 9). In contrast to the behaviourist approach, much youth and community work is indirect, with a focus on establishing participatory individual and group relationships, so that young people can contribute to the agenda setting. In such circumstances it is contrary to the nature of the work to set specific goals at the outset, as these should emerge from the engagement process. In schools, foster homes and residential units attention needs to be given to the total milieu (Chapters 8, 12 and 13). For example the extent of bullying in school is as much related to the whole environment as individual and group characteristics, whilst each member of a foster home including the other children can influence the likelihood of successful adaptation or failure (Chapter 12; Part 1993). Many family therapists also recognise that professionals should reflect on the part played by themselves and their own agency in affecting how individuals and families react to problems and possible solutions (Chapter 7).

Superficially these two major conclusions may appear incompatible. The first suggests a concentration on small-scale and precise responses to particular difficulties; the latter favours an expansive approach to tackling social issues. However, American evaluations of social programmes aimed at tackling disadvantage have suggested that just such a combination is required. Among the key characteristics of successful projects were intensive and skilled work with individuals and families within the context of a comprehensive approach, which also sought to change resources and policies to meet the needs of vulnerable people (Rosenberg and Holden 1992). This also fits with a theoretical understanding of social interaction and social problems which sees these as the product of influences at personal, interpersonal and societal levels, through an interplay of agency and structure (Giddens 1991; May 1996).

Several chapters also suggest that multiple approaches involving co-operation among different agencies or professionals can be helpful. This is particularly important for children who have been sexually abused, for example (Chapter 11).

Community-wide multi-agency initiatives have good results for those at high risk in relation to crime, substance misuse and school failure (Dryfoos 1990). Another common finding has been that those with the greatest difficulties are usually the hardest to help change or improve. In these circumstances a combination of services may be required. Thus, families with severe relationship or personal problems need a wide range of help beyond simply parent training (Chapter 2).

Services also need to work with the strengths and coping capacities of individuals and their support networks. Gilligan noted that certain children recover from adversity without or even despite formal help, sometimes as a result of good support from an interested and trusted adult (Chapter 3). Murray concludes that although sexual abuse may lead to long-lasting bitterness and unhappiness, many children and families do manage well in the long run because of their own coping capacities (Chapter 11). The notion of resilience encapsulates the fact that for many children overcoming adversity results from a combination of personal factors, informal help and agency input (Fonagy *et al.* 1994; Rutter 1995; Gilligan 1997).

A traditional concern of many professionals has been with prevention and early intervention to try to nip problems in the bud or stop them becoming major threats to children's well-being or family unity. Chapters 2, 5, 7 and 10 cited a number of examples of how programmes which give intensive support and training to vulnerable parents and/or provide compensatory stimulating care for young children can be effective in improving later development. Parent-training and support provided in the early years have been shown in several studies to improve morale and childcare (Olds and Henderson 1989; Lyons 1998). These have almost exclusively involved mothers and so far little evidence exists about programmes which work with fathers, alongside or separately from mothers – probably because few programmes like that exist (Pugh, de'Ath and Smith 1994).

Chapters 3 and 4 showed how methods of working more generally to enhance the knowledge, skills and opportunities possessed by personal and neighbourhood networks can have an important preventive impact. A good understanding of how local networks function and the availability of potential helpers can make vital connections between mobilising community action and supporting individual families (Collins and Pancoast 1976; Fuchs 1995).

Targets other than children and families

The chapters have indicated a number of ways in which particular children and families may be assisted to alleviate troubles or problems they experience by changing their thinking, attitudes, communication or actions. Yet it has also been explicit and implicit that changes are also required by other people and agencies or institutions. Indeed, much of the evidence about specific forms of intervention provide indicators about how, for example, a nursery, school, children's home or family therapy service should develop its policies, ethos, rules and modes of interaction for the benefit of children. Studies of both school ethos and residential care regimes suggest the importance of having consistent and well co-ordinated policies, rules, procedures and processes (Chapters 8 and 13).

Schools are perhaps overloaded with expectations of preventing or dealing with social problems alongside stimulating academic achievement. Nevertheless, various kinds of school-based programmes can have a wider social impact. Personal and social education has limited and variable influences. Usually knowledge improves (for example about the effects of drug-taking), but that does not necessarily impinge on risk-taking behaviour (Plant and Plant 1992). The effect of health education on smoking behaviour appears greater than on drinking alcohol (Tones and Tilford 1994). One-to-one intensive programmes in school can help children improve their reading and literacy skills, with often additional benefits in terms of greater confidence and fewer behavioural problems (Fraser 1998). A curriculum was developed in the Netherlands to help increase knowledge and skills in relation to emotions and mutual understanding, with the intention of reducing social anxiety in primary school children. Children's own scores showed a moderate reduction in social anxiety, whereas teachers' ratings showed a much bigger effect, especially for the most anxious children (Bokhorst, Goosens and de Ruyter 1995).

The evidence about the influence of family characteristics and functioning on children is very strong (Rutter and Rutter 1993; Bee 1995), but so is the evidence about the effects of material circumstances and of particular experiences outside the family. The impact of the nature of pre-school centres and schools on children's longer-term well-being and vulnerability to anti-social behaviour has been well documented (Chapters 2 and 8; Tones and Tilford 1994; Loughran 1998).

On a wider front, some people have long argued that children's outcomes are as much affected by wider actions and policies as by their family and local circumstances (e.g. Gil 1970; Holman 1988). Henderson challenges the research community to produce suitable indicators for assessing the impact on children of strategies intended to combat poverty, social exclusion and urban degeneration (Chapter 4).

Access, drop outs and families who are difficult to help

When evaluating interventions it is important to consider not only those who participate and are helped or not, but also those who never gain access or 'drop out'. Much of the evidence about success does not consider differential access. Some services and the buildings in which they operate may discourage attendance by disabled children or those from ethnic minority backgrounds. It is a common finding that even interventions which have been repeatedly demonstrated to be effective for significant numbers of families, may still fail some – because they do not gain access in the first place, cease contact during the course of intervention or simply do not experience the positive effects of the majority.

Several chapters indicate that those who do not gain help are, not surprisingly, those who are more difficult to help, but who arguably for the same reason have the greatest need. For example, children with entrenched behavioural problems are least susceptible to skills training, while rigid, hostile parents generally gain little from family mediation (Chapters 5 and 6). Many children who have been sexually abused are reluctant to engage with services and the same is true for those referred for psychiatric help (Chapters 10 and 11). One suggestion is to offer brief contact to all who may benefit, whilst giving longer term support to those willing and able to commit themselves. Conventional youth services often do not reach those who are most disadvantaged and hence perhaps in greatest need (Coles 1995; Powney *et al.* 1997; Chapter 9).

Dropping out and lack of response could be seen as resulting from family 'non-compliance' or even family deficiencies. A more positive stance is to examine the image and nature of services to see how they might be adapted so that there is a greater fit with what people want and what is on offer. This is the strategy adopted by some family therapists (Chapter 7). Also, it appears that engagement with services can be improved if providers receive training about individual, family and environmental obstacles and resistances (McKay *et al.* 1996).

Changing the location of a service may make it physically more accessible and less stigmatising, while also signifying an orientation to engage with the immediate environment of potential service-users. Thus one American study revealed a dramatic increase in referrals to a child mental health service when this was provided in school rather than in special centres (Burns 1994). Intensive personal support and counselling have been shown to be effective in helping high-risk adolescents, especially when located in familiar surroundings (Dryfoos 1990; Burns 1994).

Participation

Henderson observed the growing importance attached to children's participatory rights, with a corresponding shift in academic attitudes to accord greater respect for children's competence (Chapter 4; see also Alanen 1997; Hill and Tisdall 1997; James and Prout 1997). Similarly, Gilligan observed that one of the assets of informal network members is that their help is often more acceptable than that from formal agencies and professionals (Chapter 3). Feedback from children and young people in relation to a wide range of services and professional activities indicate the great value they place on having their views taken seriously (Butler and Williamson 1994; Farnfield 1998). Feedback about youth work makes clear that it is valued for dealing with young people on their own terms. Young people engaged in legal proceedings usually like solicitors, because their explicit role is to present the young person's viewpoint and advocate on their behalf (Farnfield 1998).

Some interventions are less participative than others. At present, access by children to help in relation to divorce is largely dependent on their parents willingness (Chapter 6). Traditionally family therapists have tended to work with whole family groups, but increasingly also work with dyads and individuals too. Young people indicate a preference for combined individual and family work (Chapter 7). A considerable proportion of young people do not like referrals to psychologists and psychiatrists, partly because of negative stereotypes, but also because of some direct experiences of poor communication (Triseliotis *et al.* 1995; Armstrong *et al.* 1998). When young people feel their preferences and style of communication are accepted, then they show willingness to discuss issues they would otherwise avoid (Chapter 9).

Duration of intervention

In recent years, disenchantment has set in with some long-term activities like traditional psychotherapy and a range of brief and solution focused strategies have become popular (see for example Chapters 7 and 8). Some studies have shown that short-term treatment can be as effective as more sustained contact (Reid and Shyne 1969; Quick 1998). As ever, it is important not to overgeneralise. Whilst in certain circumstances for some people brief inputs can be as productive as longer inputs (and hence more cost-effective), several chapters have in different ways observed the value of sustained intervention. Chapter 2 showed that early socio-educational programmes and centres have much more substantial and persistent effects if the extra structured input is maintained. In Chapter 9, Bradford noted that in youth work it is often necessary to spend much time building up close informal relationships with young people as individuals or groups before they are ready to allow attention to their 'problems'. Often the immediate benefits of residential care are undone, because after leaving young people struggle on account of the social and educational disadvantages associated with their reasons for entry to care, yet receive little support (Chapter 13). Services for families where abuse or neglect have been identified apparently work best when sustained for 6 to 18 months (Berrick 1997).

Emerging frameworks for intervention

The contributors to the book have written from a number of different perspectives. The chapters reflect sometimes contrasting orientations concerning how problems should be defined and responded to, and how responses should be addressed. Nevertheless common ground exists over the importance of systematic interventions and on the need to consider wider environmental influences and policies in addition to individualised or family-based interventions.

Particular forms of interventions need to be seen as part of a spectrum or system of responses to child and family problems. This recognises that a range of interventions are needed to reflect the diversity of problems or issues and the varied needs and responsiveness of children and families. Further, a systems framework recognises the place of strategies aimed at preventing stresses or difficulties from arising or from having significant effects, as well as interventions aimed at reducing or removing strains and difficulties. As shown by Table 14.1, various frameworks have been suggested to encompass different levels and stages of prevention and intervention.

Table 14.1 Frameworks for Prevention and Intervention				
1 *Ecosystems of child development*	*2* *Framework of child protection*	*3* *Levels of prevention*	*4* *Social policy responses*	*5* *Types of Western welfare state*
Microsystem	Values about children	Primary	Institutional redistributive	Social democratic
Mesosystem	Values about women and children	Secondary	Industrial achievement	Conservative
Exosystem	Social networks	Tertiary	Residual	Liberal
Microsystems		Quaternary		Latin

Sources: 1. Bronfenbrenner 1979; 2. Boushel 1994; 3. Hardiker *et al.* 1996; NSPCC Commission 1996; 4. Titmuss 1958; 5. Esping-Anderson 1990; Leibfried 1991; van Voorhis 1998.

Bronfenbrenner (1979) argued that children's development needed to be considered within the context of concentric circles of the socio-economic environment. The innermost circle (microsystem) comprises the child's immediate setting, like the home, day centre or school. The mesosystem consists of the interrelations between two or more settings, such as the interaction between home and school or work. The exosystem is made up of influences outside the child's immediate experience, whilst the macrosystem encompasses social beliefs, values and policies.

Boushel (1994) similarly examined the degree of interconnectedness in social relations which help keep children safe and promote their welfare. Two main elements are the support and help available from informal social networks and formal agencies. In addition, Boushel emphasised the impact of family and societal values concerning the rights, roles and status of children and women.

Implicit in both frameworks is that problems can be generated in a child's immediate environment (like the family or the school) or through wider influences or, perhaps most commonly, an interaction of the two. Whereas the immediate factors are likely to be most evident in relation to a particular child or family, broader influences can be more apparent in considering populations. These correspond with the support for both focused and broad interventions noted earlier in the chapter.

Similar ideas underpin traditional medical models of prevention, as outlined in Chapter 10. Action at a national, regional or neighbourhood level can promote *primary prevention*, exemplified by public health and health promotion strategies which seek to affect everyone (for example through hygiene, vaccination programmes, anti-smoking campaigns). *Secondary prevention* is directed at those identified as having high stress or risk, whilst *tertiary prevention* is targeted at those who already have an illness or social problem with a view to minimising the adverse effects. Hardiker *et al.* (1996) propose a fourth category of *quaternary intervention* with respect to family problems. This recognises that for some children preventive work with the birth family does not succeed or is inappropriate, so children are placed away from home. Quaternary prevention aims to prevent adverse consequences from separation and alternative care.

In terms of the topics covered in this book, some approaches may be seen as acting at primary preventive levels, though their aims can also be framed more positively as promoting welfare, participation, citizenship and so on in addition to preventing social problems. These include community work, youth work, whole school approaches and some family centres which operate in relation to all children in a particular area. By seeking to improve the welfare of all, it is hoped to reduce the stress and problems of the more disadvantaged or vulnerable. Specialist early years programmes and network-oriented actions tend to focus more selectively on vulnerable or 'at risk' children and families at the secondary prevention level. Other ways of working with children and their families typically come more within tertiary prevention, notably social learning, psychiatric and family-based interventions.

These ways of conceptualising individual, family, neighbourhood and societal influences on children's welfare and family problems can be linked to frameworks of policy responses. Several writers have classified policy approaches and welfare states according to their emphasis on universal policies (affecting or open to all) and selective policies (targeted on particular categories of people or on individual families). Most countries have a mix of approaches corresponding to different levels of problem-generation and intervention, though persistent differences in orientation can be detected (Titmuss 1958; Esping-Anderson 1990; van Voorhis 1998; Pringle 1998). Thus it may be said that the social policies of some countries (notably Scandinavia) emphasise more strongly actions at the societal, primary prevention levels to tackle material conditions and social values. Others favour a more targeted approach for government in the expectation that informal help, voluntary and private agencies will suffice for the majority. Nevertheless, all modern welfare states recognise the importance of having a range of services and levels of intervention.

In considering services delivered to families and communities, the chapters of this book have noted the complexity of identifying effectiveness, but also highlighted the kinds of activities which have been shown to work better. When acting on behalf of society to help children, professionals do have a substantial body of evidence available to inform their judgements about how best to intervene.

References

Alanen, L. (1997) 'Children and the family order: Constraints and competencies.' In I. Hutchby and J. Moran-Ellis (eds) *Children and Social Competence.* London: Falmer Press.

Armstrong, C., Hill, M. and Secker, J. (1998) *Listening to Children.* London: Mental Health Foundation.

Asquith, S. *et al.* (eds) (1998) *Children, Young People and Offending in Scotland.* Edinburgh: Scottish Office Cental Research Unit.

Bee, H. (1995) *The Developing Child.* New York: Harper Collins.

Berrick, J.D. (1997) 'Child neglect: Definition, incidence, outcome.' In J.D. Berrick, R.P. Barth and N. Gilbert (eds) *Child Welfare Research.* New York, NY: Columbia University Press.

Berrick, J.D., Barth, R.P. and Gilbert, N. (eds) (1997) *Child Welfare Research.* New York, NY: Columbia University Press.

Bokhorst, K., Goosens, F., and de Ruyter, P. (1995) 'Social anxiety at elementary school.' *Educational Research 37,* 1, 87–94.

Boushel, M. (1994) 'The protective environment of children: Towards a framework for anti-oppressive, cross-cultural and cross-national understanding.' *British Journal of Social Work 24,* 3, 173–190.

Bronfenbrenner, U. (1979) *The Ecology of Human Development.* Cambridge, MA: Harvard University Press.

Burns, B.J. (1994) 'The challenges of child mental health services research.' *Journal of Emotional and Behavioural Disorder 2,* 4, 254–259.

Butler, I. and Williamson, H. (1994) *Children Speak: Children, Trauma and Social Work.* London: NSPCC/Longman.

Cheetham, J. and Kazi, M.A.F. (eds) (1998) *The Working of Social Work.* London: Jessica Kingsley Publishers.

Cicchetti, D. and Carlson, V. (eds) (1989) *Child Maltreatment.* Cambridge: Cambridge University Press.

Coles, B. (1995) *Youth and Social Policy: Youth Citizenship and Young Careers.* London: UCL Press.

Collins, A.H. and Pancoast, D.L. (1976) *Natural Helping Networks.* Washington: National Association of Social Workers.

Dryfoos, J.G. (1990) *Adolescents at Risk.* Oxford: Oxford University Press.

Esping-Andersen, G. (1990) *The Three Worlds of Welfare Capitalism.* Princeton, NJ: Princeton University Press.

Farnfield, S. (1998) 'The rights and wrongs of social work with children and young people.' In J. Cheetham and M.A.F. Kazi (eds) *The Working of Social Work.* London: Jessica Kingsley Publishers.

Fonagy, P., Steele, M., Steele, H., Higgitt, A. and Target, M. (1994) 'The theory and practice of resilience.' *Journal of Child Psychology and Psychiatry 35,* 2, 231–257.

Fraser, H. (1998) *Early Intervention: Key Issues from Research.* Edinburgh: Scottish Council for Research in Education.

Fuchs, D. (1995) 'Preserving and strengthening families and protecting children: Social network intervention, a balanced approach to the prevention of child maltreatment.' In J. Hudson and B. Galaway (eds) *Child Welfare in Canada: Research and Policy Implications.* Toronto: Thompson Educational Publishing.

Giddens, A. (1991) *Modernity and Self Identity.* Cambridge: Polity Press.

Gil, D.G. (1970) *Violence Against Children.* Cambridge, MA: Harvard University Press.

Gilligan, R. (1997) 'Beyond permanence: The importance of resilience in child placement practice and planning.' *Adoption and Fostering 21,* 1, 12–20.

Graham, P. (1996) 'The thirty year contribution of research in child mental health to clinical practice and public policy in the UK.' In Bernstein and Brannen

Hardiker, P., Exton, K. and Barker, M. (1995) *A Framework for Analysing Services.* London: National Commission of Inquiry into Child Abuse.

Hill, M. and Tisdall, K. (1997) *Children and Society.* London: Longman.

Holman, B. (1988) *Putting Families First.* London: Macmillan.

Howe, D. (1998) *Patterns of Adoption.* Oxford: Blackwell.

Hudson, J. and Galaway, B. (eds) (1995) *Child Welfare in Canada: Research and Policy Implications.* Toronto: Thompson Educational Publishing.

Hutchby, I. and Moran-Ellis, J. (eds) (1997) *Children and Social Competence.* London: Falmer Press.

James, A. and Prout, A. (eds) (1997) *Constructing and Reconstructing Childhood.* London: Falmer Press.

Leibfried, S. (1991) 'European models of welfare and the wider international order.' In G. Room (ed) *Towards a European Welfare State.* Bristol: SAUS Publications.

Loughran, N. (1998) 'Review of literature on children, young people and offending.' In S. Asquith *et al.*(eds) *Children, Young People and Offending in Scotland.* Edinburgh: Scottish Office Central Research Unit.

Lyons, P. (1998) 'Child maltreatment.' In J.S. Wodarski and B. Thyer (eds) *Handbook of Empirical Social Work Practice. Volume 2 Social Problems and Practice Issues.* New York, NY: John Wiley.

May, T. (1996) *Situating Social Theory.* Buckingham: Open University Press.

McKay, M., Nudelman, R., McCadam, K. and Gonzales, J. (1996) 'Evaluating a social work engagement approach to involving inner-city children and their families in mental health care.' *Research on Social Work Practice 6*, 4, 462–475.

NSPCC National Commission of Inquiry into the Prevention of Child Abuse (1996) *Childhood Matters.* London: The Stationery Office.

Olds, D.L. and Henderson, C.R. (1989) 'The prevention of child maltreatment.' In D. Cicchetti and V. Carlson (eds) *Child Maltreatment.* Cambridge: Cambridge University Press.

Part, D. (1993) 'Fostering as seen by the carers' children.' *Adoption and Fostering 17*, 1, 26–31.

Plant, M. and Plant, M. (1992) *Risk Takers.* London: Routledge.

Powney, J., Furlong, A., Cartmel, F. and Hall, S. (1997) *Youth Work with Vulnerable Young People.* Edinburgh: SCRE.

Pringle, K. (1998) *Children and Social Welfare in Europe.* Buckingham: Open University Press.

Pugh, G., De'Ath, E. and Smith C. (1994) *Confident Parents, Confident Children.* London: National Children's Bureau.

Quick, E.K. (1998) *Doing What Works in Brief Therapy.* San Diego: Academic Press.

Reid, W.J. and Shyne, A. (1969) *Brief and Extended Casework.* New York, NY: Columbia University Press.

Room, G. (ed) (1991) *Towards a European Welfare State.* Bristol: SAUS Publications.

Rosenberg, G. and Holden, G. (1992) 'Social work effectiveness: A response to Cheetham.' *Research on Social Work Practice 2*, 3, 288–296.

Rutter, M. (1995) 'Psychosocial adversity: Risk, resilience and recovery.' *Southern African Journal of Child and Adolescent Psychiatry 7*, 2, 75–88.

Rutter, M. and Rutter, M. (1993) *Developing Minds.* Harmondsworth: Penguin.

Sheldon, B. (1987) 'Implementing findings from social work effectiveness research.' *British Journal of Social Work 17*, 573–586.

Smith, G. (1980) *Social Need: Policy, Practice and Research.* London: Routledge & Kegan Paul.

Titmuss, R. (1958) *Essays on the Welfare State.* London: Allen & Unwin.

Tones, K. and Tilford, S. (1994) *Health Education: Effectiveness, Efficiency and Equity.* London: Chapman Hall.

Triseliotis, J., Borland, M., Hill, M. and Lambert, L. (1995) *Teenagers and the Social Work Services.* London: HMSO.

Tygstrup, N., Lachin, J.M. and Juhl, E. (eds) (1982) *The Randomized Clinical Trial and Therapeutic Decisions.* New York, NY: Dekker.

Van Voorhis, R.A. (1998) 'Three generations of comparative welfare theory: From convergence to convergence.' *European Journal of Social Work 1*, 2, 189–202.

Ward, H. (1995) *Looking After Children: Research into Practice.* London: HMSO.

Ward, H. (1998) 'Using a child development model to assess the outcomes of social work intervention with families.' *Children and Society 12*, 3, 202–209.

Wodarski, J.S. and Thyer, B. (eds) (1998) *Handbook of Empirical Social Work Practice, Volume 2 Social Problems and Practice Issues.* New York, NY: Wiley.

The Contributors

Joanne Barton is Senior Lecturer in the Department of Child and Adolescent Psychiatry, University of Glasgow.

David Berridge is Professor of Child and Family Welfare at the University of Luton.

Simon Bradford is Lecturer in the School of Education, Brunel University. His research interests are professional education, issues affecting young people and services for young people.

Roger Bullock is Director of Dartington Social Research Unit, Totnes, a Department of Health funded unit specialising in personal social services for children in need and their families.

Robbie Gilligan is Senior Lecturer in Social Work and Head, Department of Social Studies at Trinity College, Dublin; he is academic co-ordinator of the Children's Research Centre there.

David Gough is Reader in Social Science and Deputy Director of the Social Science Research Unit, London University Institute of Education. He is secretary to the International Society for the Prevention of Child Abuse and Neglect, co-editor of *Child Abuse Review* and a member of the editorial board of *Child Abuse and Neglect*.

Paul Henderson is Director of Practice Development with the Community Development Foundation. Based in Leeds, he undertakes research, training and consultancy. He has published widely on community development practice and policy.

Malcolm Hill is Professor of Social Work and Director of the Centre for the Child and Society, University of Glasgow.

Gwynedd Lloyd is Senior Lecturer in Special Education at Moray House Institute of Education, University of Edinburgh.

Geraldine Macdonald is Professor of Social Work and Applied Social Studies at the University of Bristol.

Pamela Munn is Professor of Education at Moray House, Institute of Education, University of Edinburgh.

Kathleen Murray is Research Consultant and Honorary Senior Research Fellow in the Centre for Child and Society, University of Glasgow. She has researched and written extensively on the Scottish system of juvenile justice. She was commissioned by the Scottish Office to evaluate the use of live television link by child witnesses in Scottish criminal courts.

Helen Roberts is Head of Research in the Policy, Planning and Research Unit of Barnardo's.

Margaret Robinson is a Family Mediator and Family Therapist in Winchester. She was a founder member of the Institute of Family Therapy in London, and founded their mediation service there, where she worked as a consultant until 1997.

Arlene Vetere is Principal Lecturer, University of East London and the Tavistock Centre, London, and Past-Chair of the UK Association for Family Therapy. She is a member of the editorial board of the *Journal of Family Therapy.*

Subject Index

Author Index

Prinz, R.J. and Milner, G.E. 116

Prior, V., Lynch, M.A. and Glaser, D. 218, 231, 232

Pugh, G. 250

Pugh, G., De'Ath, E. and Smith, C. 250

Quick, E. 173

Quick, E.K. 281

Quine, L. and Pahl, J. 146

Quinton, D. and Rutter, M. 23, 30

Qvortrup, J. 25, 100

Rabinow, P. 8

Rachman, S.J. and Wilson, G.T. 51

Rae-Grant, Q. and Robson, B.E. 201

Rees, S. 27

Reid *et al.* 61

Reid, J.B. 61, 62

Reid, J.B., Kavanagh, K. and Baldwin, D.V. 63

Reid, R. and Maag, J. 174

Reid, S. and Kolvin, I. 203

Reid, W.J. 20, 21

Reid, W.J. and Shyne, A. 281

Reimers, S. and Treacher, A. 31, 149

Remschmidt, H., Schulz, E. and Matthias Martin, P.D. 205

Rey, J.M. and Walter, G. 207

Reynolds, D. *et al.* 11

Richards, M. 134

Richman, N., Douglas, J., Hunt, H. *et al.* 203

Richman, N., Graham, P., Stevenson, J. 204, 209

Richman, N., Stevenson, J. and Graham, P. 27

Rickard, K.M., Forehand, R., Wells, K.C., Griest, D.L. and McMahon, R.J. 62

Riddle, M.A., Scahill, L., King, R.A. *et al.* 206

Roberts, H. 49, 50

Roberts, H., Smith, S.J. and Bryce, C. 59

Roberts, I. and Power, C. 59

Roberts, M. 132

Robins, L.N. and Rutter, M. 153

Robinson, M. 138

Robson, C. 12, 28

Robson, M., Cook, P. and Gilliland, J. 80

Rodriguez, E. and Bowen, K.A. 27

Romans, S., Martin, J., Anderson, J., O'Shea, M. and Mullen, P. 80

Ronnen, T. 106

Rosenberg, G. and Holden, G. 276

Rosenberg, M. 27

Rossi, P.H. 10

Rossi, P.H. and Freeman, H.E. 14

Roth, A. and Fonagy, P. 149, 155

Rothery, D.J., Wrate, R.M. and McCabe, R.J.R. *et al.* 209

Routh, C.P., Hill, J.W., Steelee, H., Elliott, C.E. and Dewey, M.E. 115

Rowe, J., Caine, M., Hundleby, M. and Keane, A. 242

Rowe, J., Hundleby, M. and Garnett, L. 28, 83, 241, 245, 246

Rubin and Knox 15

Runyan, D., Hunter, W., Socolar, R., Amaya-Jackson, D., English, D., Landsverk, J., Dubowitz, H., Browne, D., Bangdiwala, S. and Mathew, R. 71

Runyan, D.K., Everson, M.D., Edelsohn, D.J., Hunter, W.M. and Coulter, M.L. 217

Rushton, A., Treseder, J. and Quinton, D. 78

Russell, R. 170

Rutter, M. 18, 140, 220, 245, 277

Rutter, M., Maughan, B., Mortimore, P. and Ouston, J. 10, 19, 166

Rutter, M., Tizard, J. and Whitmore, K. 27

Rutter and Rutter 278

Sammons, P., Thomas, S. and Mortimore, P. 166

Sanders, D. and Hendry, L. 164

Sandler, I., Miller, P., Short, J. and Wolchik, S. 73

Sandow, S. 163

Save the Children 97

Scales, P. and Gibbons, J. 80

Scannapieco, M. and Jackson, S. 82

Schachar, R. and Tannock, R. 205

Schalock, R. 10

Scheerens, J. 10, 11, 19

Schön, D. 244

Schweinhart, L. and Weikart, D. 56

Scottish Office 216

Sellick, C. 250, 252

Sellick, C. and Thoburn, J. 24, 241, 242, 244, 245, 249

Shadish, W.R., Matt, G.E., Navarro, A.M., Siegle, G., Crits-Cristoph, P., Hazelrigg, M.D., Jorm, A.F., Lyons, L.C., Nietzel, M.T., Prout, H.T., Robinson, L., Smith, M.L., Svartberg, M. and Weiss, B. 159

Shadish, W.R., Ragsdale, K., Glaser, R.R. and Montgomery, L.M. 159

Shaffer, D., Garland, A., Gould, M. *et al.* 201

Shapiro, E., Shapiro, A.K., Fulop, G. *et al.* 205